Advance Praise for
Email Marketing: An Hour a Day

"Email Marketing: An Hour a Day *is one of the best overall guides I've seen for bringing marketers quickly and painlessly to a place where email can be a truly strategic marketing channel. It is, quite simply, the on-ramp for the next generation of sophisticated email marketers.*"

 —BILL NUSSEY, CEO, Silverpop; author of *The Quiet Revolution in Email Marketing*

"*David and Jeanniey have taken their years of knowledge of the email marketing industry and stuffed them into a readable book jam-packed with little a-ha! nuggets that are certain to improve any email effort. Written to contain layers of information for all levels of email marketers, beginner to advanced, this book ensures that you will take away from it what you put into it.*"

 —JORDAN AYAN, chairman and founder of SubscriberMail; author of *Aha! 10 Ways to Free Your Creative Spirit and Find Your Great Ideas* and *The Practical Guide to Email Marketing: Strategies and Tactics for Inbox Success*

"*There is so much unnecessary mystery around email marketing. David and Jeanniey have put the myths to rest and given marketers a straightforward and actionable primer on how to build a fantastic, customer-centric email marketing program. If you read only one book on this topic, this should be it!*"

 —DAN SPRINGER, CEO, Responsys; board of directors for ITI, E-LOAN, and the Randall Museum

"*The world-renowned expertise of Daniels and Mullen is at its best here, because they break down the mysteries of email marketing into digestible nuggets that make it easy for every busy marketer to consume.*"

 —ALAN CHAPELL, Esq., chairman and founder of Chapell and Associates

"*Email marketing is a powerful tool. It is also complicated. Just when you get your strategy right, your reputation is challenged. When you fix that, your creative formats are not adhering to best practices. Email marketing could possibly be one of the most challenging and complex marketing channels out there. Knowing where to go and how to focus are key. Jeanniey Mullen and David Daniels have taken our collective challenges head-on and provide you with the solutions you need to know in this book. Read this book, and you will immediately have a better handle on your email marketing efforts.*"

 —MATT BLUMBERG, CEO, Return Path

"*David and Jeanniey are tremendous advocates for the responsible and effective use of email marketing. These impressive thought leaders understand that email marketing is the backbone of all digital communications. When others predicted the demise of email, both of these industry champions defended the medium and pointed out its evolving value to marketers and subscribers alike. Their insights are thought-provoking, are humorous, and always deliver value to marketers. I read every word that both authors write.*"

    —Scott Dorsey, CEO, ExactTarget

"*Technology evangelists are a rare breed. They not only need to be the experts in their fields—on top of every new innovation, thought, and trend—but they also need to be able to express their knowledge with enthusiasm, passion, energy, clarity, and excitement. It doesn't hurt if they are entertaining as all get out as well. I've shared more stages, rental cars, airplanes, and bar stools with David and Jeanniey than I care to remember, and I can tell you these two are the best in the business. What the heck...buy the book and find out for yourself. You won't be sorry, and you'll be a much smarter person on the last page than you were when you started on page one.*"

    —Bill McCloskey, chairman, cofounder, and chief evangelist, Email Data Source, Inc.

"*For any marketing channel to stay viable, it has to constantly improve. I am impressed with the enthusiasm and fresh ideas that David and Jeanniey continue to bring to the email industry. In* Email Marketing: An Hour a Day, *David and Jeanniey do not disappoint, because this book offers compelling and proven tactics to advance the effectiveness of email as well as practical guidance on how to prioritize and integrate emerging channels such as social and mobile communications. It's a must-have for any marketer.*"

    —John Rizzi, CEO, e-Dialog

"*While there are many books on email marketing, few come with the credentials and real-world breadth of exposure that David and Jeanniey bring to this research. Balancing vast experiences in the email marketing space with a very broad analyst reality of the dynamics in the channels, vendors, and market dynamics, they've developed a book that provides a baseline understanding of the email channel in a very logical flow and that provides the relevant context that helps marketers understand how to improve this ever-evolving channel. As two of the leading thought leaders in the email marketing space, this is a great contribution to our industry and a worthy read for anyone doing email marketing in their business.*"

    —David Baker, vice president of Email Solutions, Razorfish

Email Marketing

An Hour a Day

Jeanniey Mullen

David Daniels

WILEY

Wiley Publishing, Inc.

Senior Acquisitions Editor: Willem Knibbe
Development Editor: Jim Compton
Technical Editor: Jared Blank
Production Editor: Melissa Lopez
Copy Editor: Kim Wimpsett
Production Manager: Tim Tate
Vice President and Executive Group Publisher: Richard Swadley
Vice President and Executive Publisher: Joseph B. Wikert
Vice President and Publisher: Neil Edde
Compositor: Maureen Forys, Happenstance Type-O-Rama
Proofreader: David Fine, WordOne
Indexer: Jack Lewis
Cover Designer: Ryan Sneed
Cover Image: © Thomas Northcut / Digital Vision / GETTY IMAGES INC

Library of Congress Cataloging-in-Publication Data
Mullen, Jeanniey.
 Email marketing : an hour a day / Jeanniey Mullen, David Daniels.
  p. cm.
 ISBN 978-0-470-38673-6 (pbk.)
 1. Internet marketing. 2. Telemarketing. 3. Electronic mail messages. I. Daniels, David , 1970- II. Title.
 HF5415.1265.M853 2009
 658.8'72—dc22

                    2008040281

Dear Reader,

Thank you for choosing *Email Marketing: An Hour a Day*. This book is part of a family of premium-quality Sybex books, all of which are written by outstanding authors who combine practical experience with a gift for teaching.

Sybex was founded in 1976. More than 30 years later, we're still committed to producing consistently exceptional books. With each of our titles, we're working hard to set a new standard for the industry. From the paper we print on to the authors we work with, our goal is to bring you the best books available.

I hope you see all that reflected in these pages. I'd be very interested to hear your comments and get your feedback on how we're doing. Feel free to let me know what you think about this or any other Sybex book by sending me an email at nedde@wiley.com, or if you think you've found a technical error in this book, please visit http://sybex.custhelp.com. Customer feedback is critical to our efforts at Sybex.

Best regards,

Neil Edde
Vice President and Publisher
Sybex, an imprint of Wiley

Acknowledgments

The email marketing is one of the most supportive and tight-knit marketing communities there is. Every person in this field truly works to ensure their own programs are fantastic yet is quick to lend a hand (or a case study) to a fellow email marketer in need. Being part of this industry gives you a sense of pride that is unmatched. With that said, there are so many people we owe thanks to for making this book the work of art that it has turned out to be. So, with no further ado, here they are.

First and foremost, a tremendous amount of thanks goes to our families (Chris, Giovanna, Kristina, Cherry, Ashley, and Ethan) for putting up with us while we took on this project. It truly has been a labor of love.

David would like to especially thank his parents and stepfather, authors and educators alike, for instilling the passion of continuous improvement and the value of authoring a published book. David is also grateful to his brother Marc who started and shaped David's direct marketing and online commerce journey back in the 1980s.

Jeanniey would like to extend a special thank you to her parents, whose provided encouragement in whatever it was she set her mind out to do has helped build her undying spirit and perseverance in every endeavor.

Also a special thanks to David Schatsky at JupiterResearch, a Forrester Research Company, and the Email Experience Council for their generous offering of the use of data and their support of our efforts in undertaking such a project. Thanks to the entire Zinio and VIV teams for their continued support during the completion of this book at a time when we were also undertaking the transformation of the publishing world.

For those of you in the email world—a huge thanks to all of you. But a very special thanks to those who helped make this book so powerful, including the following:

Kathryn Waters, Stephanie Jackson, Andrea Allman, and Ali Swerdlow—not only great friends but the bestest girls in email

Jared Blank, the best tech editor out there

Alan Chappell, of Chappell & Associates, our favorite privacy attorney

Dylan Boyd, Boba Fett, and the team at eROI

Lisa Harmon and Aaron Smith from Smith-Harmon

David Atlas, Charles Styles, and Jordan Cohen at Goodmail Systems

Des Cahill, Eric Mott, and Ray Everett-Church

Josh Baer, Quinn Jolie, Dave Hendricks, Lana McGilvray, and the entire Datran
Media crew

Lizzie Maughn and her amazing team at Think Eyetracking, who knew where we really
ever looked

Matt Blumberg and the knowledgeable Return Path team

Chip House, Morgan Stewart, Jeff Rohrs, and the entire crew at ExactTarget

David Baker, Chris Baggot, Bill McCloskey, Jeanne Jennings, Reggie Brady, and the entire
old-school team of email marketing experts that contributed to this whole phenomenon

Loren McDonald and the team at Silverpop

Craig Spiezle of Microsoft and of Authentication and Online Trust Alliance (AOTA) fame

Willem Knibbe, Jim Compton, Kim Wimpsett, Melissa Lopez, Pete Gaughan, and the
entire team at Wiley

And to MP for knowing how to inspire a great final product

Lastly, we'd like to acknowledge you for taking the time to pick this book up and begin
the journey that we believe will make you a master of email marketing.

About the Authors

Jeanniey Mullen is executive vice president and chief marketing officer for Zinio, the global leader for digital publishing products and services. She holds the same position for VIV Magazine, the first fully interactive and all-digital lifestyle magazine for women. An accomplished expert in the email and online marketing world, Jeanniey is recognized as a pioneer and visionary, advocating for and driving change that redefines the impact of various marketing channels. Prior to Zinio and VIV, Jeanniey was the senior partner and global executive director of the Email Marketing and Digital Dialogue Practice at OgilvyOne Worldwide. In 2005, Jeanniey founded the Email Experience Council and currently maintains her role as its executive director.

A digital entrepreneur, Jeanniey founded and ran her own interactive agency as well as an online entertainment marketing company from 2001 to 2004. Prior to that, Jeanniey started the first agency-run email marketing division at Grey Direct. Jeanniey also held a number of roles at JCPenney, spanning an eight-year period.

Jeanniey is known as one of the most well-respected voices in the world of email, digital publishing, and online consumer brand awareness. She is a columnist for ClickZ, has published numerous white papers and best practices guides, and has been quoted in the *Wall Street Journal* and *New York Times* numerous times. She is on the board of advisors for a number of online marketing companies and events and is a frequent keynote speaker for various companies and organizations including the Direct Marketing Association, Shop.org, OMMA, IBM, NaturesMade, and the American Association of Publishing.

David Daniels is a tenured multichannel marketer, consultant, and researcher, and since 2000 he has been the leading analyst voice shaping the email marketing industry. David currently serves as vice president and principal analyst at Forrester Research, which acquired JupiterResearch in July 2008. Prior to Forrester's acquisition of JupiterResearch, David served as vice president and research director of the company's successful Operations and Industries product grouping where he authored and collaborated on market research that informed, evaluated, and accurately forecast the future of the broader online economy. David's compass-setting research studies on email marketing are familiar and cited throughout the industry. With 20 years of experience in direct-to-consumer marketing, Daniels is recognized as a thought leader in his domain, is a frequent keynote speaker, and is often quoted in the *Wall Street Journal*, the *New York Times*, and other major media outlets.

Outside of serving as the leading email marketing market analyst, David founded the Email Measurement Accuracy Coalition in 2006, and in 2008 it became the Email Experience Council's Email Measurement Accuracy Roundtable, which David co-chairs. David is also a board advisor to a variety of industry associations and events including the Authentication and Online Trust Alliance (AOTA) and MediaPost's Email Insider Summit.

Prior to joining JupiterResearch, David served as president of his own marketing and operations consulting firm (1 World Design). Before striking out on his own, David held senior-level positions at Apple Computer, Urban Outfitters/Anthropologie, MicroWarehouse, Genesis Direct/ProTeam, and CDA Computer Sales, which was one of the first personal computer catalog marketers and merchants on CompuServe.

Contents

Foreword

It is not the strongest of the species that survive, nor the most intelligent, but the one most responsive to change.

—Charles Darwin

We live in a world where our mere survival is based on our ability not only to invent but also to continuously reinvent ourselves as we find new and better ways to adapt to the world around us. Electricity, the telephone, the printing press—all are life-changing inventions that enabled our society to modify the way we experienced living. These inventions enabled us to reinvent the manner in which we approached each element of our daily rituals. Without a continuous stream of inventions, the human race cannot continue to evolve.

There have been many life-altering inventions during the past 200 years. Many of us have been fortunate enough to live during times of great invention and change rather than simply reading about them in a history book. Beginning with the first Internet experiments in the early 1970s, we were witness to one of the world's great evolutions in communications: the invention of email, an electronic mode of immediate conversation. Since that time, this communication vehicle has become a necessity, adopted by the mainstream population. JupiterResearch forecasts and data indicate that 88 percent of the U.S. online population uses some form of electronic communication, which equates to 77 million people in the United States using this new invention. That's a staggering number, because it represents three-quarters of the total households in the United States. And while email has been a driver of communication change, it has also reinvented the way we market and advertise to consumers. No longer do we rely on a one-way message push with a hope for engagement. We are not constrained to guessing about the relevancy and impact our mass message has. Email as a marketing tool has opened up a world of possibilities by enabling a two-way dialogue, personalized messaging, and data-driven analysis. This channel has grown to $1.2 billion in 2007 and is expected to continue to swell to $2.1 billion in 2012.

Recent statistics report that 60 percent of consumers admit they have made immediate purchases from email marketing messages. In 2008, the same reports concluded that 44 percent of consumers stated email marketing messages drove online purchases in the past year and 41 percent reported the same for offline purchases.

The message is clear. This new invention called *email* is a powerful personal and business tool. It's one that will live in the same life-altering invention ranks as the telephone. Understanding how to harness and direct email as a marketing vehicle is critical to every business in any industry. This book will get you started down that path.

To understand this craft called *email marketing*, I direct you to the two most highly regarded of its evangelists and experts, Jeanniey Mullen and David Daniels. Jeanniey and David not only theorize about email's role in our world, but they also apply their efforts to re-create successes that power insights and drive growth. I can say this to you firsthand, because I experience these successes daily through the marketing and advertising message employed by Jeanniey and her team at my companies VIVmag and Zinio. I assure you, email marketing is no small feat, yet Jeanniey and David make it look simple and fun.

As you read this book, you will be immediately drawn into the world of email marketing through Jeanniey and David's wit and charm. Their personalities come shining through, even as they discuss and educate you on the smallest details of the trade. This book speaks to the specifics of email marketing, but it opens your mind to a greater manner of viewing relationships with the consumer.

It is with great pleasure that I write this foreword. I hope you find this book as invigorating, enlightening, and enjoyable as I did.

Very best,
David Gilmour
Chairman, VIVmag
Chairman, Zinio

About David Gilmour

Canadian-born David Gilmour has enjoyed phenomenal success throughout his entrepreneurial career. In 1969, Gilmour and long-time partner Peter Munk founded the South Pacific Hotel Corporation (SPHC), which quickly became the largest hotel chain in the South Pacific. A decade later, the chain was sold, and the partners formed Barrick Gold Corporation, now the most profitable and largest gold-mining firm in the world. They followed this by forming a real estate company called Horsham Corporation, which became TrizecHahn and today is one of the largest publicly traded REIT companies in North America. Gilmour is also the founder of FIJI Water LLC, which in 2004 was the fastest-growing premium beverage in the United States, when he divested himself of the company.

In 1990, Gilmour and his wife, Jill, also opened the Wakaya Club, an exclusive resort on Wakaya Island, Fiji. In 2006, Gilmour founded VIV Publishing LLC, whose first product is an entirely new concept in women's magazines—a health and lifestyle publication called VIV distributed exclusively in digital form.

Gilmour was presented with the U.S. State Department's 2004 Award for Corporate Excellence (ACE) by Secretary of State Colin Powell in recognition of the international growth and success of FIJI Water together with its philanthropic endeavors in Fiji. Gilmour was also awarded "The Order of Fiji" by the president of Fiji, Ratu Sir Kamisese Mara, in 1998 for his commercial and philanthropic achievements in the Fiji Islands.

Introduction

When you stop and think about it, the concept of email as a communication vehicle is a revolutionary one. Long before email became a marketing tool, it was a communication device. The impact that email has had on our culture and our lives is tremendous. Yet, many people forget the vast change in communication that email has produced and think of email marketing simply as a cheap or fast way to sell a product. Email deserves a much higher level of respect.

This book is your guide to understanding the full marketing potential and impact that email can offer to you or your company. It strives to broaden your mind about the opportunities this amazing communication channel offers, and it provides ways to redefine the strategic uses of email as an effective marketing vehicle. And it also, we hope, conveys some of the passion and fervor that the two of us feel about our discipline and hope to share. We have dedicated more than a decade of our lives to evangelizing the role that email currently plays and has the potential to play in our personal and business worlds. Throughout this book, you will be presented with a plethora of real-world and timely examples of what works and does not work, documents and checklists to help you plan your strategy, and questions that will challenge and encourage you to redefine and rethink your approach to leveraging email as a communication and marketing vehicle.

The structure of this book was carefully designed to enable every reader, whether a newcomer to the discipline or a veteran, to walk away feeling a sense of broader understanding and appreciation for email marketing. Our biggest challenge was making sure that all the collective intelligence and insights appropriately educate you in a way that also inspires you to take what you read and build upon it. Just providing simple case studies, examples, and checklists would have been a disservice. Those of you who have experience on the front lines of email marketing know, all too well, how challenging of a craft it is. Email marketers need to understand the strategic elements that drive results and how to avoid the technical faux pas, as well as how to design creative, analyze results, and navigate trends. Email marketing is one of those rare trades that requires specific expertise in many broad categories. Therefore, this book offers an organized and unique approach to crafting a successful email program from start to finish. As you read, you will find yourself being challenged to question your current actions and compare them to our recommendations. As you apply your skills, you will be able to quickly define those areas that will help you excel. This book was designed with the ultimate goal of making you, the reader, successful in your efforts. We want to inspire you to be the best email marketer you can be.

This book strives to provide you with information easily applicable to your specific needs. If it takes you more than ten seconds to understand how this relates to your business or effort, we have failed. There are success stories and failure stories in this book. We think you need to understand both what to do and what to avoid. You should be able to learn as much from our failures as our successes. We want you to walk away from reading this book completely fulfilled.

Who Should Buy This Book

Anyone who wants to send or is currently sending an email marketing campaign should buy this book. In fact, anyone who works for a company where email marketing is being used should buy this book. It doesn't matter which of these describes you:

- Familiar with the basics of email marketing
- Currently sending email marketing campaigns
- Working for a company with a small budget
- The only person doing *any* type of marketing
- Employed by a large or sophisticated company where email plays a small or insignificant role
- An experienced email marketer looking to take things to the next level

This book was written to allow the email marketer at any level to increase their level of understanding. It will also expand the perception and increase the level of respect that email marketing gets for any reader who may not currently be on the front lines of email.

If the authors could wish for one thing to happen once you finish reading this book, it would be that you share this book with a friend or colleague who may not understand or respect what you do. Those of you who work in the field are all too familiar with the cocktail party situation where someone asks you what your job is, and you say, "Email marketing." The reply often is, "Oh, so you send spam?" The next time you hear that, give them this book, and ask them to email us. We understand there is so much more to email marketing, and we appreciate it as well. We are here to help you share in our enthusiasm and help us grow this industry's level of impact even more by enabling better conversations using email.

What's Inside

Here is a glance at what's in each chapter:

Chapter 1: Understanding Email Marketing Today begins with a basic overview of the email marketing industry: the origins of email and its uses, the evolution of the channel into a marketing vehicle, and some of the basic elements of email marketing.

Chapter 2: The Five Critical Elements of Every Email You Create provides an overview of the five key roles that email marketing plays in the broader context of marketing and advertising. In this chapter, there is a clear outline of how email marketing can and should be used to achieve different goals.

Chapter 3: Getting Ready to Build Your Email Marketing Efforts enables you to start at the beginning of the road of creating successful email marketing campaigns. It covers everything from budgeting effectively to ensuring you have the right tools to the basics of strategy design, and then carefully moves you into a comprehensive role of email marketing mastery. This chapter ensures you effectively consider all critical aspects of campaign design.

Chapter 4: What Happens Once You Send Your Email is critical to read. It ensures you know what can happen to derail your campaign but, more important, what you can do to avoid it or deal with the sometimes inevitable. This chapter is one of our favorites!

Chapter 5: Eight Key Drivers of Your Email Campaign equips you with the tactics you typically pick up in bits and pieces from industry trade publications. It provides you with checklists and best practices you can literally rip out and save. You will refer to this chapter over and over again to ensure you have the right elements in place and are following the critical government and compliance requirements.

Chapter 6: Month 1: Preparing Your Email Marketing Strategy gets into the good stuff. This chapter devotes a large amount of time to helping you build or optimize your email marketing strategy. By leveraging many of the current email campaigns in the market right now, you will be able to evaluate and apply those elements that will match your company's capabilities as well as deficiencies.

Chapter 7: Month 2: Ensuring Success as You Launch Your Campaign dives deep into the details of driving results. While Chapter 6 is built for creative and broad thinkers, Chapter 7 fits the cravings of those who love and want details. These details are often critical to driving a campaign result that delivers a strong return on investment. This is not a chapter to breeze over. It is a chapter to spend time with and fully digest.

Chapter 8: Month 3: Adding Bells and Whistles kicks it into high gear. Now that your campaign is out the door and you have some results, this chapter persuades even the most advanced email marketers to rethink their efforts and expand email into new areas. It provides insight into the ways in which consumers have adapted technology into their lives and the most important roles email plays as a personal management vehicle. This chapter is one the bloggers will blog about for years to come.

Chapter 9: Getting Ready for Year 2 and Beyond brings us back to the realities of the real world and sets expectations for what will come next. This chapter will keep you on the right track to ensuring your email marketing efforts not only succeed but are sufficiently supported for continued growth.

In addition, you'll find a remarkably thorough glossary, which will get you up to speed on all the terminology you'll encounter in this book and in other print and online discussions of email marketing; and two appendixes, which list the URLs for every vendor and other resource mentioned in the book and provide two checklists from a series created by the DMA/EEC's Email Design Roundtable.

Finally, from this book's web page at www.emailmarketinganhouraday.com you can download several Excel spreadsheets for calculations discussed in the book as well as a remarkable PDF example of dynamically generated content discussed in Chapter 8.

Throughout the entire book we offer guidance that will hold true regardless of how the technology, the economy, or even the industry changes. We are thrilled to be able to share our passion with you and encourage you to share those areas of the book you enjoy with others. Oh yeah, we love feedback. Good or bad, critical or supportive, we want to hear from you. Please make sure to drop us a line when you can. Thanks, and enjoy your reading!

How to Contact the Authors

We welcome feedback from you about this book or about books you'd like to see from us in the future. You can reach us by writing to experts@emailmarketinganhouraday.com. You can also reach us via our profiles on LinkedIn or Facebook or at either of our day jobs.

Wiley strives to keep you supplied with the latest tools and information you need for your work. Please check its website at www.wiley.com, where we'll post additional content and updates that supplement this book should the need arise. Enter **Email Marketing, An Hour A Day** in the Search box (or type the book's ISBN—**9780470386736**), and click Go to get to the book's update page.

Understanding Email Marketing Today

1

Email marketing *means different things to different people. Some see it as a critical communication link between consumers and the brands they trust and love; others see it as a thinly veiled, intrusive marketing tool. Either way, the email marketing you conduct today faces stiff competition from the email communication that is now the backbone of our digital lifestyles. This chapter starts with a brief history of email marketing and then looks at the value email marketing offers companies today.*

Chapter Contents

How We Got Here

In the early 20th century, noted English mathematician and philosopher Alfred North Whitehead said, "Fundamental progress has to do with the reinterpretation of basic ideas." The progress in communication, both in scope and velocity, that is embodied by the prevalence of email is at its core a reinterpretation of a new way to communicate through the written word.

Email is progress. It is an integrated and indispensable part of all our lives. Its widespread distribution, made possible by the advent of the Internet, lowered the economic barrier to global communication and has made it a vital link to our families, friends, and communities. Just like the printing press 500 years before it, email is an effective and efficient means of mass distribution. Email also provides an easy way to conduct personal one-on-one dialogue.

 Write This Down: Today email is considered the backbone of all digital communications.

Email is the most popular form of asynchronous communication; it touches hundreds of millions of people around the world every day. Consider for a moment that, as of 2008, 73 percent of the North American population has email. In the United States, consumers spend as many hours online as they spend watching television. And out of all the many benefits that such pervasive Internet connectivity affords us, the primary activity that individuals use the Internet for is communicating with others via email. According to the JupiterResearch/Ipsos Insight Individual User Survey (July 2006), 87 percent of consumers in the United States cites email as the top reason for connecting to the Internet.

 Write This Down: In 2007, 234 trillion emails were sent. (Source: Omniture)

Seventy percent of U.S. Internet users has two personal email accounts, indicating that we need more than one email address to keep up with the many benefits of its purpose. The pervasiveness of email is underscored by the volume of messages a person receives. On average, each day email users in the United States receive 41 messages in their primary personal inboxes, with 37 percent saying they receive 31 or more messages daily. Based on the composition of messages they receive in these accounts (Figure 1.1), email users get an average of 10 promotional messages per day in their primary personal inboxes. These numbers are in addition to hundreds of email communications that people receive each week at work.

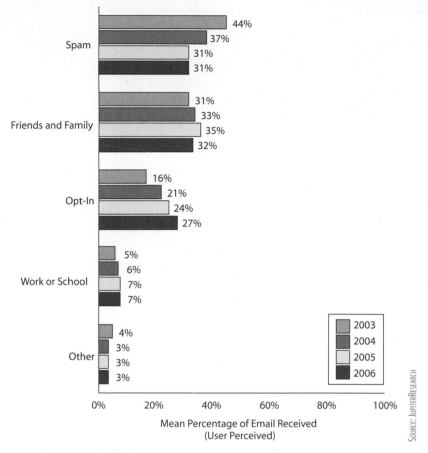

Source: JupiterResearch

Figure 1.1 Share of email by type in a consumer's primary personal inbox, 2003–2006

To summarize those statistics, the share of opt-in permission email in the consumer's primary personal inbox is increasing, and the amount of spam in the inbox is decreasing. According to JupiterResearch, opt-in permission email—mail that consumers have explicitly signed up for—accounted for 16 percent of the email in the consumer's primary personal inbox in 2003 and increased to 27 percent in 2006. During that same time period, the share of spam decreased from 44 percent to 31 percent.

Note: See the glossary for a complete definition of *opt-in* and other email marketing terminology you'll encounter in this book.

Email has brought tremendous efficiency to our lives. For example, it lets us confirm our purchases and it enables us to communicate with merchants. Spending in online retail in the United States will grow at a combined annual growth rate (CAGR)

of 11 percent to reach $215 billion in 2012, which will generate 5 billion pre- and post-sale email contacts for U.S. retailers by that same year. Consumers can easily archive their transactions, and email can be a more efficient form of customer service than calling a merchant and sitting on hold. The value that we place on email cannot be dismissed.

 Write This Down: In 2006, 49 percent of all personal communication in the United Kingdom was written via email. (Source: Forrester)

With the massive amounts of email that we now receive and rely on daily to communicate, you might wonder, How did we get here? How did email become so powerful that it has changed the way the world communicates?

It did not start with Al Gore creating the Internet; he simply brought the U.S. Congress's attention—and funding—to this new communication medium when it was still in its infancy. Email originated with a group of inspired and hardworking individuals as a forum where professors, technology luminaries, and government officials could share ideals and conversations. As with all great ideas, their efforts started small and have now created a connected, global, worldwide society.

We can trace the roots of the commercial Internet and email marketing to 1969, during the Cold War, when the U.S. Defense Department created ARPANET, a computer-based messaging system designed to survive a nuclear attack. In its earliest form, this network was nothing more than what is commonly known as a file system where one person could post a note for another person to see in a folder.

By the early 1980s, the network had expanded to a small group of universities, all sharing the power of connected digital messaging. Getting connected to an early Internet service like Usenet was no simple matter (Figure 1.2). The computers they used in those early days were "mainframes," much bigger but much less powerful than the desktops and laptops we have today. At about the same time, the development of increasingly smaller and more powerful microprocessor chips was beginning to make the first personal computers available to the masses. As we all know, the PC quickly became essential to businesses of all kinds, as modern user-friendly software was developed. In the late 1980s, the first commercial providers emerged, such as CompuServe and MCI, and the consumer face of what would be forever known as the Internet soon followed.

This new phenomenon in personal connectivity quickly resulted in conversations around the water cooler such as, "Are you online?" and, "You can find me in the moondance Usenet group." This created a new world of communication, opening the Internet up not just for personal communication but for businesses as well. Email marketing soon emerged as one of the most profitable and effective forms of marketing.

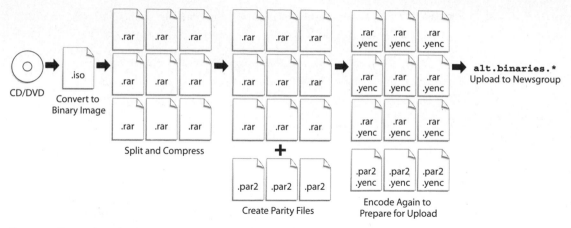

Figure 1.2 The complicated process of uploading content and messages to Usenet

Over the past ten years, email marketing has grown into one of the most flexible and in-demand applications and disciplines of the Internet economy. According to a study by comScore in August 2007, the worldwide web mail market includes more than half a billion people. The Radicati Group projected that there were nearly 1.2 billion hosted email inboxes worldwide as of October 2007, a number that is expected to rise to 1.6 billion by 2011. Email is still an emerging marketing medium, and the industry is young. It's not too late to start leveraging email, and you can use this book to optimize your current practices.

Although few people might have expected it in the beginning, email is now an integrated part of hundreds of millions of lives. It is more than marketing; it is a link to family, friends, and community. It is the lifeblood of the Internet.

What Email Means to Your Audience

Now that you know the history of email and its potential growth implications, you are ready to consider what email and email marketing mean to your audience. This is a critical element to master. Most consumers do not think in terms of marketing emails they receive and personal emails they receive; they differentiate in terms of personal value and relevancy. In fact, the term *email marketing* may not even resonate with your reader. Consumers love email messages that they feel enhance their lives; here's what one said at a presentation we gave:

> *My favorite types of emails are the notices from my online photo-sharing program letting me know my friends have posted new photos. It makes me feel really connected to them and makes me happy.*
>
> PARTICIPANT, Email Experience Council keynote presentation:
> "The Value of Email, in the Eyes of the User," 2008

To a smart marketer, understanding and embracing the way our readers consume and relate to email are critical in helping drive success for our marketing programs.

The Five Types of Email

Spending time improving the "in-business" tactical elements will not significantly improve your email marketing efforts if you have not first effectively defined *why* you are embarking on an email marketing campaign, *what* the ultimate message you want to resonate with your reader is, and *how* your reader will be able to demonstrate that they have not only understood your message but also acted on it.

Are you ready for the five key types of email you need to know about to create a marketing success? OK then, let's get down to business.

We believe that out of all the thousands of types of emails you can design, or hundreds of thousands of permutations of creative, i.e. images and markting copy, for your messages, you will ever create only five key types of email messages:

- Awareness
- Consideration
- Conversion
- Product usage
- Retention and loyalty

As shown in Figure 1.3, these types represent different stages in the overall email campaign. Although the stages are generally distinct, they may overlap over time as your customer and prospects move through the various stages.

As outlined in Table 1.1, each type plays a unique role in helping a company drive home its brand or marketing message with a customer; each incites one of five types of actions. You can effectively choose which type of emails you should send to a customer only once you have identified *why* you are sending that customer an email. To help you understand this point better, the next sections explain in more depth the five types of email that can be sent.

Figure 1.3 The five types of email

▶ **Table 1.1** How the Five Types of Email Work

Type	Communication Goal	Email Purpose	Example of Email Usage
Awareness	To make customer aware of Company X by building imagery	To bridge media (online and offline) to identify interest	Ad placement in email publications (and other email-based initiatives), or using co-registration to deliver high brand-value messaging to the inbox
Consideration	To bring Company X into the consideration set (top two or three brands in the category) by consistently promoting the tangible benefits	To accelerate interest and qualification through benefits immersion	Capture opt-in from media interest; use email to push people through the tunnel to conversion faster
Conversion	To close the deal through a dialogue that overcomes barriers to purchase	To drive customers to sales channels (for example, call center) for conversion	Embed a click-to-call-in email communications that drive customers to call center
Product Usage	To stimulate interest in other products and services	To drive engagement with brand, establish advocacy, and set the stage to up-sell/cross-sell	Dynamically populate email offers based on business rules
Loyalty	To broaden and deepen the relationship to promote renewals	To foster and deepen the relationship for lifetime value (LTV) impact	Deliver value-added information (for example, winter driving tips for an auto company) via email

Awareness

Forget email marketing for a second, and think about the goal of creating brand or product awareness with your consumer. At this stage, you are simply trying to create awareness that you exist in a consumer's mind-set.

Now let's get back to email. Think about how your email campaign—from segmentation to creative and copy design to the call to action and even reporting analysis—will change if the main goal of the email is not to sell but to drive awareness of a brand, product, or service. Awareness-focused emails often do not work alone. They are meant to drive a recipient to another location, offline or online, to get more information, or to be engaged with the brand or product. Apple does this really well, as you can see in Figure 1.4. Recently, Apple launched its latest version of the iPhone. You can see from this creative that the iPhone is not going to be ready for one month. Therefore, the purpose of this email is simply to make consumers aware of something they may be interested in and put the thought into their heads that more messaging is coming so that they will be more receptive to the next message.

The main goal of our first-tier email programs is to drive someone to the call center to get more engaged with one of our representatives.

We don't expect a closed sale on first contact.

SYD JONES, director, IBM

Figure 1.4 An awareness-building email from Apple before the release of the iPhone

Consideration

Once you have a consumer's attention (usually at the point where they have been exposed to your product or service multiple times), you need to think about a new type of email: email messages that create and drive consideration. Unlike awareness-related emails, consideration emails contain educational elements that actively move the reader toward taking an action to buy or try your product. These emails focus on specific benefits of the product and in many cases provide a means for people to self-qualify themselves as viable prospects. Chapter 2 discusses the most successful elements of these types of emails.

Zinio Labs, the innovation division of Zinio, which is the digital publishing services company that one of the authors works for, creates new ways to read digital publications in a mobile environment. When Zinio comes out with a new product, it is often free to test. The purpose of its emails is to drive consumer awareness *and* consideration for a new way to read publications. The email in Figure 1.5 is a great example of a message sent with the latest upgrade of its mobile application.

> *Drive all the potential candidates you want; if they aren't qualified, I consider it a waste of marketing dollars.*

> FIONA CONNEL, account director, Ogilvy One Worldwide

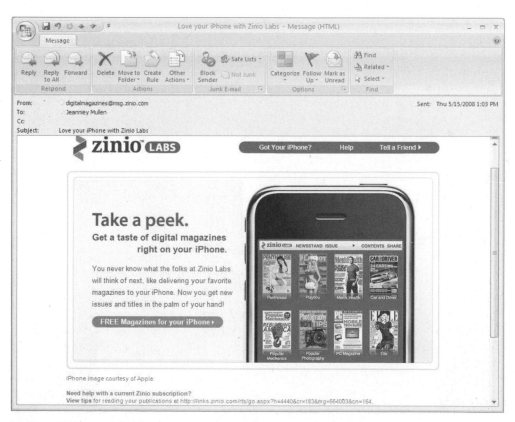

Figure 1.5 Zinio Labs consideration email

Conversion

Conversion emails are the most common form of email marketing messages that a person receives (outside of personal communications).

These messages are your standard, hard-hitting, "Buy it now" and "Sign up today" emails. But email marketer, beware! These emails can be the worst performers when you evaluate your return on investment (ROI). Conversion emails work well when the reader is already in the mood and mind-set to purchase something from your company. Send this message to them at any other time, and you run the risk of alienating them from engaging in a future conversation.

 Write This Down: The secret of an effective conversion email is that it is sent only after you receive a "buying signal" from your reader. Even in the world of email, these buying signals exist; you just need to know what to look for.

Most companies that send conversion-based emails effectively either have a well-known product or service or are offering something price-sensitive or as an impulse buy. Catalog companies typically send these types of emails to subscribers who have purchased from them in the past. Travel and leisure companies also send many of these types of emails in an attempt to get people to buy when they are in the mood. Figure 1.6 shows a great example of a direct-marketing conversion email from Hotels.com.

Product Usage

After the initial sale has been made, many email marketers get lazy, stop working, or flip the responsibility of emails to another department within the company. Don't fall into this trap!

For example, when you purchase something from Amazon, you immediately receive a confirmation email. Inside that email are some recommendations of other products that people who bought the same thing you did also purchased. A week later, you receive an email asking you to complete a survey about how happy you are with the product you have purchased and, again, subtly recommending products "others like you" have tried. This sneaky but clever service-oriented approach to the email cross-sell/up-sell works more times than you can imagine.

The bottom line is, once someone purchases your product, they are going to use it. And whether they like the product or not, they will be talking about their experience, possibly online. Your best bet is to keep the lines of communication and influence open and capitalize on this effort; by sending emails as they are using the product, you can help soothe upset consumers or expand the reach of loyalists.

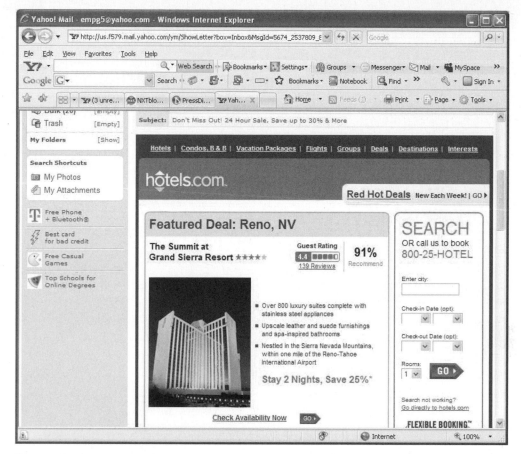

Figure 1.6 Hotels.com conversion email

Write This Down: Consumers are 127 percent more likely to purchase something else from your company immediately after they have completed their initial purchase. (Source: DMA)

If you are looking for a leader in this category, look no further than Amazon. The email shown in Figure 1.7 is a fantastic example of not only confirming a purchase but also inviting feedback and setting someone up for a cross-sell and/or up-sell email. Conversion emails do a fantastic job of creating a feeling of a true reciprocal relationship between the customer and the company. Pair this with the recent good feeling a customer gets when they buy something they love, and you have the makings of a win-win situation.

Figure 1.7 Usage email from Amazon

Loyalty

Similar to usage emails, loyalty emails are sent only after a sale or transaction has taken place between you and your customer. The difference is that usage emails drive the customer to use the product or service they just purchased, and the emails encourage the reader to share their resulting feedback with friends and family. This helps capitalize on the "high" of buying something they value to leverage viral marketing. Loyalty emails, however, have a much longer life span. They need to keep someone engaged with your product or service for the life of your relationship with them (or until it is time to make the next purchase).

Is this type of email important? One thing is for certain: With more than 41 emails popping into your consumer's inbox on a daily basis, you need loyalty email to keep your brand on your consumer's mind.

The role of loyalty emails is simple: keep your company and your company's sense of value on top of the consumer's mind. Often referred to as *e-newsletters*, loyalty emails don't sell, they celebrate!

> *My monthly email newsletter is a critical component of reducing attrition and driving exhilaration.*

> RICHARD MAGGIOTTO, CEO, Zinio

Women's lifestyle e-magazine VIVmag does a good job of setting up loyalty emails in between issues. In the email shown in Figure 1.8, you will notice that the content is not too sales-oriented but more focused on building the relationship and reinforcing to readers that they made a good choice in purchasing this product or service in the first place.

Figure 1.8 Loyalty email from VIV

Recapping Three Key Points

Before we move on to talk about the economic impact email marketing can have on your business, we'll recap what you've learned so far:

- Email did not start as a marketing channel; it was a way in which to create real-time communications that eliminated geographic barriers.

- Email, in a consumer's mind, is not about marketing; it is about personal relevance. Personal and business messages are combined inside an inbox and fight for attention based on how effectively they can positively impact the reader's life.

- When all is said and done, effective email marketing doesn't start with the most beautifully designed message; it begins by getting one of the five types of email into the consumer's inbox and driving the right reaction from the reader.

Understanding the Economic Impact of Email

Let's talk money. As you'll see while learning the nuts and bolts of it throughout this book, email marketing is a demanding, high-energy effort. Does it really have a strong payoff?

We have a secret to share with you here: Email is driving your offline and online growth! It's true. Although many marketers have focused on revenue and sales being driven from other channels, such as the Web, stores, and even direct-response TV ads, it is email that has evolved over the years to be the "super influencer."

 Write This Down: People who are registered to receive email marketing messages from your company will purchase an average of 167 percent more than those people in your marketing database who are not receiving email. (Source: Ogilvy)

Email is the most cost-efficient marketing medium available to organizations today. For example, marketers who leverage subscriber behavior and use that data to segment and target their subscribers deliver mailings that are nine times more profitable than their peers who simply broadcast. The Direct Marketing Association reports that every $1 spent on email marketing drives more than $48 in revenue. A different study in 2008 by Datran Media found that 80 percent of marketers report email is their strongest-performing media buy ahead of search and display advertising.

However, the lesson here is not to see the profitability of email simply as a means of generating revenue; you can also leverage email to reduce operating expenses.

For example, brokerage firm Charles Schwab discovered that by sending out personalized end-of-market-day summaries to their clients within 90 minutes of the market call, it could reduce the massive number of inbound calls to its call center. Schwab sends hundreds of thousands of personalized email messages to clients, including details about stocks in their portfolios and relevant news about those holdings. Since rolling out this campaign, Schwab has reduced calls (costing from $5 to $10 apiece) and raised the profitability of its online customers by more than 30 percent. To date, this program has delivered an additional $635 in profit per subscriber per year to the company.

Although Schwab improved profitability, it used email primarily as a cost-reduction lever and not purely a revenue generator. To understand what types of tactics and effort you should put into your email marketing efforts, you must first understand what the value of an email address is to your organization.

> **Write This Down:** Based on a mailing of 4.1 million messages and typical response metrics, the value of an active email address is $118.09. (Source: Email Experience Council ROI calculator)

You can calculate this number in several ways, including the following:

Acquisition Cost as the Email Address Value One simple way to determine the value of an email address is to use the cost of acquiring that address. Flipping that cost to a positive value will tell you the value of that email address.

Monetary Value per Client Another popular method that retailers use to determine email value is to look at the monetary value of that client. Using the total annual spending of an email subscriber will highlight their spending value. Dividing the total revenue generated from your email subscribers by the total number of recipients will provide you with a per-subscriber revenue number that you can use as a proxy for value.

Ready to get going? We are, too. But to help reinforce what you've learned about email marketing so far, we're concluding this and subsequent chapters with a brief self-test.

Test Your Knowledge

We've just thrown a lot of terminology and other information at you; check your progress by seeing how many of these questions you can answer correctly. A score of 4 out of 4 will ensure you are on your way to email marketing success.

- What percentage of the U.S. online consumer population cites email as the top reason they connect to the Internet?

- Who is credited with creating email in 1972?

- What are the five roles of email?

- What is one way you can measure the economic impact of your email marketing program?

The Five Critical Elements of Every Email You Create

2

In the first chapter, we explored the five categories of email messages you will send: awareness, consideration, conversion, usage, and loyalty. This chapter focuses on the critical elements to consider for any of these types when designing an email campaign. To become a skilled email marketer, you need to understand how to continue improving results over time. This chapter will help, and we hope it quickly becomes one you bookmark for future reference.

Chapter Contents
Creating Brand Impact
Adding Intelligence to Your Design
Driving the Purchase
Creating Transactional/Service Messages
Adding Viral Marketing Elements

Creating Brand Impact

How much brand impact does your email create? Regardless of the purpose of your email message, one thing is for sure: your email message is going to have an impact on, and be impacted by, the strength of your company's brand. If this impact is good, your email program will enhance credibility and create a sense of trust with your consumer, which are major components of brand equity. This moves them one step closer to engaging with your organization. If this impact is bad, you could very well have single-handedly ruined the chances your reader will ever do business with your company again.

How Strong Is a Brand? A Lesson from History, Matey

As Captain John Smith looked out the starboard side of his ship, he felt his heart beating faster. Land! He saw land! What a phenomenal feeling. He knew it would only be a matter of days before he could see his baby daughter again, kissing her and holding her in his arms. Captain John Smith turned and walked to the other side of the ship.

As he looked out the port side of his ship, he felt his heart beating faster. But this time, it was for a very different reason. *This* is what he saw:

No words, no tag lines, not even a sound—just a brand image. This image very quickly registered in the captain's head: death and destruction. The brand of the pirate was very clear: "We are here to kill and rob you. We will succeed. And with every success, our brand will grow stronger."

The example we just shared with you would have occurred long before email even existed. But it is the clearest representation of the power and reach of an existing brand's influence that we can imagine. The brand expectation and influence that is carried into your reader's inbox is no different. At the first sight of a company name or logo, the reader will make a certain set of presumptions about the purpose and strength of the content contained within the email. This is a critical element for every email marketer to remember. Email design will influence your broader brand equity, and your company's brand equity will influence engagement with your email campaigns. You can't separate the two.

Determining How Much Brand Equity Your Emails Carry

Every email that reaches an inbox will be given some sort of consideration. Typically, a recipient will look at the From name and/or the subject line to determine whether the message is worth opening immediately, later, or not at all. Although many studies have been conducted to attempt to determine whether more attention is given to the From name or the subject line, their results remain inconclusive. Many factors are involved. For example, the devices on which emails are read and the surrounding environment in which emails are read both play roles in determining which of these two critical areas of the email receive attention. That said, determining how much brand equity your emails currently carry is a critically important element of your email marketing success.

Heatmapping to Determine Your Existing Brand Equity

It's nearly impossible to determine existing brand equity in a "live" manner; you will need to develop a test. One cost-effective way of determining brand equity is by conducting an eye-tracking test called *heatmapping*. In this process, a sampling of representative readers is exposed to an email inbox containing multiple messages. The order in which they look at different items in the inbox and the length of time the readers spend looking at each are noted by recording the viewing behavior using eye-tracking machines. The results are aggregated, and a *heatmap* is created, clearly showing areas of influence. Essentially, heatmapping shows how long people spend looking at your contents to determine whether they are interested in your brand. Although you cannot calculate the level of brand equity you have with them from this, you will find out whether your brand resonates with your viewer—whether it has equity/value.

In the example shown in Figure 2.1, you can see how people process the inbox for a series of emails sent.

Regardless of the types of messages listed in this inbox, the name of the company consistently gets attention. Well-known company names generate strong brand equity for their target sector. If you were looking to increase your skills in a target area and a well-known company in that sector sent you an email, without knowing what it is said inside, wouldn't you give higher consideration to opening it than to an email from an unknown sweepstakes verification company?

Figure 2.1 An inbox heatmap

The cost of heatmapping services can range anywhere from a few thousand dollars per test to more than $100,000 annually depending on the size of the study, the specialized audience requirements, and the number of tests you want to run. That said, even if you opt for a small study, we can promise you the ROI will be worth it. If you do decide to move forward with heatmapping, we offer you one caution: Although a number of companies claim to provide heatmapping services, you really need to ask what this entails. In this chapter (and throughout the book), we refer to heatmapping as the service provided by companies that actually captures the reflection of viewers' retinal activity as they look at pages online. Some companies will tell you they provide heatmapping services but will do so by aggregating click activity and showing you heatmaps of where people click. Although that information is helpful, it is not what you want.

An effective heatmapping study relies on the results of being able to capture where people look and in what order they see your page elements. Currently, the top two companies providing heatmapping services around the world are Think Eyetracking (www.thinkeyetracking.com) and Eyetools (www.eyetools.com).

Why Understanding Brand Equity Matters

Understanding your brand equity prior to designing an email marketing efforts is key. It lets you know how much of a challenge you will face to get your email opened, let alone read. Much of the success of your email marketing efforts depends on getting your emails opened. A company with a low level of brand awareness or equity (aka trust) will have a lower open rate. A big mistake many people new to email marketing make is to think that the offer is the most critical part of your program design. In reality, the most important part of your campaign is going to change based on the level of brand awareness and equity. If no one opens your email because they do not know or trust your brand, your email marketing program cannot succeed.

What to Do When Your Brand Equity Is Low

If your brand equity is low, it's most likely for one of two reasons:

- Your company is new and does not have an established brand.
- Your brand carries a sense of low value/trust.

New companies have an interesting challenge. They have low brand equity simply because they are not known products. Whether a new company is a new player in an existing field (for example, a new retail store) or a new company introducing a new concept to the world (for example, when ATM cards first came onto the market), it must follow the same strategies as an existing company that has low levels of equity with the consumer base.

The bottom line is, if your brand equity is low, your approach to email must be very different than if it were higher. Since you cannot rely on your email getting strong open rates, you will need to focus on establishing brand equity and a connection when people are opting in to your email programs. In this case, a combination of a preference center and a welcome email is critical. That is, on the web page where someone is about to provide an email address, you should clearly show the options for email types they have and the frequency of those messages; this will help rebuild trust and credibility. Following up with a welcome email that clearly restates the value proposition for agreeing to receive the emails and the expected frequency will also help increase response.

> **Write This Down:** Do not expect strong results where there is low brand equity or awareness.

Travel and leisure retailers seem to be the furthest along in building equity enhancement programs. American Airlines is one of the best in its class when it comes to reinforcing brand equity through its preference center and welcome emails. As you can see in Figure 2.2, the airline follows all the critical best practices.

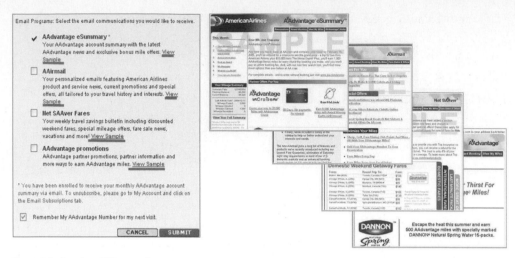

Figure 2.2 American Airlines preference center

Adding Intelligence to Your Design

Once you get beyond the inbox and your email has been opened, your brand equity is still important. Every time a reader opens an email, they have an expectation for content or offers based on prior online and offline brand experiences. Your job at this point is to make them feel like you've read their mind, anticipating exactly what they need. This is a challenge you need to be prepared for when you enter the world of email marketing. How can you be ready?

Basic Elements of Intelligent Email

Creating an effective email requires that you start with a clear understanding of *consumer reality.* What is consumer reality? It is what the consumer is thinking/expecting when they open your email. It is *not* what the marketing department, or people who work for your company, assume will happen.

You should keep in mind four basic elements of effective email whenever designing an email marketing strategy:

- **Don't assume your email recipient has seen your TV, print, or in-store ad.** Cute extensions of a TV spot or print ad in an email, without reference to the original ad, can confuse the reader and hurt the brand. Once, a high-tech company running a business-to-business (B2B) campaign had a funny TV spot showing a forklift emptying a roomful of servers to make way for the server of the future. The company followed this with an email showing a photo of the forklift by itself, next to the company logo. When this arrived in the prospects' inboxes, the readers wanted to know whether the company was selling forklifts now.

- **Your email recipient doesn't read all your emails.** Jeanniey once learned this the hard way. The organization she founded, the Email Experience Council (EEC), sends weekly emails. Each week, the staff would slave over creating new content so it would seem fresh and new. Little did they know that the people who receive these emails have lives. Some weeks, the recipients were on vacation and didn't read their EEC email; other weeks they were out sick or working on a big project. In any event, once the EEC staff saw that key messages and offers were receiving low response, they did some testing. The average email recipient needed to receive a key message in three emails in a row in order to actually view the content once; this garnered the highest response. Remembering that your email subscriber doesn't read your emails is a tough reality to swallow, but it pays off in the end.

- **The copy in your email might not work.** This is one of our favorite elements to share with people. Often, you or your copywriters will work hard to ensure that the copy flows well and has a rhythm to it that invigorates your reader. Email copy is poetic, right? Reality check: If the copy you are using in your email does not align with the search phrases people are using when they visit your site, you are missing the significance. For example, when IBM first launched its laptops, it decided to call them ThinkPads. This was a brand name that gave IBM a perceived competitive edge. Much of the marketing referred to the product simply as a "ThinkPad," not as a laptop computer. But outside the IBM walls, when a person was looking for a laptop, either on the Web at large or on the IBM site, they mainly typed in the search word *laptop*. Since the ThinkPads weren't referred to as laptops, the search results were minimal.

> **Note:** Put a bookmark in the book here, and call the person who has your search engine results. See how closely they align.

The phrases received in your search box on your website, or even through paid search, reflect the phrases that people associate with your brand. Keeping this in mind when you are writing email copy will move the impact of your message up a few notches by creating a synergy between what your reader reads and what they were thinking.

- **The first time your email is read, it may not be read in the email inbox.** With the proliferation of devices people carry with them to enhance their digital lifestyle, there is an increasing chance that your email message will not be first viewed in the email inbox. An RSS notification may be sent to a reader; an SMS alert may be sent to a mobile device; a BlackBerry, iPhone, or other handheld unit may hold the message; or your message may be diverted to a social networking application. Handheld devices process email content much differently than your computer inbox does. This can cause reading and clicking challenges. In addition to the device-specific challenges, consumers who are reading "on the go" often give a different level of attention and focus to their messages. Keeping these elements in mind can be helpful to you.

A 2007 survey by JupiterResearch asked consumers what technologies they had used in the past year for personal communication, instead of email:

- Eighteen percent stated social networks.
- Twenty-seven percent stated SMS texting.
- Currently only 4 percent of email users in the United States subscribe to RSS feeds.

When creating your content, know that size restrictions, the ability to read or interact with messages, and simply the amount of attention given to the content being read "on the run" all play a role in the way the reader digests your email message.

Using This Insight to Your Advantage

To help you gain an advantage from the insights we have shared so far, we would like to ask you to start thinking about your email campaigns differently. Do not assume that your email message will be viewed by your reader in an inbox setting, where they can give your message full attention. More and more people are reading emails in a mobile environment. Also, you should assume that by the time someone receives an email from you, they have probably already seen or heard about your company through some other media element. Maybe it was your website or an ad banner through a search. Yes, when designing your email effort, begin with the assumption that before your email arrived, your recipient may have been influenced by other media pertaining to that particular product or service, whether online, or via search or mobile. Also assume that once they read your email, they are not going to buy right away and will go to the Web to search for customer reviews, competitive products, and more.

Now, use these assumptions to take your email program up another notch and create an email that resonates with your reader as not just effective but insightful. After you read the next section of the book, you will be able to, so keep reading.

Email/Search/Display Integration

Not only does the recipient have certain expectations about your email just by looking at the From name and subject line, but once they open it, they are reading the content with biases relating to what they may or may have not been exposed to through other marketing and advertising elements your company is running.

That said, you might not even recognize that you hold the key to looking like a rock star in your customer's mind by integrating your email program with your search and display programs. There are two approaches to creating this success: you can start with your in-house file or start with your display ads. Either way is phenomenal. Here is how they work.

Starting with Your In-House File

To help visualize this process, pretend you are sending an email to recipe enthusiasts:

1. When someone receives an email from you, drop a non-personally identifiable tracking cookie onto their computer (not the same cookie you use to detect whether an email has been opened).

2. When this reader goes to your sites search, conducts a web search, or clicks a display ad, you will find out what they are engaging with (for example, fried chicken recipes).

3. Use this information, including the words they used in the search box and/or the copy on the banner they clicked, to create a dynamic content block in your next house email that offers them access to the content they have been searching for (for example, "New fried chicken recipes now available.")

Starting with External Intelligence

This process is similar to the previous process, but it begins with the cookie drop on the search landing pages and/or display ads:

1. When this reader goes to your site search, conducts a web search, or clicks a display ad, you will see what they are engaging with (for example, fried chicken recipes).

2. When they land on your site and sign up for your emails, what you've learned is passed along and included in the welcome email. You can now speak with certainty in the welcome email to create expectations and offers that appear to have read the new subscriber's mind. (For example, "Thanks for signing up for our recipe emails! We hope you are a fried chicken fan, because that is our feature recipe this month.")

Figure 2.3 illustrates the workflow for both scenarios. Based on proprietary research the authors have conducted in this area, companies that use this type of strategy are seeing results increase more than 300 percent compared to less targeted content strategies.

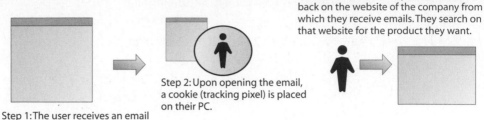

Step 3: Later, the same user goes to the Internet to search for a product and ends up back on the website of the company from which they receive emails. They search on that website for the product they want.

Step 2: Upon opening the email, a cookie (tracking pixel) is placed on their PC.

Step 1: The user receives an email to which they have subscribed.

Step 4: The company uses the search intelligence it captures to insert a dynamic image that matches the recent search results.

Step 5: The user receives this email and buys because the content appears to match their current needs.

Figure 2.3 Integrating email and search

Driving the Purchase

The content in the email isn't enough. Intelligent emails will go a long way toward making your reader feel as though they truly have a relationship with your brand and your company, but by themselves they are nowhere near enough to make your email marketing program successful.

An interesting phenomenon is taking place in the world of email these days. As an email marketer, you need to not only be aware of it but also learn how to master it. We have finally hit the point where the volume of emails in our personal and business lives has surpassed our ability to digest the content with any high level of comprehension.

Write This Down: JupiterResearch reports that 26 percent of the emails consumers receive in their primary personal inboxes are marketing messages that they opted in to receive.

JupiterResearch says the average person receives 41 emails a day in their inbox. We are going out on a limb to say that anyone in the email marketing field probably receives three times that number (on a good day). Email readers are now challenged with going through their emails as quickly as they can, whenever and wherever they can, just to keep up with the deluge.

Sadly, the effect of this barrage of email content is that it's much more difficult to conduct a quality conversation with your reader. This phenomenon is often referred to as *email ADD*, as in "email attention deficit disorder." It is estimated that for every three words you type in an email, only one is read or retained. This is a scary reality for consumer marketing emails, and it's even scarier in the business world.

Reality Check: Email ADD and the Impact on the Industry

Here's a story from Jeanniey.

After recently accepting a new job and traveling on business, I received an email from a colleague inviting me out to dinner. I was thrilled.

The invitation was in an email that came as a reply to a thread we were in on an email user group. The header information looked like this:

```
From: John Doe  [mailto:jdoe@mymailsystems.com]
Sent: Thursday, February 14, 2008 10:15 PM
To: davidandjeanniey@gmail.com
Subject: RE: [Inbox Insiders] So...How'd everyone like the show
```

I was so excited to receive the invitation that I did not even realize that the subject line was not specifically about dinner. Later that day, when the same colleague emailed me the location and time to meet, he simply replied to the same string, with the same subject line.

Being extremely busy in the new job, I decided to read the user group emails later and went on with my day. At the end of the day, I figured he had gotten busy and couldn't meet, because I hadn't gotten an email with further details about dinner, so I made other plans.

One week later, while cleaning out my old emails, I actually read the rest of the email thread and saw a phenomenal evening event planned for a group of us. Needless to say, I missed it.

After emailing him to apologize profusely by sending a subject line with this header:

```
From: Jeanniey Mullen
Sent: Sunday, March 02, 2008 1:29 PM
To: 'John Doe'
Subject: I changed this subject line -
```

I received this email in reply:

```
From: John Doe [mailto:jdoe@mymailsystems.com]
Sent: Monday, March 03, 2008 4:48 PM
To: Jeanniey Mullen
Subject: Meeting up — WAS: RE: I changed this subject line -
FYI we have a little convention we use internally which I should start using
more — when a thread (like "so how'd everyone like the show") takes on a
different direction (like "meet for drinks"), MyMailSystems people tend to
change the subject line as above, w/ the new more relevant one first, then a
dash, and "WAS:" in front of the old, no longer meaningful subject line.
```

Noting the change to the subject line so people understood what was being discussed was a fantastic suggestion and one that could have saved time and effort—and kept me from missing a fantastic evening.

Waging the War Against Email ADD

In our digitized world, email ADD is not going to get better. Gaining an understanding of the implications of email ADD is only the starting point. Knowing how to work within constraints to define effective and successful messages is the only way to gain control of the conversation back.

Here are three important techniques:

- **Always put new content in context before the user hits Delete.** If your email reader has no context for the message they are reading, your message equity is at risk. In other words, if you send an email to Joe with fresh content and no mental notes for him to refer to (reminders of prior conversations, links, and so on) and Joe scrolls through the email on his BlackBerry while boarding a train to D.C., your message equity has dropped to 33 percent or less.

  Conversely, if your message has associated notes (content callouts, links, or other information), you stand a much higher chance of having your message resonate and be responded to.

- **Define the email's benefits in terms of the reader's long-term goals.** If your email does not clearly and concisely state why the message will help the reader achieve their long-term goals and fulfill future needs, it is at high risk for low comprehension. Good examples might be, "Get access when you need it" or "Save this message for when you need to…"

  Creating language that is clear and concise and that conveys how your reader will benefit in the long run will pay off many times.

- **Leverage attention nodes.** An *attention node* is some type of formatting in the email that clearly grabs the reader's attention. In marketing messages, this is most commonly done with a callout box, action tag/button, or other imagery. In a text for personal email, attention nodes can be any creative use of spacing or character keys that help clearly drive where the attention needs to be placed. For example, you can use three asterisks (***) to signify importance. Generally, we are lucky if more than the content in the attention node is read.

Combine these efforts by also leveraging the power of three, and you will succeed. Based on proprietary testing we've done over the past ten years, three is the optimal number of times you should put a message in front of your readers to maximize clicks. Three is also the number of emails a new subscriber will read to determine whether they will stay engaged with your brand's email program. And finally, three is the average number of email subscriptions a reader opts in to for a given category.

Acknowledging that every email (personal or business-related) will need to not only battle reputation, relevance, and delivery but now also email ADD, and understanding how to leverage the power of three to help you do that, can move you three steps ahead in creating a successful conversation.

Beyond the Email Content: What You Need to Know

Once you master the ways you can battle into and then within the inbox and have your message read, you still are only halfway to success. The key to a completely optimized email program is to remember that the main purpose of your email is to drive action at another location—a physical location, a virtual location, or even a location someone visualizes in their mind.

In any event, you need to remember a critical element here: The branding and content in your emails must match the same type of branding and content on the final destination pages. The entire user experience needs to be consistent in order to maintain interest and action.

Figure 2.4 shows an email from the cable service Optimum that demonstrates how doing it out of context can turn a great email into a poor driver of performance. The creative content of this email is strong; it has a clear message and purpose. However, when you click the link, you become lost in the landing page, which has ten links and a different logo, which makes you feel like you've landed in an entirely new and unrelated location.

Figure 2.4 This email (top) promotes a sweepstakes, which links to a rewards microsite (bottom) with a different logo and nine other choices that could distract the reader.

In some cases, these types of inconsistent user paths have generated up to an 80 percent loss in sales. Abandonment is high when your reader isn't guided in a simple and consistent manner. The right way to guarantee success is to maintain consistency between images and copy. And above all, remember that your email creative has to match the creative and messaging of your broader brand. This is the link that holds strong as people leave your email and move into your website or retail store.

In some cases, this can be difficult to do. Figure 2.5 shows an example of a high-end women's digital e-magazine that does a phenomenal job of driving from one location to another and back again.

Vivmag Cover

Vivmag Email

Vivmag Website

Figure 2.5 VIV successfully drives the reader from email to home page to magazine pages.

The take-away from this section is that compelling content alone isn't going to maintain success in your email program, even if it is combined with intelligence and targeting. Using imagery that maintains, manages, and boosts the brand imagery of your email experience is crucial.

Creating Transactional/Service Messages

If you had a wise old marketing mentor, one thing they probably told you was, "Hit them while their credit card is still out." Although the clear and consistent combination of intelligence, copy, and creative are critical for most email messages, one type of email message allows you to stray, just a bit, from the harsh standards of strategic, creative, and tactical design. This email is the *transactional*, or *service-based*, email.

Transactional/service-based emails are not used primarily for marketing purposes. Their purpose is to inform or confirm the reader that an action they have taken has actually happened. The intent of these messages has always been more in line with the types of messages you receive from a customer service division of a company than a marketing division. To maintain this distinction and make sure the content inside these emails remains focused on service intent, the federal government enacted the CAN-SPAM Act of 2003. This law, which took effect January 1, 2004, and was amended effective July 7, 2008, is discussed in detail in Chapter 5, but we can summarize its most important requirements here:

The CAN-SPAM Act requires that businesses do the following:

- Clearly label commercial email as advertising
- Use a truthful and relevant subject line
- Use a legitimate return email address
- Provide a valid physical address
- Provide a working opt-out option
- Process opt-out requests within 10 business days

Although the intent of these emails may have been service-oriented, many crafty marketers use these emails to drive cross-sell or up-sell purchases. Why? It's because, in the reader's mind, these messages confirm an action or purchase recently made. Therefore, they are read faster and at much higher rates than marketing messages. In some cases, these emails are read to confirm that the purchase activity just conducted was recorded appropriately. Could you imagine not opening the email from your favorite airline confirming your purchase of a ticket to Hawaii, only to find out when you arrive at the airport that your ticket is to Newark? Federak Express seems to have figured out how to manage the fine line between marketing emails and transactional emails. In Figure 2.6, you can see an example of a transactional message that also showcases other ways you can work with Federal Express without crossing the line and making it appear that the main purpose of the email is to sell you additional products and services.

Write This Down: Seventy percent of transactional emails are opened and read within three hours of receipt.

Transactional emails may not be the most beautiful emails, but they do seem to garner the highest level of attention from readers. Combine that with the legal requirements to keep the content focused and to the point, and these messages can be quickly viewed and filed or deleted. This helps battle the user's ongoing fight with the inbox email overload that can lead to email ADD.

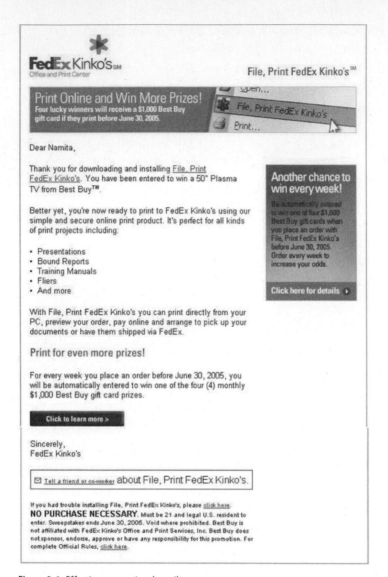

Figure 2.6 Effective transactional emails

While transactional messages are typically sent when a purchase is made, one other type of service email is worth mentioning because of the impact it has on your brand equity. This email is called the *welcome* email.

Like confirmation emails, welcome emails have historically had significantly higher open rates than regular emails. These messages are key to setting expectations with new subscribers and communicating the brand promise. Yet 28 percent of major online retailers still don't send welcome emails. In late 2007, the Email Experience

Council conducted a study of welcome emails sent by 122 major retailers. Here are some key findings from the study:

- Thirty-two percent of welcome emails included a discount, reward, or incentive.

- Sixty-two percent of welcome emails asked the subscriber to whitelist them by adding an email address to their address book.

- Seventy-nine percent of retailers sent HTML welcome emails. The remainder sent text-only welcome emails. That said, most of the HTML welcome emails were "HTML lite," making extensive use of HTML text to ensure that the content could be read even when the recipient has blocked images in their inbox.

- Fifty-three percent of welcome emails included links to the retailer's privacy policy.

- Seventy-five percent of the welcome emails included the retailer's brand name in their subject lines.

Welcome emails hit a reader right after they have raised their hand to let you know they want to engage in a dialogue with you. They are critically important to establishing a profitable relationship with your company. Not only that, but welcome emails and purchase-confirmation transactional emails can also play another key role; they can help turn a reader into an advocate by instigating viral email activity.

In Figure 2.7 you can see a sample welcome email from Petco.com that manages to cover each of these key elements. After receiving this email, you may want to provide additional information about yourself, as well as send this to a fellow pet lover.

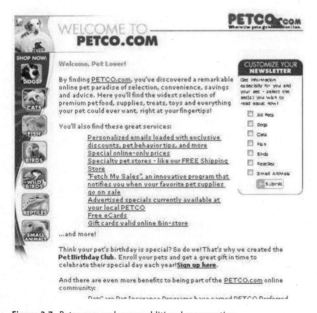

Figure 2.7 Petco.com welcomes additional conversation.

Adding Viral Marketing Elements

A few years ago, one of us was in a meeting with about six clients from the same company. The discussion was about the recommendation to send viral emails. After a few minutes into the overview, a senior client stopped the conversation and said, "I absolutely do not want to send viruses to our customers." It was at that point that the rest of us realized we were all speaking using "inside business" terms. Since that time, the term *viral* when pertaining to marketing efforts has become fairly mainstream. If you are not familiar with it, we can assure you it is not a bad thing. A *viral email*, or *viral effort*, means it is something that resonates so effectively with readers that they share it with many others quickly, something like the way a virus spreads.

The true value of including viral elements in your existing email programs has been a hot topic of debate for a few years now. Advocates of viral email remain solid in their belief that an appealing email, sent to a reader who has a high opinion of your company, can and will be sent to at least five members of that reader's social group. In many cases, these readers are the key stakeholders and influencers your brand desperately wants to reach out to in order to build a relationship and eventually make a sale.

Naysayers of viral email believe it simply doesn't have an impact on future sales at a level of any significance. This group believes the efforts can't be tracked because many people would rather use their Forward button in their email client instead of a form inside an email. Sadly, for email marketers, technology has not developed to a point where elements outside the email content can be tracked and reported on. Although some companies, such as Iconix, are developing ways to enable marketers to track what happens to emails once they reach the inbox, most people are not able to know whether an email marketing message is deleted, forwarded, or filed.

This group also believes that the only effective type of viral marketing is non-sales-related. They think people will forward funny emails or emails with no sales or marketing included.

We're in the first group. We believe that, if used correctly and offered at appropriate times in the relationship, viral elements will drive concrete responses, and therefore they deserve to be recognized as one of the key influencers of your email programs.

Here are some statistics that may help convince you:

- According to management consulting firm McKinsey, about two-thirds of all economic activity in the United States is influenced by shared opinions about a product, brand, or service.
- According to KnowledgeStorm, just more than half of B2B buyers researching IT solutions cite word of mouth as an important decision-making source, and almost 40 percent specifically cite online forms and communities.

- Influential people (meaning those people in your life whose opinions you value significantly) are particularly likely to be sought out for computer purchasing decisions (34 percent vs. 16 percent of the general population).
- About half of all online marketers are involved in some form of word-of-mouth or viral activity. In fact, many Fortune 500 marketers like those at Coca-Cola have been quoted as saying that viral marketing efforts allow them to connect with their targets in ways that would never be approved for "traditional" venues.

Two Ways to Define Success of Your Viral Marketing Efforts

As you create any email marketing strategy (and later chapters of this book will get into more detail on this), you will always be looking for a way to justify your efforts. With viral marketing, the thing to remember is that you can leverage two types of success. There is no easy or uniform way to measure the influence of word-of-mouth marketing; you should try both quantitative and qualitative measures. The first type measures clicks and pass-alongs; the second type measures community buzz.

Quantitative Measures

- Monitor the activity of all pass-along materials including emails, videos, and other viral content. (As discussed further in Chapter 8, you can track an embedded Forward to a Friend link, but that is of limited value because so many people use the email client's own Forward button, an action that can't be tracked.)
- Track pass-along rates, click-throughs, open rates, registrations, and downloads.
- For registered users, track their engagement levels with each piece of content. This information can be ported back to a central data repository in order to qualify customers and enact business rules for appropriate follow-up communications.

Qualitative Measures

- Although it's not email-focused, this often works as a multichannel approach: Employ technology that scours open community platforms such as blogs, chats, message boards, email lists, and newsgroups to capture valuable consumer data in which consumers are communicating their experiences, opinions, and beliefs—positive and negative—about brands and their associated products and services.
- By analyzing this data, estimate the general buzz around a product or campaign as an indicator of its word-of-mouth success.

Best Practices for Creating a Buzz Using Viral Efforts or Word of Mouth

When you're looking to create phenomenal results in your email marketing programs, start with the end in mind. Is your campaign meant to drive interest in your company or product at a high level, or does it need to drive hard-core sales or registrations? Once you have an ultimate goal in mind, you can begin to create the way that your viral efforts will integrate with your current messaging strategy. Adding viral elements does not always require a stand-alone email. Many successful email marketers have found that their best viral successes are created when the viral "ask" is just one element of a larger email. For example, a transactional email might say, "Thanks for your recent purchase. If you tell five friends about this site, we will give you free shipping on your next order."

To help make you as effective at creating wildly successful emails as early on in this book as possible, we thought it would be best to end this chapter with seven best practices tips from the Word of Mouth Marketing Association (WOMMA), which does nothing but focus on viral marketing efforts. Be sure to read the rest of the book, though; we have more great content, tips, and tricks coming up. When you're done, tell your friends and colleagues how helpful it is.

WOMMA offers these tips for developing effective viral efforts:

- **Take off your corporate-marketing-speak hat.** Speak in customer language. Refrain from the usual practice of carefully crafted copy that will immediately be identified as such and ignored. Think of how you would talk to a friend or family member versus an "end user" to whom you are marketing. Even more important than speaking directly is speaking honestly. Be up-front, or you'll create mistrust and potentially damage your brand.

- **Identify opinion leaders and make friends with them.** For every category, there are people who have expertise and are influential in sharing their knowledge with others. These people have a wide circle of influence and can efficiently spread your word to huge numbers of interested parties. Find these *influentials*, and arm them with relevant information about your product or service.

- **Make it easy to spread the word.** Do whatever possible to facilitate the diffusion of your message. From email, instant messaging, and Forward to a Friend buttons to text messages and events, employ tools that remove all barriers to facilitating dialogue.

- **Start with the Big Idea.** Don't make the mistake of starting tactically, as in "We need an email viral campaign" or "What kind of video can we create that will get passed around?" Concentrate instead on your core marketing objectives, and focus on coming up with the Big Idea or core strategy that will resonate with your target. The best ideas are often the simplest and ideally incorporate a key piece of insight about the consumer.

- **Connect to your overall marketing strategy.** Viral and word-of-mouth efforts can do wonders on their own, but they're far more effective (and you'll get greater efficiency) if they're tied to other elements in your marketing campaign.

- **Be responsive to the two-way dialogue.** Because viral marketing is often "uncharted territory" for marketers, we can forget that we have a responsibility to listen and respond to consumers on their own terms. This means you are no longer responsible just for the messages you deliver but also for listening and appropriately responding to the messages from thousands of customers and prospects.

- **Measure it all: the good, the bad, and the ugly.** In all cases, consumers will tell you what they're thinking. In fact, this is one of the primary reasons many marketers struggle with the idea of viral marketing in the first place. Every program must be carefully monitored to not only register the impact of a program but also to appropriately establish an effective two-way dialogue. From specific clicks to community discussion, effective measurement can make the difference in how useful your program becomes and the depth of impact it provides to your company.

Test Your Knowledge

There's a ton of information in this chapter that will be important for you to know. A score of 5 out of 5 will ensure you are on your way to email marketing success.

- How many reasons can there be for a low brand equity score?
- Does heatmapping work from clicks or eye movement?
- What are two key roles that the welcome email plays?
- What year was CAN-SPAM first introduced?
- Do viral or word-of-mouth email efforts take place only inside the email using the Forward to a Friend link?

Getting Ready to Build Your Email Marketing Efforts

In the previous chapter, we explored the importance of brand and how you can leverage email intelligently across the entire consideration and purchase cycle. What we will explore in this chapter are the tools and resources to execute email marketing well. To become a skilled email marketer, you also need the right tools to complement your strategy, and these tools come at a cost. We will provide some useful examples of how to justify these expenses and get the most out of your marketing dollars.

3

Chapter Contents

Aligning Your Strategy with Your Tools

Although dozens of applications and vendors offer email tools and services, many are better for particular types of email marketing purposes than others. To determine which tools and application features you require, you need to assess your category of email and its purpose as it relates to your marketing strategy. The category of marketing email to be used often depends on the type of business doing the marketing. For example, newspapers and other publishers may want to do only newsletter email marketing. For them, maintaining a relationship with their readers is sufficient. Another category is promotional email, where products and services are advertised; this is used mostly in the retail sector. Banks and utility companies are focused more on transactional and service-based email. These categories of email require different tools, or at least utilize email marketing features such as personalization on a more regular basis. Newsletter marketers, for example, typically send the same daily or weekly newsletter to every subscriber, reducing the need for tools such as dynamic content or the ability to trigger messages based on a subscriber's behavior. A strategy that is aligned with your promotional endeavors will require tools that allow you to segment your list into different types of subscribers and change the content within an email to ensure that it best matches the subscriber's profile. Regardless of your email category, the following strategy guide applies to all types of email.

 Write This Down: A May 2006 JupiterResearch executive survey found the top challenge for email marketers was "knowing where to begin to optimize their mailings." (Source: JupiterResearch)

Determining Your Tools: A Ten-Point Strategy

Based on the considerations we've just outlined, every email marketer needs to perform ten important steps to determine which tools are appropriate for their marketing strategy:

- **Begin with the end in mind; incorporate testing and use frequency caps.** Ensure that email marketing mailings focus on goals by incorporating regular testing into marketing campaigns. Tests should focus on variables that are levers (for example, frequency, time of day, and content) for attaining target goals (for example, conversion). Working backward from a specific goal will ensure that optimization practices such as testing are part of the mailing process. Additionally, determine the maximum number of messages subscribers will receive in a given month. This is referred to as a *frequency cap*. Typically, marketers mail once per week; however, you should develop a contact strategy that incorporates frequency rules to avoid "burning out" subscribers. In Chapters 5 and 7 we provide you with real-world examples of how to incorporate testing into your email production process. For now, however, begin to identify those goals and message attributes that you may want to test down the road.

- **Place value on email addresses.** As discussed in Chapter 1, unless you understand the value to the organization of email addresses or email subscribers, you will have difficulty making a strong case for additional investments in email marketing programs (for example, dedicating more site real estate to email acquisition or using offline resources to collect and/or reactivate email addresses). Determining the value of an email address requires understanding email acquisition costs and metrics such as the average revenue per email subscriber. A more detailed approach can mirror customer lifetime value calculations, incorporating customer-specific recency, frequency, and monetary values. A recency, frequency, and monetary score or value is commonly referred to as *RFM analysis*. This approach is used to segment customers into different groupings based on their (monetary) spending, the frequency of their purchases, and the recency of their last purchases. Marketers will often use this to create groups of six-month buyers, meaning those buyers who have purchased in the past six months. This approach can also be applied to email clicks and/or site visit behavior, as in those subscribers who may have clicked within the past six months. Chapter 5 provides you with several recipes for calculating email address value.

- **Develop acquisition, retention, and reactivation programs.** Although most marketers immediately jump to developing ongoing retention- or newsletter-oriented mailings, our experience indicates that acquisition and reactivation programs are not well thought out. Unfortunately, you must anticipate that many of the email addresses in your file are going to go bad (that is, *churn*), with one-half to two-thirds of lists not being responsive. Surveys and sweepstakes (if brand appropriate) work well to elicit a response from dormant subscribers. Use the value of an email address as an arbiter when determining appropriate and cost-effective reactivation tactics (for example, call center intervention or postal mailings). Map out a subscriber preference center page to determine the manner in which new addresses and unsubscribe requests will be processed. Keep in mind that you want email to be a two-way conversation with your subscribers; you want to create a dialogue. In future chapters, we will discuss optimal subscriber preference center pages.

- **Develop key performance indicators.** Although rates for open, click-through, conversion, and delivery are useful to know, they are also the necessary ingredients for developing an engagement metric to trend the health of a mailing list or segment over time. Along with these metrics, add the unsubscribe rate, spam complaint rate, new subscriber rate, and hard bounces to a quotient that directionally indicates the quality and performance of the mailing list. Each submetric can be individually evaluated, but rolling all of them up into one metric is an easy way for marketers to gauge the health of subscribers over time. See the "Calculating an Engagement Metric" sidebar for an example of combining submetrics into an engagement metric.

Calculating an Engagement Metric

A representative calculation for an engagement metric is as follows: Take all the key performance indicators and score them on a three-point scale, with the value of 1 when you are below your benchmark average, the value of 2 when you are at or within 2 percent of your benchmark average, and the value of 3 when you are 2 percent or more over your benchmark average. Apply this approach to all your major key performance indicators, and sum them up. The higher the number, the better your list is performing. It signals that your audience is relatively engaged with you. For the purposes of illustration, your engagement metric calculation may look like the following. (Please do not use these metrics as benchmarks; they are here for illustrative purposes only.)

Delivery rate = 95%	Score=3
Open rate = 24%	Score=1
Click-through rate = 12%	Score=2
Conversion rate = 1.5%	Score=2
Percent of list clicking within past month = 50%	Score=3
Opt-in rate = 3%	Score=3
Spam complaint rate = 10%	Score=1
Unsubscribe rate = .01%	Score=2

(Note: With the spam complaint and unsubscribe rates, the higher the number for these metrics, the lower the score should be.)

The overall engagement score in this example is 17.

Although each metric is a key performance indicator, rolling up the metrics in a scoring system like this will give you a quick snapshot of the list's performance. If there is a big change from mailing to mailing, it is easy to identify which individual key performance indicator is dragging you down. In the coming chapters, we will provide more insight into best practices for measuring and analyzing your mailing performance.

• **Focus on behavior.** Subscribers' behavior should be central to your segmentation strategy. Create engagement rules (for example, the number of subscribers clicking at least one link during past three or four mailings versus those clicking more frequently and those not clicking at all). This approach will create a behavioral segmentation framework to drive subsequent mailings and remarketing campaigns, and in turn provide an completely effective means of targeting. For example, Travelocity sends subscribers email based on their last actions on the site, whether it was saving a trip itinerary for a possible future purchase or making a purchase. We will provide more detail on how to go about managing segmentation later, but for now, ensure that you begin to map out how you will break your subscribers into different buckets and how that will impact the application tools you require.

- **Develop/tailor landing pages.** Driving subscribers to the primary website is generally the preferred tactic of most marketers. However, some programs—including welcome and reactivation campaigns—could require the development of specific landing pages. Tailoring landing pages to reinforce email content that further drives subscribers to a desired outcome could be necessary if organizations choose to tailor the site experience by subscriber segment or persona. For now, consider that you may need to have a few static landing pages added to your website. These will cover campaigns such as welcoming new subscribers and reactivating dormant ones. You'll find examples of these pages in Chapters 5–7.

- **Optimize content.** Managing content and creative often represents the largest part of the production process. Consider the manner in which your messages render in a variety of email clients, including provisions for Wireless Application Protocol (WAP)—enabled devices such as handhelds with email. Tools such as free HTML-to-WAP converters that can be found with a Google search can make this effortless, but understanding content and rendering as a part of your email strategy is critical to succeeding with the brand-oriented aspects of your email, as discussed in Chapter 2.

- **Develop seed lists.** Find some individuals within your company to place on seed and proof lists. This ensures that you and your colleagues will get test versions of the mailing for proofing as well as the actual email when it is sent. Additionally, develop seed lists that incorporate a wide variety of Internet service providers to measure delivery and message placement (for example, the bulk folder) across a large number of domains. Vendors including Pivotal Veracity, Return Path, and Lyris offer seeding solutions to monitor delivery (see Appendix A for contact information).

- **Determine use of multichannel marketing in early stages of planning process.** Some companies may turn to email marketing first because it is relatively inexpensive and make coordinating and integrating email campaigns and data with marketing in other channels a long-term goal. Even if that is your strategy, it's important to determine how you will use multichannel marketing as early as possible in the planning process. For example, the manner in which email marketing data are stored and organized could have particular bearing on the amount of work required to implement integrated multichannel marketing. Accordingly, marketers might want to use something other than an email address as a unique record identifier. Using a generic customer ID number as the unique record number will provide data management benefits if data from other channels and applications are integrated with email marketing data. It also allows for *householding* (the ability to roll up either multiple customers to one email address or multiple email addresses to one household), because if the record identifier is not an email address, you can have multiple email addresses associated with one household customer record identifier. You should plan for your email marketing efforts to become a central and integrated part of your overall corporate marketing. Mapping out the data you want to collect and how it will be organized is vital to ensuring success and efficiency down the road.

• **Map out continuity campaigns for leverage.** An ancillary benefit of using sequenced strings of messages is that much of the work involved in creating individual messages within campaigns can be leveraged and reused. Allowing your mailing to be triggered by an event, such as a customer click-through or an elapsed timed event, is referred to as a *triggered mailing.* Once you tie multiple triggers together, this is referred to as a *continuity campaign.* Coupling this approach with the aforementioned behavioral segmentation strategy will allow you to craft mailings triggered by behaviors and/or events, thus reusing messages designed for other subscribers. This approach is typically used in welcome campaigns for new subscribers, which can consist of three or four stock messages that apply to all new subscribers. (You'll learn more about welcome campaigns in Chapter 6.) This approach is also applied to some of the transactional and service opportunities that we discussed in the previous chapter. With the exception (for most email marketers) of welcome campaigns, triggered continuity campaigns are something to aspire to and not necessarily required on a day-one launch. Still, understanding the role of triggered campaigns as a tactic in your email strategy will aid in creating an effective vendor-selection process.

Evaluating Vendors

Once you have the essential pieces of your strategy mapped out, it is time to begin seeking a vendor or an application that can execute your email program. There are many vendors in this sector, and collectively they are referred to as *Email Service Providers* (ESPs). These vendors offer a solution that is hosted and accessed via a web browser. Some ESPs also offer strategic and production-oriented services, allowing you to outsource all your email marketing to an ESP.

ESPs can be broken down into the following categories:

Self-Service Solutions for Small to Midsize Businesses These ESPs provide little in the way of strategic and tactical services but allow you to log into a simple application and upload your subscriber list and creative into their applications. Depending on your list size, these solutions can cost as little as $20 a month, or if you require more features or have larger lists, they can average $400 a month. ESPs that cater to marketers looking to spend less than $100 a month include Constant Contact and VerticalResponse. ESPs that cater to medium-sized businesses include EmailLabs, SubscriberMail, and many others such as ExactTarget that also cater to enterprise clients.

Self-Service Solutions for Enterprise-Class Businesses These ESPs offer flexible strategic and tactical services so that you can utilize their services as needed or simply use the application in a self-service fashion without any vendor production support. What makes these vendors different from those catering to smaller businesses is their ability to integrate with other applications and data sources, as well as the number of features that their applications offer. Typically, these vendors cater to large retailers and banks and provide the capability to do highly personalized mailings. Some of the vendors in this category include Responsys, Silverpop, and WhatCounts, which is a vendor that also offers the ability to implement its technology on-premise.

Full-Service Solutions These vendors primarily cater to enterprise companies, and their clients are often consumer-packaged goods companies and media organizations since historically these companies have little internal customer relationship management (CRM) technology. These vendors can do email in a full-service manner on your behalf or in some form of collaboration with you. Vendors in this category include e-Dialog and CheetahMail.

Write This Down: Email spending in the United States will grow to $2.1 billion in 2012. (Source: JupiterResearch)

Usability, personalization capabilities, and account management support justifiably top the list of reasons why marketers selected their current ESPs. However, few of them focused on integration capabilities and the ability to automate mailings. Although you should absolutely focus on the usability of the application, you should equally analyze areas that will improve efficiency, including time-intensive tasks such as repeatedly cloning mailings versus automating recurring mailings.

A Checklist to Maximize Your Vendor Selection Process

With this basic understanding of the vendor categories in hand, you can further your selection process with this ten-point vendor selection checklist. However, consider the following elements only when questions about prospective vendors' reputation, scalability, reliability, and security have satisfied your internal and corporate comfort level.

Account Management Based on the level of account service required (for example, full or collaborative), determine whether service is included or whether additional fees will be incurred. If you require comparatively greater strategic and tactical services, inspect the size of the account management team, develop service-level assurances, seek dedicated/consistent account support, and inquire about the experience and training of the account management staff.

Asset Movement Understand both the manner in which data and content are uploaded into the system and the provision for exporting post-campaign results for further analysis or information sharing. More than one-third of the ESPs reviewed annually by JupiterResearch lack the provision to simultaneously upload multiple images into the system, and one-third lack file-transfer protocol support.

Automation Control The power of email marketing lies in its ability to act quickly on information and trigger follow-up mailings based on performance and behavior. Find out an ESP's approach to triggering and automation; in particular, determine whether automation triggers are constrained to events internal to the ESP or can be defined by external events (such as the user abandoning a shopping cart or other information from a commerce engine) and/or a fixed calendar interval. The ESP's ability to automate items can often be linked to its integration capabilities, further underscoring the need to clarify how assets are moved into and out of the system.

Compliance Support Determine how the ESP helps to ensure messages will be compliant with CAN-SPAM and the related Federal Communications Commission's wireless domain registry (see Chapter 5 for details on these legal requirements). Although the burden of compliance resides with you, the marketer, systematic approaches can be used to ensure compliance with necessary regulations. For example, the CAN-SPAM requirements mandate that an opt-out is placed in the footer of every promotional message. Ask the potential ESP partner whether their system has the ability to ensure that the required element is in the footer of those messages. Although this is necessary for promotional messages, an opt-out is not required for service-related messages, which requires flexibility from the prospective ESP to provide different compliance support for different message types, (e.g. promotional and transactional).

Data Interrogation Although all ESPs include standard behavioral-based reports (for example, opens and clicks), you should ascertain how data in the system can be queried if they're not presented in a desirable format. For example, determine the ESP's custom reporting capabilities and the availability of response data for use as segmentation attributes. Several ESPs collect polling data but do not append the data to customer profiles, rendering the data useless as a segmentation attribute.

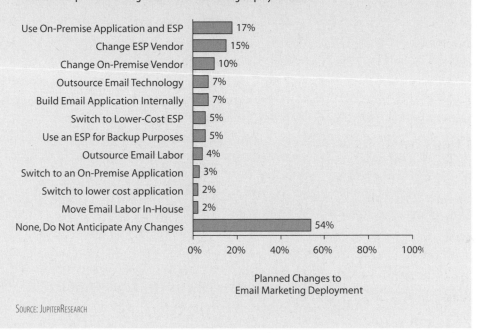

Statistics on Email Marketers and ESPs

In 2007, JupiterResearch surveyed companies doing email marketing to see what deployment strategies they were currently using and what changes, if any, they were planning in the next twelve months. In 2007, 56 percent of companies were working with outsourced ESP provider.

Here are the planned changes to email marketing deployments:

Category	Percentage
Use On-Premise Application and ESP	17%
Change ESP Vendor	15%
Change On-Premise Vendor	10%
Outsource Email Technology	7%
Build Email Application Internally	7%
Switch to Lower-Cost ESP	5%
Use an ESP for Backup Purposes	5%
Outsource Email Labor	4%
Switch to an On-Premise Application	3%
Switch to lower cost application	2%
Move Email Labor In-House	2%
None, Do Not Anticipate Any Changes	54%

Planned Changes to
Email Marketing Deployment

SOURCE: JUPITERRESEARCH

Data Orientation Many ESPs house their data in relational databases, allowing comparatively easier data replication and repurposing. Even with this infrastructure, however, many work with subscriber data primarily as one big list. Such an approach makes it more difficult to create segments because it requires additional lists to be created, compared to creating the database in multiple segments that can be recalled at will. Although a list-based approach works well for many marketers (for example, newsletter marketers), this approach can become unwieldy for marketers who plan on doing deep segmentation. Determine whether subscriber data should reside in a single record that gets appended as the data set grows or whether the subscriber record should consist of data stored in multiple tables, each focused on a single type of information and linked only by a unique record ID.

For example, if subscriber contact information is stored in one table, it should contain a primary key to link to the client's purchase history, which in this example would be stored in a separate table and linked through this common record key or through a mapping of one table to another.

Deliverability Focus Inspect the ESP's approach to deliverability tools and the possible premiums associated with them. Volume senders must insist on sending from a dedicated IP address, and all marketers should ensure that the ESP they choose offers domain-level response reporting, identity records (for example, sender policy framework), bounce cadence flexibility (the ability for you, the marketer, to change the rate and number of times that bounced messages are re-sent before being recognized as a failure), and table-stakes delivery tools such as content scoring, inbox seeding, and compliance/bounce handling. In future chapters, we will provide you with detailed information related to the technical ins and outs of email deliverability. At this stage, you just need to understand that it is necessary to evaluate a potential vendor's deliverability capabilities.

Feature Depth When assessing an ESP's value, be sure you know the breadth of features it offers. However, understanding the depth and usability of these features is equally important. For example, focus on the manner in which dynamic content mailings are assembled, proofed, and measured—not on the existence of dynamic content. Similarly, items such as a Forward to a Friend link and a Click to View button (so a subscriber is able to view the email in a web browser) are relatively common, but large differences exist in an ESP's ability to personalize these features or alter forwarded messages to reset opt-in and opt-out verbiage. For critical features such as testing, be sure the ESP offers a sound methodology and testing flexibility (for example, the ability to test items within dynamic content elements). There are many different schools of thought when it comes to testing methodologies. Although you don't need to be a statistical-modeling expert, you should familiarize yourself with the concepts of multivariate testing and split-path testing. We will show you how to apply these concepts in practice in the coming chapters, but for further reading on the methodologies embodied in these forms of modeling, seek out references on the Internet, such as Wikipedia.

Recycling Flexibility Although nearly all vendors allow previous campaigns to be recalled and copied, the real value in salvaging existing mailings is often restricted to their parts, not their wholes. Ascertain the manner in which the ESP allows mailing components to be saved and reused. For example, only one-half of ESPs (53 percent) reviewed annually by JupiterResearch allow content elements and rules associated with them to be saved and recalled independent of the mailing. Seek out systems that have provisions for reusable templates and template elements.

The Selection Process Employ a standardized selection process that includes a scenario-based demonstration in which the prospective ESP must create a sample mailing using dummy data you provide. Keep strict controls on this process, such as monitoring the time a vendor takes to compile and send the mailing as well as compiling a standard list of questions that will expose the ESP's approach to the aforementioned nine items.

Beyond this ten-point checklist, many other valuable resources can help you select a vendor. Industry analyst firms, marketing associations such as the Email Experience Council and the Direct Marketing Association, and online discussion groups such as the email marketing roundtable on Yahoo are all wonderful resources to help you determine whether you have selected the best vendor for your email needs.

Organizational Readiness: Resources Required for Success

Email marketing has many elements. Upcoming chapters will give much greater insight into the various elements of email marketing and their impact on the organization. However, let's quickly explore the pieces that make up the email marketing continuum.

Strategy This embodies the totality of the email production process, but from a tactical perspective, *strategy* here applies to list segmentation and targeting. Targeting is the marriage of the segmentation of your list to the content or offer being placed in front of this segment. Additionally, in this tactical context, the strategic role defines the purpose of the email program and the manner of email acquisition, reactivation, and testing. You'll learn more about strategy in Chapter 4.

Creative Design In most organizations, this role is shared with other interactive marketing endeavors such as the website creative, but in larger organizations where email is mission-critical and tailored, this is a dedicated role within the email marketing team. (Expedia, for example, employs this model.) Although creative elements (logos, and so on) can often be leveraged from other content stores within the organization, email increasingly requires the creative elements to be optimized for a variety of different email clients (for example, Outlook, Gmail, and AOL) and platforms such as mobile devices in order to ensure that the email creative renders appropriately. In Chapter 5, we provide you with the creative and markup basics as well as highlight vendors and tools that aid the creative process. Lisa Harmon of Smith-Harmon has a blog, Make It Pop! (http://blog.emailexperience.org/make_it_pop/), which is a good reference for staying abreast of the latest creative best practices.

Production Production is where the mailing all comes together. The person handling this should be well-versed in HTML coding and database scripting, because they assemble the email. (Note that coding HTML in email is different from coding an HTML web page. Although the tasks are similar enough that it is helpful for the coder to have HTML web page development skills, you should seek out someone who has experience working with HTML in email.) This person will be responsible for everything from pulling the list and tying segments to offers, to proofing the email to ensure that all the links function properly. This person will also set up the tests, such as subject-line testing, that have been prescribed for the mailing. Depending on the scope of the email marketing program, production tasks can be dedicated to specialists (as with creative) or to partners. For example, some marketers simply outsource the database scripting requirements (which are used to drive personalization and targeting) to their vendors, where others rely on more usable or simpler applications that do not require such detailed programming skills.

Deployment Often when working with an ESP, this task will actually be handled by the vendor. This task embodies any final proofing and seeding as well as deploying the actual tests (such as subject-line tests, and so on) in advance of the mailing being deployed. Lastly, this role is tasked with scheduling and sending the final mailing.

Reporting and Analysis One of the wonderful things about email is the immediacy with which you can view the mailing results. After a few hours or a few days, you will begin to pull a variety of reports and do analyses on your mailing's performance. Much of this will be used to feed segmentation strategies, evaluate template and content performance, and perform more operationally oriented tasks such understanding how your email deliverability performed to your top domain recipients. Reporting on delivery as well as the delivery implications in production and deployment may require further specialization and outside expertise from the aforementioned vendors, such as Return Path. We will discuss the issues of email delivery and give you some tips and tricks to avoid the spam folder in later chapters.

We've just described five roles. Does that mean you need five people to execute email well? No. In fact, most organizations execute their email marketing programs with just two-and-a-half full-time equivalents. Although companies such as Wells Fargo have dozens of people responsible for email marketing, other companies, such as Petco, have just one-and-a-half full-time equivalents managing and executing their email programs. However, to be successful, you must take staffing levels and internal email expertise into account. Marketers with fewer resources are typically less likely to use personalization and targeting tactics that drive results higher, simply because they do not have the resources to create the multiple content versions and segments that such an approach requires. Marketers working with ESPs generally have relatively less staff because they can tap into an ESP's expertise and resources as needed.

Figure 3.1 shows average annual salaries for dedicated email marketing staff for B2B versus B2C marketers and for companies with annual revenues of more than $500 million versus companies with lower revenues. Figure 3.2 shows the percentage of the total number of marketers at different salary levels, as reported by JupiterResearch.

As you can see, email salaries and budgets are relatively small compared to other marketing disciplines and channels. The good news is that this makes email even more affordable, and because email is still a relatively young industry, this makes it possible to find qualified resources without breaking your budget. A 2007 JupiterResearch study found that the average amount companies spend on personnel budgets for email marketing is $182,067—up from $169,710 in 2005. The positive news for email marketing professionals is that salaries have increased from an average of $50,526 in 2005 to the current average of $63,547.

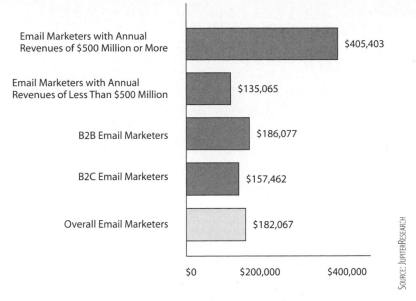

Figure 3.1 Average annual salary for all staff dedicated to email marketing

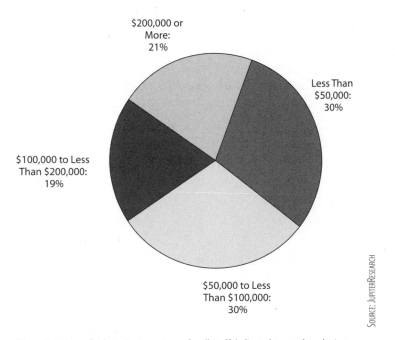

Figure 3.2 Annual salaries in percentages for all staff dedicated to email marketing

The coming chapters will arm you with the expertise to master each piece of the mailing process in order to set you and your company on the road to email success.

Budgeting for the Future

How much money should you allocate to the various email functions?

Email budgeting can be a tricky thing if you do not yet have a house list of email subscribers or know the size of your list. Your budget is driven primarily by the staffing costs and requirements covered in the previous section and by the size of your list. Email is typically priced on a cost-per-thousand (CPM) basis. Average CPMs for email marketing from the ESP vendor community are also not very consistent from vendor to vendor, so be careful not to base your budget solely on what your peers might be spending. These cost discrepancies between vendors are primarily because of the way application features and services are priced. However, for an average business-to-consumer promotional email marketer, a ClickZ/JupiterResearch survey found that list sizes were on average about 3 million subscribers and that the average pricing for a typical self-service email marketing deployment via an ESP was approximately $4.80 per thousand subscribers (costs nearly double for full-service engagements). CPM will decrease as list volume increases, but average marketers that might send 1 million email messages in a month would spend approximately $4,800 dollars a month to send that much email. It is important to understand all the costs associated with a vendor's solution. For example, many ESPs have additional monthly charges for adding users to the account. In this example, two application users would raise that $4,800 monthly fee to approximately $5,200 a month.

Figure 3.3 compares the annual budgets in 2007 reported by companies surveyed by JupiterResearch for email acquisition, retention, and creative. Email marketing is highly effective and efficient, but as you can see, budgets do not match the strategic importance organizations place or should be placing on email marketing. The majority of marketers annually allocate less than $250,000 to each of the discrete email functions of acquisition, retention, and creative. Also, market studies indicate that budgets for email marketing have remained relatively consistent year after year. For example, the share of companies annually budgeting $250,000 or more for retention email remains constant at 6 percent.

 Write This Down: According to Internet Retailer, 50.6 percent of Internet retailers report that 6 percent or more of their sales come from email marketing, while another 25 percent say the proportion is more than 11 percent.

It is important that you establish up-front what the goals for your email marketing program are; these goals can include branding impressions, revenue, store traffic, conversion, retention, reduction of paper-related costs, and so on. Setting up these goals will allow you to measure the incremental progress in attaining them over time.

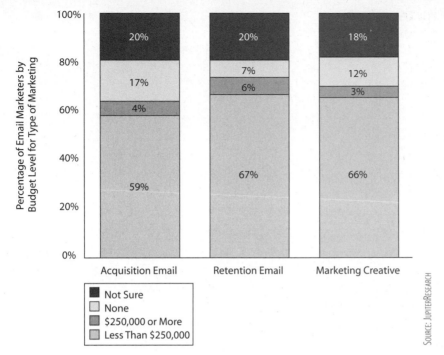

Figure 3.3 Annual budgets in 2007 for email acquisition, retention, and creative

To determine your budget, you should assess your list size and staff necessary to execute the programs you desire. Use the aforementioned benchmarks as guides to setting your budget, but keep in mind that the Direct Marketing Association has found that email returns $57.25 for every dollar spent on it. Wow!

Justification: Selling Your Boss on the Return on Investing in Email

Your boss will want to know just how much money can be derived from email marketing. Start with explaining that the cost to send just one email is a fraction of a penny; even for marketers starting out with smaller lists, this amount might add up to only a few hundred dollars per month. Explain that the real costs are in the people necessary to execute and optimize these mailings, but that the variable expenses related to the email technology and sending of email will accelerate in relation to the growth of your email list and overall sending volume. Then hit your boss with some of the following statistics—these are gems to get the bean counters' attention:

- According to JupiterResearch, 90 percent of users will use email to engage in and define the value of a relationship with a company. ESP Merkle reports that 40 percent of email subscribers will go "out of their way" to patronize a company whose email programs they like.

- Half of online buyers make online or offline purchases based on the email they receive. That's right—email is just as effective for driving offline, in-store purchases as it is in driving online purchases. Additionally, Forrester Research reports that email subscribers spend 138 percent more than those who don't buy through email.

> ### Case Study: Borders
>
> The bookstore chain Borders uses email to drive its loyalty rewards program. To increase the number of Borders Rewards members, Borders placed incentives on the percentage of Borders Rewards transactions for each cashier in its stores. Cashiers at the point of sale were therefore encouraged to collect email addresses, enroll customers in the program, and prompt customers to use their cards each and every time they transacted. The company has five full-time associates working on the Borders Rewards program, handling the planning and production aspects of the mailing. Since the program's inception in 2006, more than 12.5 million customers have enrolled. Each mailing is responsible for driving millions of dollars of store revenue every week. Email has become a wildly successful tool for Borders.

- A study that David did for JupiterResearch in 2005 found that when marketers begin to target their subscribers and leverage subscriber behavior to the end, they can generate 11 times more profit from their email mailings than those marketers who simply broadcast the same message to all the subscribers. Even when factoring in the additional staff necessary to do more segmentation and targeting, these programs were found to generate more revenue and be more profitable than those broadcasting one email to all of their subscribers. The subtle point here is to petition for additional staffing resources, if not immediately but in six to twelve months out so as your email program matures, you can begin to add the necessary staff to employ these tactics that drive email ROI even higher.

Finally, explain to your boss how email can be leveraged to meet other corporate goals such as collecting additional data about customers via the surveys to further customer relationship goals and reduce costs related to communicating corporate announcements, such as service and transactional messages.

In subsequent chapters, we will share techniques on how to cut the waste out of your email spending as your email list grows, such as determining when to stop mailing non-responders and underperforming names.

Test Your Knowledge

We've just thrown a lot of terminology and other information at you—check your progress by seeing how many of these questions you can answer correctly. A score of 3 out of 3 will ensure you are on your way to email marketing success.

- What is a frequency cap, and why should you use it?
- What size does JupiterResearch forecast that the email marketing market will be in 2012?
- What is the engagement score, and which key performance indicators should be included in the score?

What Happens Once You Send Your Email

Before you can launch your first campaign, you need to know what to expect once you hit the Send button. This chapter will help you ensure that you have the right reporting and analytics framework set up and that you have the right amount of money in your email marketing budget. We also introduce the five most common disasters for new email marketers and show how you can avoid them—or at least have Plan B in place.

Chapter Contents

Defining the Analytics Framework

The previous chapter focused on determining what you need to consider when selecting an email marketing vendor or service and how to set up your program and staff. All the elements you read about are important to the success of your program. However, you cannot afford to lose sight of how email marketing fits into your organization and the elements of analytics that you will need in order to determine not only the effectiveness of your email marketing efforts, such as open rates and click-through rates, but also the effectiveness of email marketing on your organization's comprehensive efforts.

Case Study: Great Email Marketing Results Add $0 to the Bottom Line

A small nonprofit organization we have worked with decided to launch an email marketing program to help the organization build membership sales and increase reach. The employees did everything right in terms of finding a technology provider, creating campaign plans, and staffing the team. However, they forgot one thing: they never built a process to assess how closely the email marketing behaviors impacted behaviors of other organizational efforts. For example, did frequent readers become members?

After eight months of having a great email campaign in the market, the organization found that readership of messages was high, but any action requiring involvement with the organization, or monetary commitments, was low. Not sure of how this was possible, this organization hired an analytics firm to help determine what was happening.

The resulting findings concluded that the types of people signing up for the email program were people who were interested in following the organization's efforts, but they were not the level of decision makers who could commit to a monetary investment at this time. In other words, their email program was targeting the wrong people.

Having spent most of the marketing budget and resources on powering this email program, this organization found itself challenged on how to meet its annual goals.

In the end, the organization's email program was split into two groups. "Lurkers" continued to receive weekly emails with news and updates, but a new program was launched that matched the overall organization target audience and membership growth activity. Within six months the organization was back on track, and what the staff learned, they felt, could be "transformational" to anyone getting involved in email marketing.

Start with Your Email Marketing Plan, and Expand It to Include Your Companys Growth Plan

We've talked about the importance of integrating your email marketing plan with other marketing channels in your company's overall growth plan. The following tasks are essential:

- Make a map of entrance and exit points into your email database.
- Determine how you will analyze the impact that email marketing is having on your overall results.

Mapping Entrance and Exit Points

Asking you to make a map may seem kind of silly, but it will help your email efforts tremendously. Email marketing is often misunderstood. Many people seem to believe that email marketing performs best when it is not integrated with other advertising ands marketing efforts. In fact, it is also the entry and exit points for almost all marketing channels. It has an impact and is impacted by everything else happening in your offline and online marketing efforts.

The average website has at least seven entrance or exit points where someone can provide an email address, contact a company, or share other contact information. Figure 4.1 shows an example of two such entrance points near the top of VIVmag's home page. Your email marketing database should connect with these fields at some point to ensure that a conversation can be maintained, that you can continue to communicate with the reader via email, and that the reader can continue to respond via clicking. Ask for the visitor's email address on every page of your website!

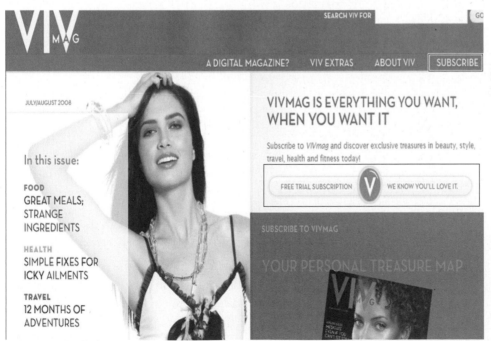

Figure 4.1 Sample entrance points from media to email

The Analytics Plan

Once you have a map (either mentally or visually) drawn that includes your entrance and exit points to start an email marketing dialogue, you will see that it broadens the impact of your email marketing efforts pretty significantly. Figure 4.2 shows an example.

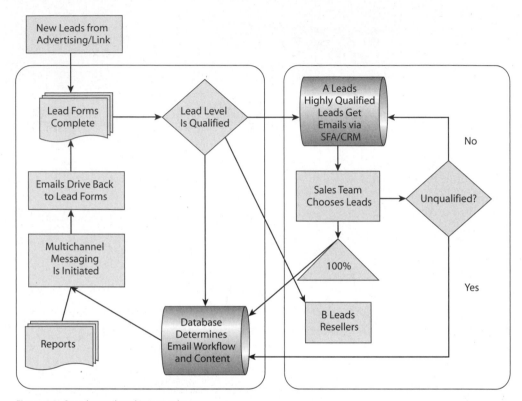

Figure 4.2 Sample email marketing road map

Suddenly, it is no longer enough to determine whether your current email efforts are effectively set up; you must also ask whether you have the right email marketing programs in place at all. The answer to this question lies in the results of a good analytics program that runs behind your email marketing database and establishes a broader line of impact.

What Your Analytics Program Should Tell You

A good analytics program for email marketing efforts does not have to be expensive. It just needs to provide five critical elements of functionality:

Dashboard An analytics dashboard like the Google Analytics example shown in Figure 4.3 lets you view campaign results based on a number of elements that are critical to your business. Most analytics packages allow you to customize a dashboard so that you can determine what top-line elements appear up front, and that you don't need to search, cut and paste reports together.

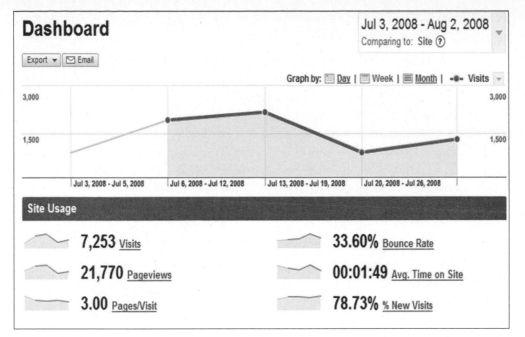

Figure 4.3 Google Analytics Dashboard

Funnel Regardless of which business you are in, you will rely on a significant number of visitors to your website turning into leads, which ultimately turn into customers, who then buy more, or more frequently, from your company. A good analytics program will provide this funnel overview to you, showing what percentage of visitors progress to each stage.

Geographic Targeting Understanding where the visitors who come to your website originate (both location and time zone) is a critically important element for you to understand from an analytics perspective. Many times your product or service offering will be more appealing if you can advertise it during a time when your prospect or consumer is considering your services, such as advertising cereal around times when people will be hungry. In the United States, for example, those times will be different on the East Coast than on the West Coast. Another example is general appeal; for instance, people in the southern United States might be more responsive to different words in copy than those in the western United States.

Website Activity Your analytics program will tell you what the site traffic looks like, specifically, how many pages people see on your site, what type of paths they go through when visiting your site (how many pages before they leave), and what pages they enter and exit on.

Visits to Purchase / Search Engine Marketing (SEM) Analytics programs now commonly tell you not only how people use your site but also what keywords they used to get there and what types of words they type in your internal search box to navigate (this is known as *SEM* or sometimes as *organic search*). This is one of the most impactful reports you can utilize as part of your email efforts moving forward.

These critical elements help you ensure your email marketing program is on target to drive needed business results for your company. Understanding who is coming to your site will enable you to target the timing and delivery of your messages. Knowing what words people type or click to get to your site will enable you to update your copy with relevant phrases that will drive more clicks. Furthermore, seeing exactly how and where people navigate through your site will ensure you can get those much needed conversions or email campaigns that can educate or nurture people to move down your sales funnel faster, or for higher dollar amounts, than previously.

Choosing an Analytics Program

For many people just getting involved with email, deciding which analytics program to choose can start to get complex and expensive quickly. This often leads to questions of, "Do I need an analytics program at all?" and, "Why do I need to know about it *before* I start my email marketing?"

As the authors of this book, we answer the first question with a resounding "Yes!" You need an analytics program *before* your email marketing efforts begin. These programs will help you determine how effective your current efforts are and increase effectiveness for all email-related efforts, from opt-in list rental targeting to landing page effectiveness and dialogue efforts. And beginning with analytics doesn't have to be difficult or expensive. In fact, Google Analytics, illustrated earlier, can be a great starting tool for free.

Case Study: BuildDirect Increased Sales 50 Percent Using Google Analytics (Source: Google Business)

BuildDirect is a global online merchant wholesaler and specialty retailer of building products. Founded in 1999, and based in Vancouver, B.C., Canada, the company does business in 40 countries on 6 continents with a portfolio of products in flooring, roofing, siding, decking, and countertops. Orders consist of container quantities shipped to ocean ports or inland terminals, as well as pallet quantities shipped to any postal code or ZIP code address in North America. In 2004, *Profit* magazine ranked BuildDirect as the second fastest growing company in Canada.

BuildDirect is an entirely virtual organization, which allows for lower overhead. The company credits much of its success to savvy use of online marketing and advertising.

Challenge

Although the company was growing rapidly, management was eager to improve the efficiency of its online spending—especially with a marketing budget that approached $1 million per quarter in the first years of operation.

Case Study: BuildDirect Increased Sales 50 Percent Using Google Analytics (Source: Google Business) *(Continued)*

BuildDirect had a marketing mix that consisted of a combination of search engine advertising, email newsletters, and online website customer sign-ups. The challenge was to improve performance through better tracking of which tactics worked and which didn't.

In 2004, BuildDirect turned to Google Analytics to replace an existing analytics package. In a matter of months, Dan Brodie, the director of operations, said he could see the email marketing channel was not converting as well as he would have liked. And the company wasn't getting sufficient value for its spending on third-tier search engines for traffic that converted poorly.

Results

"Web analytics are essential for any online company, and they have been key to dramatically improving our operation," says Brodie. Using Google Analytics, he was able to see which ads were working and how effective newsletters and site design were in driving sales. "Our online sales volume has increased 50 percent—all without anyone picking up the phone. This is a tribute to BuildDirect's continual site design and market testing, as well as the actionable information Google Analytics provides."

He adds, "With Google Analytics, we learned that many of our search engines were not delivering sufficiently targeted traffic. Higher visitor volume is great, but we needed to focus on conversions—traffic that leads to sales."

Better Results from Search Advertising

BuildDirect focused advertising spending on the top search engines and immediately saw conversions increase by 37 percent, even while reducing its overall search marketing budget by 33 percent. The company has since increased its search ad spending on high-converting sources, and it continues to maintain very strong conversion rates.

More Effective Email Advertising Campaigns

In addition to improving search advertising, BuildDirect was able to judge the effectiveness of email campaigns designed to drive traffic to its site. Even though the company had purchased email lists of "confirmed-interest" home renovation prospects and sent 600,000 to 800,000 emails at a time, the ROI was still low because of a low conversion rate. After using Google Analytics for campaign monitoring and tracking, BuildDirect doubled its email marketing conversion rate. "Once we began using Google Analytics cross-segment performance analytic tools to identify our customer demographics, we were able to design specific creative tailored to our buyers," says Brodie.

Continues

Case Study: BuildDirect Increased Sales 50 Percent Using Google Analytics (Source: Google Business) *(Continued)*

Improved Customer Engagement

By using Google Analytics Marketing Optimization reports, BuildDirect found that sample purchases were a powerful way to drive more sales. "Home buyers who purchase a sample have a 60 percent likelihood of returning to the site within the next 30 days and placing a full order," says Brodie. In addition to tailoring the message to each customer segment, BuildDirect uses Google Analytics' A/B testing capabilities to perfect its marketing approach. "We test different versions of creative on each newsletter and track results using Google Analytics, so we know the open rates, click-through rates, and conversions for everything we try."

Streamlined Site Design

Finally, BuildDirect was able to optimize its website design based on Google Analytics report data. "Using the Google Analytics Site Overlay and the Defined Funnel Report, we found we were losing almost half of our customers on the three-stage process between cart and payment confirmation," Brodie says. "We reduced this process to one step. By simplifying to a single page, we increased sample orders by 100 percent and expect that to contribute to a significant revenue increase within a few months." BuildDirect will continue to test and monitor online marketing programs with web analytics.

"Before Google Analytics, we basically guessed how we should be spending marketing dollars. We now know how much campaigns pay off and how well they work," Brodie says. "Google Analytics has had a huge positive impact on our business."

We discussed performance indicators in the previous chapter, but it's so important it bears mentioning again. Once you have your analytics program set up, you are truly ready to launch your email marketing efforts. You will have a holistic view of who has an opportunity to see your email opt-in efforts and how qualified they really are, the best types of engagement programs and phrases to use to kick start your efforts, and how well your conversion tactics are at getting someone to buy or convert.

Congratulations on setting up a great and well-thought-out program; you are ready to hit Send and start seeing results.

What to Do If Something Goes Wrong

Yikes! Did you *really* send your first campaign while you were only on Chapter 4 of this book? We hope not. Why? Because we have not had a chance to share with you the most important elements of an email campaign: what to do when something goes wrong.

A newbie to email might think they can actually be an effective email marketer without anything ever going wrong. That is not the case. Ask anyone who has sent out an email campaign about what can go wrong, and you will get a tremendous list of items that can and do go wrong.

Things that can go wrong with your email vary from small errors to large errors that can even result in legal issues. In fact, you shouldn't worry about *when* you will make the error. Instead, you should feel confident that you will be able to handle it when it happens to you.

We took a look at all the stories people sent to us over the years about "email oopses" that have occurred and wanted to share the following Email Experience Council blog posting from Chad White and the resulting comments with you.

From the Arsenal of Oopses (Source: Email Experience Council)

In one Email Experience Council newsletter, Jeanniey confessed that she's no deployment expert: "I am notorious for sending emails with typos, links that don't work, image hosting paths that work only on my PC, messing up segments, and more." She shared her favorite oopsy and said that the mistakes that she's made have all taught her phenomenal lessons. And then she asked whether anyone had a "disastrous email story" to share—and many brave souls stepped forward to share their lesson learned.

My two cents on this is that mistakes in emails are difficult to avoid because of the complexity of the medium and volume involved. All you can do is try your best and learn from your mistakes—and the mistakes of others.

Without further delay, here are the "oops" moments our subscribers shared with us.

—Chad White, Editor at Large

* * *

"You are definitely not the only one! I have an arsenal of "oops," but I'll share my favorite of all time. I was adding the physical mailing address and associated contact details to the bottom of an email for a B2B campaign. The phone number I needed to add was spelled out, and because I was translating the letters to numbers by looking at my phone and using my keyboard—forgetting that the layout of the numbers are different—I inadvertently transposed two numbers. The correct number would have pointed someone to a help desk for product support; the incorrect number pointed to a phone sex line. There were only a few reports of people actually calling that number. I believe one was a CEO.

"Naturally, I learned from this and physically dial all of the phone numbers on anything I ever send out! (And I learned that phone sex lines are not limited to 900 numbers!)"

—Amy Gabriel

So, What Do You Do When It Happens to You?

As you can see, mistakes of all shapes and sizes happen with anyone's email marketing campaigns. The key here is to know what to do when it happens to you. As with most things that go wrong, the first rule of thumb is, Don't panic. Errors happen. Instead, be ready to assess the situation to determine the impact and your next steps. To help prepare you for the steps to take when an email marketing error occurs, we will walk you through a mistake that really happened.

(This is a true story—the names have been changed to protect the innocent).

The Background

An email campaign had been in place for a number of years. It was a fairly simple campaign: a personalized email (first and last name) was sent to a prospect within seven days of asking for more product information and providing their personal contact information, including mailing address.

The Mistake

Someone new to the program (on the service-provider side) sorted the file before loading it into the system by one of the columns. Inadvertently, they left the first and last name columns out of the sorting. This caused the email names to be mismatched with the names. When a recipient opened the email with the subject line of "Your personal follow-up," they saw someone else's name.

The Call from the Client

The client received a call to customer service questioning this email. The client immediately called the service provider to find out the scope of the issue.

The Response

The response from the provider (and our recommendations for you) consisted of the following steps:

1. **Ask for details and a copy of the email to be sent to you.** Many times, the origin of the issue requires needing the header information to track down or solve the problem. This information is not available if the email is forwarded to you. Figure 4.4 shows what header information looks like.

2. **Determine the impact of your error from your email reports.** In the case of this example, the email sent to the recipient showed that it was a legitimate email, sent by the email provider's system. All technical aspects checked out; only the names were off. A quick check in the email database uncovered the error of the column formatting. The next step was to check the reports to see how many people had opened the email so far. It was 40 percent. Normally, a 40 percent open rate would be seen as great news for this client. In this case, it meant that 40 percent of the list has been exposed to inaccurate data that could potentially make them lose faith in this client.

Figure 4.4 Full header information

3. **Make a recommendation for response.** Email marketing errors that are not fol-
    lowed up with a response to those affected tend to do more damage than those
    who just come out with a statement. A reply of silence can often generate blog
    backlash. In this case, though, understanding that 40 percent were affected was
    key, because it enabled the service provider to recommend *not* sending a blanket
    email but sending one only to the people who had opened their email to date.

    The recommended response to the client was an email with a subject line that
    referenced the last email they received, without causing more panic.

4. **Monitor the results of your email response rates, as well as your analytics.** Of
    those people who received and opened the email with the inaccurate informa-
    tion, only 25 percent of them opened the follow-up email. Interestingly, though,
    a quarter of those people ended up buying the company product. Compared to
    the typical response to these programs, this program actually ended up perform-
    ing on par with the standard campaigns. Crisis averted for this instance!

    Although this story had a happy ending, there are some important take-aways
from this section of the chapter. Not only do you need to take a realistic and methodi-
cal approach to handling email mishaps, but you need to have your "ducks in a row"
before you send your campaign so you are well prepared to solve the challenges you
are dealt. A good email strategy, strong analytics, and a solid budget will often reap
rewards far beyond the implementation of a few emails.

Revisiting Your Budget

Now that you have a handle on the core elements needed to get your program up and
running, have selected an email service provider or technology, have organized your

analytics efforts, and know what to do when something goes wrong, you are ready to send, right? Not so fast. Before you execute your program, you should really stop and revisit your email budget one more time. Do you *really* have enough money?

So, at this part in the book, now is a good time for you to get your budget checklist out and make sure you have accounted for all that you will need to spend.

Write This Down: Regardless of how much money you have in your email marketing budget, many marketers do not think they have enough money to enhance their programs, attract new email marketing subscribers and battle loss through attrition from the previous year. Many people are looking for more funds to replace email names and attrition.

In the previous chapter, we discussed the average costs to send email and recommended building your budget needs from an assessment of the list size and the staff necessary to execute the programs you desire. Those are important numbers, but they may not include some more of the tactical spending you might have missed inside your budget—items that could create challenges for you down the road. This checklist should help ensure you have everything covered:

List Replacement Fees Forrester finds that 30 percent of email addresses will "go bad" every year because of bounces, people changing addresses, people starting new jobs, and unsubscribes. Ensure you devote enough of your budget to replacing 50 percent of your list (to account for blocked new subscribers and nonresponsive emails).

Design No matter who you are, or how many resources you have, outsourced design fees are going to raise their heads at some time within the year. A mandatory cost from a list rental company for design edits, a "crunch time" project in which the design can't be managed in-house, a special fee for design from a partner program—these elements can all come into play. Although this isn't a big budget line, it should be accounted for.

Testing Frequently, the second-largest missed item on the budgeting line is testing. You don't realize how much you need it until you launch an email campaign that just doesn't work. Although internal testing is great, make sure you have $5,000 to $10,000 set aside for landing page optimization, heatmapping, or list rental source testing to validate some theories.

Data Support Regardless of the email service provider or analytics engine you have, you will need to bring in "the big guns" quarterly or at least two times per year to help identify trends in data movement. Although your in-house team can probably manage it well, you could end up with a project sitting on the books for four to five months waiting to be given high priority. In the meantime, your email campaign could suffer. Plan to save a few thousand dollars a month to enable data support.

Mad Money There isn't really an appropriate name for this category, but our moms said it best: "Stuff some money under your mattress for when you need it." Every year, a new, hot technology related to email comes out that your company or provider doesn't yet support or believe in. (In 2008, it is social networking email campaigns, discussed in Chapter 8.) But you still want to test it. It is always a good idea to have a few thousand dollars stuffed away for a rainy-day test to ensure you are still thinking sensibly.

To ensure you have your budget set up to support growth, focusing on growing learnings and fueling incremental success are key. Kudos to you if you took your high-lighter out on this chapter. Although the recommendations many seem small, they will pay out big time down the road.

The Email Marketing Database and Future Multichannel Efforts

A good bit of this chapter has focused on what you need to do to ensure that your email marketing efforts are successful and that you look like a rock star within your company. From analytics support to disaster recovery to budgeting for the unexpected, the focus has been on supporting direct-email marketing efforts. That said, your email is the backbone of every other marketing channel. At some point in time, people will encounter an email from your company, even if they have never sent you one. This phenomenon is not new to marketing yet is often treated like it is. It is called *multichannel marketing.* And with email, multichannel marketing is something you should consider at the same time you are putting your analytics and budget in place. How do you ensure that your initial email marketing database setup will enable you to create multi-channel efforts down the road?

Although there are many different theories of how visitors become customers for any company and different graphical representations of those ideas, we are especially drawn to one graphic. Shown in Figure 4.5, it is called the *four phases of consumer activity.*

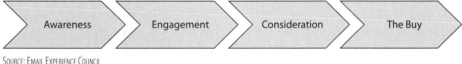

Source: Email Experience Council

Figure 4.5 The four phases of consumer activity

Regardless of whether your company is large or small, regardless of whether your focus is B2B or B2C, and regardless of what industry you represent, your customer will go through the four phases of consumer activity in determining whether they should be associated with your company. The interesting thing about each of these phases is that email plays a critical and unique role depending on what other media vehicles are in market. This multichannel messaging impact can completely change the effect of your email marketing program.

To ensure you are achieving the biggest impact with your email marketing efforts, you need to ensure email is being used appropriately at each phase of the buying cycle. In many cases, this could mean that email is the secondary influencer or even plays a tertiary role to other media. The specific role that email marketing plays doesn't matter. What does matter is that it plays that role in a way that increases ROI and customer satisfaction.

Phase 1: Awareness

When a potential or current customer is becoming aware of a product or service you offer, the truth is, it's most likely not happening through email. One of two elements will pique a person's awareness of your ability to service their needs:

- They woke up with an issue they needed to solve (for example, the car will not start).
- A friend told them about something they *had* to get or look into because it would change their life (for example, a George Foreman grill).

In each of these two scenarios, your prospect will go online and search for information about this product or service or potentially even go to a store where it is offered. The key media at this stage in a consumer's life is probably not email. This email isn't a direct response element. Instead, email marketing efforts here work to aid other forms of media, such as online, TV, and print, to help bring the product or service to the top of a prospect's mind. They help build the brand of the product you are offering.

Phase 2: Engagement

When someone is ready to "try but not buy" your product or service, they want to engage with the brand. Testing to make sure a company is "right for them" is critical to getting someone to make a purchase. This phase of the life cycle is one of the areas where email marketing can take the lead, but not by being delivered to the inbox. Instead, the multichannel role of email is to support the website or customer service group's efforts and therefore simply sit there and ask for the permission to continue a dialogue. Here, the role of email is to entice someone to opt in to future messages. It's very valuable to a company, because it opens the door to direct and results-driven messaging. The critical role of email at this stage is to accept the data and respond with a welcome email that will get people excited. Keep it simple and engaging, and offer something of value. People who read this email will want to learn more about the different types of flowers you sell for the next special occasion, for example.

Phase 3: Consideration

Although the first two phases are really supporting roles for outbound email marketing efforts, the third phase is where email starts to take more of a frontline role. When someone is considering a purchase, nothing is better than a well-timed email to help seal the deal. In fact, Forrester reports that once someone buys something via an email marketing purchase, they are likely to spend 138 percent more with your company than those who decided to buy through other channels.

Email marketing at this stage drives sales. A recent Ipsos study found that consumers are more likely to make purchases based on email offers from businesses they know and trust and have purchased from before. This is critical in the consideration phase. Getting your message in front of a potential customer needs to coincide with the time when they are considering a purchase in your product set. Since there is not a perfect predictor of this timing, continuous, valuable messaging makes email the messaging channel of choice.

Phase 4: The Buy

Woo-hoo! A purchase was made! Email marketing has to kick things into high gear now to make sure the excitement from the purchase is being used to drive a positive experience. Sometimes known as *transactional messages*, this type of email message reinforces the value of the purchase the customer just made and makes them feel good about it. But remember, email marketing doesn't act alone at this point in the customer's buying cycle. The multichannel reach through sales associates and word of mouth plays a heavy role too!

The truth is, without our customers, we'd be nothing. And email at this point in a customer's life cycle is critical. Asking for feedback with surveys and polls and making it simple to share one's love of a product or service with friends make these messages an invaluable source of future sales and lifetime value.

Making the Most of Your Email in a Multichannel Environment

Emails that you send at different points in a customer's life cycle either have an impact or are impacted by all the media the customer sees. The more media vehicles in place, the higher the response potentially is.

Figure 4.6 is a graph from the Email Experience Council that does a great job of illustrating how to ensure that your emails are surrounded by the strongest forms of media.

What This Means When You Are Setting Up Your Initial Email Database

Now that you are an expert in the theory of multichannel email marketing (and more will be discussed in the next chapter), you need to apply that theory to the email marketing database you have.

More often than not, just like missed opportunities with budgets, many times the best email marketers limit themselves through missed opportunities with database integration. Ensuring your email marketing database can support multichannel marketing signals (for example, updating a record to show that someone called customer service six times) doesn't have to be costly or time-consuming. It just needs to be done up-front.

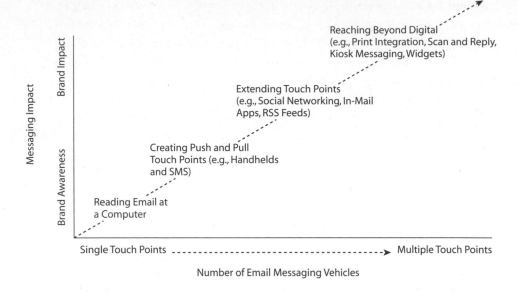

Figure 4.6 Email marketing in a multichannel environment

Overnight Shipping Company's Email Program

As an illustration of the impact of multichannel efforts and email at its best, we'll share this story with you.

When you go to the Overnight shipping company website and want to place an order, a series of multichannel efforts kicks off that are very sophisticated.

These include the following (not in this order):

- A real-time query to the database to see whether you are a returning customer

- A check to see whether the email address or IP you are entering from is a larger or target customer (if so, you get a special offer)

- A special offer for the type of credit card you are planning on using (based on another real-time lookup and partnership with credit card companies)

- An email sent to your account, which will determine how potentially responsive you will be in the future

- An email to a sales rep if you end up representing a large or key prospect account

- Retargeting banners on and off the site based on your actual purchase or non-purchase

- And more

Believe it or not, all these multichannel effort happen in real time and require very little human intervention. This is the result of a well-thought-out strategy and a very strong and nimble set of databases that speak to each other.

Your email marketing efforts can be just as powerful and just as impactful with a little preplanning.

As authors who have "done it the hard way" many times, we can say that making sure your email marketing database can support additional and customized field headers is key. You should also ensure that your email marketing database and/or service provider has a solid FTP service as well as the ability to support APIs. In many cases, large companies cannot afford to have all their customer data live outside of their firewalls and must use secure APIs to transmit multichannel data back and forth in real time to generate the next step in email efforts.

Asking these questions now will save you precious time and money in the future.

The Top Five Ways You Can Mess Things Up If You Are Not Really Careful

The majority of this chapter looked at the benefits of dotting the i's and crossing the t's before launching your email marketing efforts. You will find that these suggestions, although seemingly a bit excessive, will ensure your program delivers peak performance from the start.

With that said, as you move into the tactical elements of creating your actual email strategy, content plan, and messaging plan, here is a quick recap of the top five ways you can turn all your hard work into disaster it you are not careful:

- **Undercutting your budget.** You can have the best email results around but lack the ability to grow without the right budget in place. Worse yet, you could run into real problems with your email campaign (deliverability issues or data concerns) and have no way to address them without a budget to support the work.

Write This Down: The authors' budgeting rule of thumb is to make your email budget and then add 30 percent on to it for the "unknowns."

- **Forgetting to design your email database.** Although many email service providers or technology suppliers will tell you their database is "standard" and "adequate," don't believe them. Also, turn a deaf ear when your technology team tells you they have the data needs all covered. Make sure your database supports all entrance and exit points for customers to share information with you. Make sure it is simple to share this data with all the other databases your company leverages.

Write This Down: Your email marketing database should enable you to define the primary key, support APIs, and automated FTPs without additional fees and, most important, should allow the simple importing and exporting of custom-designed queries to support your business.

- **Not planning for disasters.** Everyone makes mistakes. At some point in time, we promise you, an email marketing program you are responsible for will go wrong. Keep a level head about yourself when this occurs. It could be the downfall of your program, or it could be a chance to show your customers you are human too and win their loyalty and trust at a higher level than you have ever expected before.

Write This Down: The best open rates on email campaigns actually happen in campaigns that are mistakes. Empty subject line fields or fields that say, "This is a test," typically garner open rates of more than 75 percent.

- **Not realizing that email is only *one* element of your multichannel marketing campaign.** Email marketing is great but is not the only channel influencing your customer. TV ads, print ads, online ads, your website, your search, and word of mouth also play key roles. Respect the role that email plays given the various other elements your marketing team has launched. Build a strategy that supports the holistic approach, or run the risk of being seen as the "oddball out."

Write This Down: Seventy-two percent of the time, email marketing templates and landing pages fail to be redesigned when new large branding campaigns launch, creating a disconnected communication. (Source: Email Experience Council)

- **Expecting your email marketing efforts to work from day one.** Email marketing is difficult. Now that you have a handle on all the high-level and strategic thoughts you need to consider, in the next chapter you will dive into the tactical elements required for creating success. Do not take the availability of email addresses and low cost of deployment technology for granted. As you have read, email drives significant revenue for those who get it right. Similarly, it can tarnish a brand beyond repair for those you get it wrong. Approach email with caution and attention to detail. Follow this book, and you will be pleased with your results.

Test Your Knowledge

Understanding what can and may happen once you send your email is important. Make sure you are ready to click the Send button by asking yourself these questions. A score of 5 out of 5 will ensure you are on your way to email marketing success.

- Why is it important to have an analytics program set up that goes beyond your email marketing service provider's reports? Name a free and simple program anyone can use.

- Does your email budget have a role in the companys growth plan?
- Provide two different recommendations for when something with your campaign goes wrong.
- Define the four phases of a multichannel campaign where email plays a role.
- Name the top five ways you can "mess up" your campaign if you are not careful.

Eight Key Drivers of Your Email Campaign

In this chapter, we will review key drivers to building a successful email campaign. Make sure you have that highlighter in hand because we'll show you how to apply general email tactics to specific types of businesses and business models. Underlying all the key macro drivers is your overall email marketing strategy. We will continue to reinforce the strategy guidance that we laid out in previous chapters, but now it is time for you to examine the nuances of the tactics that will be the foundation of your email marketing program.

5

Chapter Contents

Key Driver 1: Email Address Acquisition

Acquiring an email address can be one of your easier tasks as an email marketer; however, ensuring that you are adhering to best practices to leverage your site traffic to its fullest for email acquisition will take some trial and error. Besides your own website traffic, you can use a variety of channels and sources, such as list rental, to grow your email list. Additionally, it is necessary to capture the source of the email address—did it come via your website, via your call center, or through some other means? You can capture this information with a simple code that is hidden to the user but that allows you to measure the effectiveness of your different acquisition sources. Paramount to your email marketing success is balancing the quantity of the email addresses that you will acquire with their quality. Simply acquiring or renting a large list of email addresses may not deliver the return that you are seeking compared to methodically growing your own list over time. Both methods serve a purpose, and this section will provide you with all the necessary tactics to understand acquisition.

Your Website

Site registration and email acquisition should be a prominent part of your website. Many successful marketers, such as Lands' End (Figure 5.1), dedicate a portion of their home pages that is "above the fold" (meaning the primary area of focus on a web page that does not require the user to scroll down) to highlighting and promoting the link or form to acquire email addresses. Others, such as The Home Depot (Figure 5.2), ensure that email address opt-in boxes are on every page of the website. Both approaches can be successful as long as you put those acquisition links at the top of the web page or a place of prominence on the landing page.

Figure 5.1 The Lands' End website places an acquisition link near the top of its home page.

 Write This Down: As of April 2008, 40 percent of online consumers in the United States opt in to receive email newsletters. (Source: JupiterResearch)

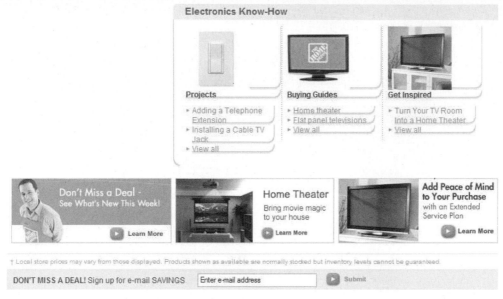

Figure 5.2 The Home Depot site includes an email opt-in box on every page.

When building email acquisition on your site, keep these tactics in mind:

- **Ask for and collect only the data you will use to segment your subscribers.**
  Consumers are leery of providing too much personal information, particularly
  for a brand with which they are just beginning to form a relationship. Although
  data such as geographic information can help multichannel retailers target email
  subscribers who live close to their stores, for others such information may never
  be used. Map out the three to five pieces of information that will inform your
  email segmentation strategy over the next twelve months. Common data points
  to collect on the registration form are email address, name, address, and gender.
  We recommend you take an incremental approach to data collection: capture
  what you need up-front without presenting more than five fields. Later you can
  use surveys and polling questions to capture additional information that can be
  used for more detailed segmentation.

- **Ensure that your site registration complies with the Children's Online Privacy
  Protection Act (COPPA).** For sites that cater to children or an "online service
  that is directed to children," COPPA requires that sites do not collect personally identifiable information from children younger than 13. The Federal Trade
  Commission governs this law, and you should become familiar with these guidelines particularly if your business caters to or could potentially attract children.
  For additional information, see www.coppa.org.

- **Leverage traffic from search engines and dynamic landing pages.** When consumers use search engines to find websites, they are increasingly being exposed to results that take them to dynamic landing pages, which are pages that are specifically engineered to display the product that is being queried. In these instances, whether they are dynamically generated or static, landing pages ensure that email registration is a noticeable component of that page. A best practice is to leverage the search phrase that is used to drive the dynamic landing page and use that search phrase in the context of the promotion of your email registration form. For example, if the search phrase is *flat-panel TVs*, as in Figure 5.3, use that language to suggest that the site visitor sign up for a newsletter on selecting and purchasing flat-panel TVs. Such an approach also recognizes that the online consumer rarely makes an impulse purchase and makes repeated site visits before purchasing.

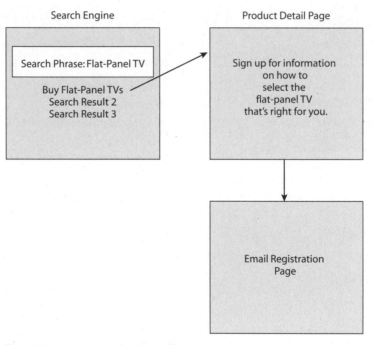

Figure 5.3 Leveraging search engine traffic

- **Use standard form field names.** When building your email registration form, ensure that you are following the guidelines laid out by Microsoft and standards bodies, such as the HTML Writers Guild, to name the fields using the standard names. This allows autocomplete features in Internet Explorer or the Google Toolbar to populate that form easily, thus improving the site experience for the visitor.

- **Ask for permission.** When combining email registration with shopping or site registration forms, ensure that you add a check box that allows the visitor to opt into the email newsletter or marketing piece. This single check box should be unchecked, allowing the visitor to express their permission to receive such messages.

- **Provide expectations.** This is where you begin selling the subscriber on the notion that they should be subscribing to your email newsletter. Give them a general idea of how often they will receive email messages from you.

- **Provide an example.** To show potential subscribers exactly what they are signing up for, provide a link to your most recent email newsletter or a thumbnail snapshot of the newsletter. As you can see in Figure 5.4, National Geographic is a good example of a marketer that provides subscribers with insight into what they will be receiving.

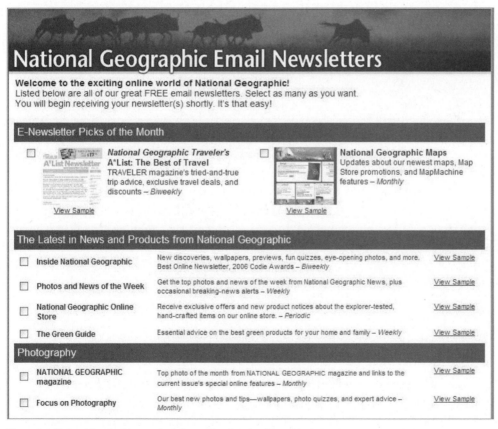

Figure 5.4 National Geographic provides links to examples of each type of subscription.

- **Provide a link to your privacy policy.** Although industry research from Jupiter-Research and others has found that consumers are clearly concerned with privacy, few actually take the time to read privacy policies. Nonetheless, provide a link to your full privacy policy, and to allay concerns, highlight key elements in the policy. For example, state you will not share data with third parties on the email subscription form.

- **Build a list-scrubbing routine to remove harmful addresses.** It is not unheard of that malicious site visitors will attempt to register with `abuse@` or `complaint@` email addresses, which will likely land you in the spam folder. Check with your ESP to ensure that it has a standard scrubbing procedure that automatically suppresses harmful names or allows you to add domain-level suppression to your email list to remove, for example, competitors from joining your email list. Additionally, your email service provider should be scrubbing your list against wireless email domains, as mandated by the FCC. (Note that this restriction does not apply to domains that consumers may pull down on their wireless device, such as an AOL account on a BlackBerry, but it does prohibit messages to wireless email boxes, including domains such as `@mail.verizonwireless.com`. This provision does not ban transactional messages, but "sending unwanted email messages to wireless devices" applies to all "commercial messages.")

Later in this chapter we will provide additional information about regulations related to permission and what can be done with the email addresses once you acquire them. In some instances, companies enlist *double opt-in* (see the glossary) to further underscore legal requirements and embrace best practices. Double opt-in is not a legal requirement, and marketers who have used it have indicated in interviews that as much as 30 percent of the initial registrants drop off—that is, they fail to confirm their permission the second time. It may be worthwhile for marketers who have had list hygiene and delivery issues to explore double opt-in to improve list quality as well as qualify for reputation management and accreditation services. It is also important to ensure good delivery practices, such as list seeding, on the confirmation messages to ensure that they are not getting blocked and that consumers do receive them.

Other Channels

If you have a call center, physical store, or kiosk, or if you run events or have other offline means of interacting with your customers and prospects, then email address acquisition must be part of that strategy. Here are a variety of helpful examples of how you can integrate email into those channels:

Call Center Asking for an email address adds five to ten seconds to a phone call, but the value of an email address can offset the cost of the longer phone call and justify the decision. Call center phone agents should be scripted and trained to ask each client for an email address and to ask them for permission to send emails. Most call center client interaction systems can easily facilitate adding such a field, and extracting that data from those systems does not require direct integration with your email marketing software. Simply pull a text file of that information daily or weekly and merge it (while suppressing duplicates) into your email house list. In some call centers, the representatives are spot-checked and graded to ensure that they are asking for the client's email address on every call.

In-Person Email Acquisition This can take a variety of forms, including at the point of sale, at a self-service kiosk, or at a marketing event such as a trade show. With all these forms there is a cost of adding the email address request to the transaction time or infrastructure that is required to achieve it. Multichannel retailers such as Borders and Office Depot do a good job at the point of sale of asking for or confirming the email address that they might already have on file for the customer. In these instances, the email address is so valuable to these companies that they actually give incentives to the cashiers to ring up sales that are accompanied by the customer's email address. In these instances, the email address is often used as the primary customer identifier to run loyalty and rewards programs. Evaluate the costs, and do not dismiss the awesome opportunity that face-to-face interactions with clients and prospects offer to grow your email list.

Print and Magazine Advertisements A useful way to gauge the effectiveness of print campaigns is to promote email registration. As you'll see in Chapter 6, the cosmetics manufacturer Sephora runs ads in major fashion magazines promoting its newsletters that detail a URL to a specific landing page (or micro site). This allows Sephora to maximize its advertising spending, and at the same time it provides a directional measure of success to that print ad, which is quantified by the number of email subscriptions that were generated by the advertisement.

Texting on In-Store Banners "In-store" means any place where both your customers may be found and a banner can be placed. For example, US Airways puts the banner shown in Figure 5.5 in the bag collection area of a major airport, where one of us was a captive audience. It simply asks people to text their names and email addresses to a short code in order to get miles for the trip they just completed. Even though the only camera we had was a cell phone, it was such a good use of text messaging to support email address acquisition that we had to capture it for this book.

Service-Related Email Messages Consumers largely use email to contact customer service on pre- and post-sale bases. Although these email addresses can be captured for the purpose of outbound email marketing with the customer's consent (in other words, opt-in), the outbound service reply should include a reminder in the footer that promotes email registration for marketing messages and/or newsletters.

Figure 5.5 US Airways' use of a text banner for email address capture

Third-Party Sources

There are multiple means to acquire email addresses from other sources, including co-registration, email appends, list rental, and sponsorship. Although these forms of email address collection can all be effective, a 2006 JupiterResearch study titled "E-mail Acquisition: Aligning Budgets to Effective Acquisition Opportunities" found that these forms of acquisition were less satisfying in terms of quality to marketers than their own site registration. In each of these third-party forms of email acquisition, you must scrutinize the source where the provider is getting the email addresses, the manner in which they are collecting the data, and the age of the email data you would be acquiring. Quality can be a costly drain here because a high number of bad or old email addresses can drive your bounce rate so high that it may end up blocking your email messages on particular ISPs. To guard against this, you should send your mailings from a different IP address and over time migrate the email addresses that are responsive to your primary IP sending address. Even in this instance, however, you should continue to maintain these email addresses on a separate list so that you can monitor the quality and performance over time. With those caveats in mind, here are some options to acquire email addresses from third-party sources.

Write This Down: Email service provider ExactTarget reports the following co-registration results on programs that its clients ran in 2004 and 2005:

- Open and click rates are consistently less than half those for in-house lists.
- Recipients acquired through co-registration unsubscribe from the email programs faster.
- Co-registration conversion rates are much lower than those for in-house lists.

Co-Registration

When your email opt-in box rides alongside another advertiser's, usually on a publisher's website, that is *co-registration*. Examples can be found on portal and news publisher sites. On the MSNBC.com weather page, for instance, you will see an opt-in box from an advertiser such as the Weather Channel to get its forecasts sent by email. The Weather Channel is also a publisher, and on its opt-in page, you will see relevant offers from retailers that sell products dependent on the weather, such as lawn care products. As you can see, it's a best practice to pick a co-registration partner that is contextually relevant to what your newsletter or email marketing offer provides. In these instances, co-registration can be effective. However, based on our experience, the cost can be as high as 50 cents per name, so in many instances co-registration results do not provide the necessary return on the money spent to acquire the names because the results typically underperform the names acquired directly from your own website. There are many fine co-registration vendors; for example, Prospectiv focuses on business-to-consumer co-registration, and Return Path has a Postmaster Direct offering oriented more toward business-to-business marketers.

Write This Down: As of April 2008, 54 percent of consumers in the United States have provided their email addresses as part of a sweepstakes. (Source: JupiterResearch)

Sweepstakes

This is a subset of co-registration, where the publisher provides a sweepstake for the advertiser to drive email subscriptions. Although consumers will participate in them, these sweepstakes typically underperform other methods of acquisition. You should be leery of using sweepstakes (for example, "Free iPod") to entice subscribers to participate in your co-registration program, because people tend to use secondary email addresses to sign up for those types of programs. A 2006 JupiterReseach study found that sweepstakes programs performed the worst compared to other forms of email acquisition.

Email Appending

Email address appending is the process of adding a consumer's email address to the consumer's record in your database. The email address is obtained by matching records from the marketer's database against a third-party database to produce a corresponding email address. The number of addresses that match your data is called the *match rate* and is a point of negotiation with email appends vendors. Vendors will charge based on how many of those names opt into your mailing. This fee can be similar to the price of co-registration or as high as $4 per email address if the vendor refreshes its email list more often, which should result in newer email addresses. Like co-registration, append programs often underperform the email addresses you would acquire through your own means. It is important to understand a potential appends vendor's acquisition source of email addresses and the age of these addresses. For customers with a very high lifetime value or for companies that do a high amount of postal direct mailing, such as credit card companies, appending additional customer data can be a valuable tactic to employ. Consult your ESP for vendors that provide this service.

List Rental

Renting third-party lists is one of the most common ways to acquire customers and/or build an in-house email list. However, this is also one of the more common ways that you can get into spam trouble if the list you are renting was built in a less-than-pristine manner. You should insist that any list you rent was built using either confirmed opt-in or double opt-in.

You should only rent names of people who have already expressly indicated to the source that they want to hear from a third party. As with other third-party forms of acquisition, be sure to find out from the prospective vendor the source of the email addresses, the age of the list, and how it processes bounces (how many times an email address bounces before it's removed from the list). Additionally, determine what level of targeting can be achieved by selecting lists that match only the demographics or segments you are seeking to acquire. The price should be determined by the quality of these addresses. Email to this list should be sent from a separate IP address than your primary house list. In most cases, the list provider will send the email for you, making it necessary to investigate its reporting capabilities and reputation as a sender. You can usually find this information publicly via tools such as www.senderbase.org. In recent years, list rental has fallen out of favor because of the high number of spam complaints that are associated with the practice. Consult your ESP to determine whether list rental is an appropriate way for you to grow your list as well as determine the most suitable appends vendors.

 Write This Down: According to an email marketing forecast for 2007–2012, spending on sponsored email will total more than $600 million in 2012. (Source: JupiterResearch)

Email Newsletter Sponsorship

This is one of the most prevalent email acquisition tactics, with email sponsorship accounting for nearly half of the billons of dollars that will be spent on email marketing in the United States over the next five years. Rates for advertisements in a publisher's newsletter vary dramatically based on the distribution size of the list and the degree to which it is aimed at your target market. Newsletter sponsorship is typically charged on a performance basis, with contracts built around cost-per-open, cost-per-click, cost-per-registration, and cost-per-thousand emails sent. The registration model is the most relevant approach to defining the value of acquisition campaigns. Vendors such as Datran Media offer a variety of these performance sponsorship opportunities across a wide variety of publishers' newsletters. Your advertisement in these newsletters should be compelling and informative, but keep the subscriber guessing just enough to drive interest and thus propel them to click through. Landing pages for your ads should prominently highlight email registration.

Welcome to the Campaign!

A key part of email acquisition is the follow-up mailing or set of mailings that happen immediately after the subscriber opts in. In bricks-and-mortar retail, a store merchant will treat a returning customer differently than a new prospect who walks into their store for the very first time; you should do the same. This simple analogy provides the primary lesson that you should follow when acquiring new subscribers via email. A common mistake of marketers is immediately lumping new subscribers in with old subscribers and sending them the same weekly email communication. A better practice is to set up a string of three to four messages that ease the subscriber into the typical mailing flow. This is commonly referred to as the *welcome campaign*. Here are some ideas on how to approach and build a welcome campaign:

Welcome Message This message should be sent immediately after the subscription takes place and should serve to both confirm the subscription and welcome the subscriber to your email marketing program. It should also contain the following elements:

> **Add to the Address Book** To further protect their subscribers, most ISPs and email client software, such as Microsoft Outlook, turn off the images in emails by default. Image rendering issues impact the ability to accurately measure open rates and certainly undermine the creative aspect to email marketing. These image-rendering issues and the erroneous labeling of messages as spam plague all email marketers. To minimize image rendering issues, ask the subscriber to add your email address to their address book. This should be an element in every email marketing message, but with the introductory welcome message, more creative emphasis should be placed on this part of the message. One important consideration with this tactic is to not change the From address across your email marketing campaigns, because the benefits of a subscriber adding your address to their address book can be leveraged only if you continue to use the same From address across all your mailings.

> **Click to View** An additional way to get around image-rendering problems is to include a "View This Email in Your Web Browser" link at the top of your email.

This link will take the user to a hosted version of your email newsletter. Your ESP should offer this functionality by default, typically as a link that can be added just before you deploy your message. As with the Add to the Address Book feature, this element should be in every message but highlighted with a bit more prominence in the welcome message.

Set and Reinforce Expectations As with the subscription page, best practices remind your subscribers how often they will be receiving your email messages.

Federal Compliance We will cover CAN-SPAM requirements in greater depth later in this chapter. Your welcome message should contain the federally mandated opt-out provisions.

Welcome Message No. 2 This should be a slight variation on the message that the customer signed up to receive. In a retail or newsletter context, it should emphasize that the subscriber can forward this message to friends, making them a conduit to further grow your list. Some marketers experiment with placing new subscriber incentives on this second welcome message, such as free shipping on the first order or 10 percent off for new subscribers. For business-to-business marketers, the call to action in the email creative may be to download a white paper or request further information from a salesperson. Such an approach helps to further qualify the business prospect as more engaged or "hot" than a subscriber who chooses not to click.

Welcome Message No. 3 At this point, you should be integrating the new subscriber into the normal weekly flow of your marketing messages, but this additional message offers an opportunity to collect additional feedback. As described in our registration best practices, such a message provides you with the opportunity to collect incremental demographic or other valuable segmentation data from the subscriber. You can do this easily by embedding a polling question or a link to the subscriber's preference center that requests additional information.

As you can see, there are many components and options to getting email acquisition correct. Your ability to test these concepts through mailings such as the welcome campaign will ultimately determine the success of your email marketing program.

Key Driver 2: Creative/Copy

Beauty is in the eye of the beholder, and that concept is nowhere more important than in properly designed email creative and copy. There are many moving parts when constructing email, and using colors, images, and HTML are often the first things that can trip up an email marketer. The wonderful thing here, however, is that you have the ability to be creative, to strive to make your message stand out from the pack, and to illuminate and reinforce your brand image. Achieving all of this starts with a strong From field and subject line.

The From Line

We've already mentioned the importance of the From line and the need to keep the address the same in all your mailings. It's also crucial to have a "friendly" From address. Make sure your From line does not look like acmeemailstore@bugs.servrctz04.bunny.com, a practice that would certainly lead to delivery headaches. Use your brand name, and in a business-to-business context use personalization fields to insert the salesperson's name into the From address so that the email appears to come from the salesperson and not the corporation (for example, BugsBunny@AcmeEmailStore.com). Once you have settled on a From line, stick with it.

Subject Lines

With most images turned off by default, email recipients begin forming their opinions about the relevance of your message based upon the subject line. Use this line to summarize the email content. You want to tell the email content, not sell the email content. Here are some subject line do's and don'ts to keep in mind:

Do's

- **Limit.** Keep your subject line to 50 characters or less. Keep it simple; less is more when it comes to the subject line.

- **Test.** Test the effectiveness of multiple subject lines by using A/B split testing techniques. For example, retailers will often test a subject line by sending half the list a subject line that includes the words *free shipping* and the other half a subject line that includes the words *10% off*. Testing is important, but be careful not to sound too much like a stereotypical used car salesperson, and be particularly cautious with words such as *free* because they can often raise the content's spam score.

- **Use personalization.** Although putting the person's first name in the subject line may provide a slight improvement, over time the effectiveness of this form of subject line personalization often diminishes. Multichannel businesses, such as retailers, may want to experiment with location instead, such as "One-day sale this weekend in Albany."

- **Convey urgency and importance.** Airlines have higher open rates when using simple subject lines, such as "Trip Alert" or "Special Weather Advisory."

- **Make it personal.** "Your order confirmation" and "Your May statement is now available" are two transaction-oriented subject lines that often have high open rates.

- **Make it special.** "Be the first to see our new fall collection" or "Must have styles for spring" teases the reader but makes the product and subscriber feel special, like an "email insider."

- **Reinforce the From.** Use your brand name in the subject line, such as "[Company Name] April Newsletter."

- **Be honest.** Set expectations that are appropriate, and be clear and concise. Put yourself in the subscriber's shoes, and think of what would make you consider taking a look at this message. Stay true to the expectations that you set up on your registration page.

- **Be smart; stay relevant.** As an industry we talk a lot about relevancy, and we will dig into this secret sauce more in upcoming chapters. However if you are promoting purses to a list that is largely made up of men and it is not Valentine's Day, Mother's Day, or the holiday season, chances are your audience will not see it as relevant.

Don'ts

- **Don't use any capital letters.** Avoid writing your subject text with capital letters.

- **Don't use symbols.** Avoid symbols or exclamation marks that overhype your message. Often these punctuation characters will raise the spam score or "spaminess" factor of your message that could send it to the junk folder.

- **Avoid repetition.** Avoid using the same subject line on repeated mailings; keep changing it. This is one case that when you find something that works, don't always stick with it. Continue to test new variations.

- **Do not mislead.** Never be misleading with your subject line or header information. This is particularly important because it is mandated in the federal CAN-SPAM guidelines described later in this chapter. For example, a subject line that reads "Your Order Details" for a message that is nothing but a promotion is deceptive and breaks the letter of the law.

 Write This Down: According to 2007 data, 69 percent of consumers decide to click the Report Spam or Junk button based on what is in the subject line. (Source: Email Sender and Provider Coalition)

The Spam Check

In the early part of the 21st century, *spam*—unsolicited commercial email—was at its peak. To combat the spammers, ISPs began to score the content of message by using tools such as SpamAssassin to read the message and look for trigger words that matched previous spam messages they had already identified. These trigger words include the likes of *Free*, *%*, *!*, *Winner*, and many, many others. If the program sees too many of them, it will deem the message spam and change its disposition, either blocking it or sending it to the junk folder. Most ESPs offer tools to screen your message for these words and give you a score using the same technology that the ISPs use.

Additionally, tools from such providers as Return Path, Pivotal Veracity, Lyris, and Habeas go further and score your message on a number of other attributes, including the formation of links and your sending infrastructure. These valuable tools also provide you with data on how many of your messages made it into the primary inbox. However, content-based scoring, although still important, is no longer the primary tool that ISPs use to determine your "spaminess" factor, because spammers have matured.

Although we cannot provide you with the entire history of spam here, you know that the tactics that we must use as legitimate marketers to ensure that our messages render correctly and reach inboxes are required in part because of the ever-increasing safeguards that the ISPs need to put in place. Spammers have gotten increasingly smarter about getting their emails delivered. For example, they began to fool content-based filters by using HTML tables—putting words like *Viagra* into columns, the *V* in column 1, the *i* in column 2, and so on. When that no longer worked, they simply started using images to get around the content-based filters. To combat that, ISPs began turning off images by default, which certainly has a huge impact on us as marketers, because, after all, what marketer doesn't love a pretty picture?

We suggest you explore the necessary best practices for avoiding spam traps with your ESP or one of the aforementioned delivery service providers, because that topic is a moving one, and it's one that is likely to morph again and again as the market continues to mature. So with those basics in hand, you are ready to dig into some creative best practices that encapsulate the body of the message.

The Width of Your Email Template

Although most consumers use monitors with resolutions of 1024×768, email readers often do not take up the entire screen. This is in part because of vertical ads running down the side of the inbox in environments such as Yahoo or the way applications such as Outlook are laid out on the screen. The first thing to consider when building an email template is the width and length of that template. Consider the following when mapping out your template.

The newest version of Yahoo Mail overlays a vertical ad starting 601 pixels from the left side of the email, which means recipients have to scroll to view the right side of the email. So if your email is wider than 600 pixels, these recipients have to take an extra step to view the content.

So, is a 600-pixel width the right answer? Maybe—and certainly yes if Yahoo domains account for the majority of your email list. If your list is like most marketers', domains such as AOL.com, Yahoo.com, MSN.com, Hotmail.com, and Gmail.com will make up the bulk of it. A simple solution but one that involves quite a bit more up-front work is to segment your list by domain and format each template to the appropriate domain. However, we do not recommend this because you have no guarantee that the subscribers using these domains are actually reading the email in the online client such as Yahoo Mail. That is, all these webmail services allow their users to pull their email to an external email application (for example, Outlook or Thunderbird) or to an external device such as a Treo or BlackBerry.

 Write This Down: A 700-pixel width is acceptable for Apple users, but that is only about 5 percent of the population.

The best way to determine the width that is most appropriate for your list is to test. Gary Bauman, former email marketing director with Red Envelope, suggests splitting your file into two, three, or more groups and testing, for example, 600 pixels versus 650 pixels versus 700 pixels across several mailings, rotating the three groups so that each group gets one of each size. Then look at the aggregate results and the results by email domain. The revenue you lose from having the right side of emails covered by ads in Yahoo might be outweighed by having more content above the fold in other email clients. If there's a huge drop-off when Yahoo recipients get wider emails and a huge pick-up when other domains get wider emails, then it might be worthwhile to deliver separate creative for Yahoo subscribers. Let the return on this test mailing decide the best strategy for email template width.

Another tool for optimizing your email template is to seek out the aforementioned delivery service providers (DSPs), such as Return Path, Pivotal Veracity, or Lyris, because they offer applications that can render your email across multiple email clients. See Appendix A for contact information for these and other vendors.

The Length of Your Email Template: Work Above the Fold

As for the length of your email template, brevity is best here. We suggest doing what you can to fit it all on one page, two pages maximum. Use hyperlinks to cut down on verbose content to send your subscribers to your website to gather more information. Again, email is the trigger to inspire the recipient to learn more about a topic or begin a transaction. Think of your email like the front page of a newspaper, where the headline is the most important piece of information. Work above the fold, ensuring that your call to action is clear and near the top of the email; or at the very least, make sure the primary focus is on your creative.

Email Creative Best Practices

Considering the image-rendering challenges that are presented by today's email inbox environment, it is necessary to adhere to the following best practices.

Multipart-MIME A multipart-MIME message is essentially a package of your message—your HTML markup and a text version. The assumption here is that your subscriber's email client will determine which one it can render and display the message because it is best formatted for that email client. This works particularly well in today's environment given the increasing number of people who use their handheld devices (Treo, BlackBerry, and so on) to access their primary email accounts. Although multipart-MIME might sound terribly technical to pull off, in practice it is quite easy because most ESPs and email marketing applications provide you with the simple ability to create a text version of your message and an HTML message. Once you input those versions into the application, the provider and/or software stitches these versions to create one multipart message. In most cases and deployments, *multi* means two. However, the language provisions allow you to write and form the version that is best.

Alt Tags Ensure that all images have alt tags. These tags should include action-oriented text that paraphrases offers captured in images. Additionally, avoid using images for critical elements, such as federally prescribed CAN-SPAM language.

> **Write This Down:** As of 2007, fewer than one-quarter of online users (21 percent) turn on images in email messages, creating mailing measurement and performance issues for marketers. (Source: JupiterResearch)

Click to View and Add to Address Book Options As mentioned earlier with welcome campaigns, ensure that your email creative includes reminders to add senders to the address book and provides a hyperlink so that the entire email can be viewed in a web browser.

Key Driver 3: Making the Data Work

Your ability to segment and target your list will help to make your mailings more successful. Additionally, you need to ensure that your organization is collecting data consistently across all touch points throughout the organization to normalize the data that is collected. Here are some best practices to ensure that your data strategy is effective:

- **Use a unique customer identifier other than the email address.** Using a customer record key other than the client's email address will allow you to have a unique number in which to roll up a variety of customer data. For example, when linking to offline customer data, or enlisting address correction or appending services, it will give you a unique identifier to match the customer record against in the event the subscriber's email address is different from the one you have on file. Additionally, this will allow what is referred to as *householding*—rolling up a variety of email addresses in order to understand that they represent the customer or a number of customers who are residing at the same address. This is becoming increasingly necessary because most customers have at least two email addresses.

- **Collect exactly the same information from your customers and prospects at every acquisition source.** Always collecting the same amount and type of information ensures that you will be able to normalize your segmentation schemes across all those customers.

- **Understand language and subscriber location.** Increasingly, email addresses from around the world are being added to email marketers' mailing lists. Use the country domain information that is embedded in the email address, or simply ask what the customer language preference is. This is particularly necessary when launching localized language versions of your website for use in foreign countries. Having language associated with this data will allow you to tie it to the most appropriate foreign language character set when your message is deployed.

- **Use customer behavior as a segmentation attribute wherever possible.** Although the addition of website clickstream behavior to your email segmentation can be very useful, it is necessary to at least use the email click behavior as an attribute to segment customers over time. You will begin to see patterns emerge of subscribers who are repeatedly clicking your links and those who are not. This will highlight a level of engagement and can be an effective way to create groups of subscribers—those who are engaged and those who are not. Tailoring your message to the list of subscribers who are not engaged is a good tactic to spur your subscribers into action. Popular methods to get this segment's attention are to send them polls, contests, and more discount-laden messages. Although contests and sweepstakes typically don't garner great results, they can be effective with dormant subscribers as a means to spur these inactive recipients into action. This approach should be tested cautiously to determine whether contests can drive a high number of valuable subscribers back into action.

Your email service provider and/or technology will have a standard data mapping scheme as well as additional best practices to ensure that you are collecting appropriate data and that they are formatted correctly. However, ensure you are working with them to craft your segmentation strategy because targeted email mailings consistently perform better than broadcast (that is, one message to all) mailings.

Key Driver 4: Multichannel Integration

As you've seen, there are many strategies to collect and validate the customer's email address at the point of customer interaction. However, several additional steps after acquisition can dramatically engage your audience when done correctly. The Internet is a massive driver of influence because it is the primary tool that consumers use to make purchasing decisions regardless of channel. In fact, JupiterResearch reports that by 2012 the number of dollars actually spent online will be dwarfed by the number of offline dollars that are influenced from this online research.

Write This Down: According to a 2007 email marketing consumer survey, nearly half of email subscribers make at least one offline purchase every year that was influenced by an email marketing offer. (Source: JupiterResearch)

The primary goal of shoe retailer Nine West's email marketing program is to drive the consumer into its stores. Nine West has realized that its average order value is higher for those people who shop in their physical stores and that return rates are lower for those customers. Accordingly, Nine West has had success in its email marketing by offering coupons that are redeemable only at its offline stores. Similarly, Borders uses the same tactic to drive customers into its stores every week with discounts that are larger in store.

As mentioned previously, it's particularly important with multichannel integration to organize your database around a unique record identifier other than email addresses so that additional offline data can be associated with the subscriber, such as geography. One of the main data elements that you will use here is the customer's geography. Keep this in mind particularly if you sell items online that might not be appropriate for every region. For example, one multichannel retailer recently sent an email advertising spring lawn care products and lawnmowers to subscribers living in Manhattan. Oops! Clearly this was a wasted marketing expenditure and further underscored how out of touch the retailer was with the needs of that particular customer segment.

Perfecting the use of multichannel data depends on the capabilities of the marketing applications that are being used. To integrate online and offline data successfully, you need all of the following: a marketing platform that can automate the receipt and storage of this data so that it can be analyzed and used as a whole rather than separately, a set of processes to enable this efficiently as an ongoing activity, and experts who have done this before and know what the hurdles and issues are. Expertise can be acquired through consultants and vendor services, but your processes and platform will make the most difference.

Consider the following when mapping out your multichannel strategy:

Process At what interval will offline and online data be aggregated? Most marketers run these routines daily, but some merchants have near-real-time capability to make this data actionable across channels. Seek out your competitors, walk into their stores, and see what they are collecting from the customer at the point of sale and how quickly they are acting on it. Office Depot, for example, stunned us when minutes after signing up for its email loyalty program at its cash register, it sent a welcome message to us before there was even time to get to the car and load its goods in the trunk.

Which Data? Again, using our rules of acquisition, there is no need to move and aggregate client data that you have no immediate plans to use. Be sure to focus only on the data that will be immediately actionable to you.

Break Down the Silos Often multichannel integration and coordination is stymied by political issues of competing interests or different factions within an organization. Speak with the offline peers, and understand how your email program can help them. What would they really like to know about your customers? We often find that the offline marketers are in search of survey data on their clients or cannot analyze their offline marketing tests as quickly as they would like. Surveys and testing are two key areas where the email marketer can help their offline counterpart. In both cases, the results from an email marketing change will be back and available for study long before anything could ever be achieved in an offline store.

Technology This is a critical key to ensuring multichannel data success, so much so that it is the fifth key driver to your email marketing success.

Key Driver 5: Technology (Delivery, Deployment, and Design)

In previous chapters, we provided a good deal of insight into selecting an email service provider or email marketing technology. You should expect the vendor evaluation stage to take at least three months; for many organizations, it can take as long as six months to ensure that the solution meets all organizational requirements. Once you have selected a vendor (and particularly if it is a hosted ESP-based solution), the deployment can take as little as a month. In some cases, based upon your requirements, it can be deployed in a matter of days. On-premise technology—software or hardware that will reside at your company—can typically take up to a month to deploy and configure. However, one of the key drivers that will aid in the faster selection and deployment of your solution will be how well you have designed your requirements. Accordingly, keep these design requirements in mind:

User Rights and Privileges Determine how many people will be using the application and what their roles will be in using it. For example, you will likely want individuals on your senior management team to have access only to reporting, while other members of your team will require access to the entire application. Make sure one of your selection criteria is that the solution has the ability to provide different user rights and privileges based upon the tasks that user is responsible for.

Integration to Key Applications If you are a business-to-business marketer, you likely are already using a customer relationship management tool such as Salesforce.com or Microsoft Dynamics CRM. You will at some point want to integrate the behavioral data from your website into your email marketing application, or vice versa, to better inform segmentation schemes. Integration is a key part of technology deployment that marketers often fail to emphasize enough in the selection process. Investigate the prospective vendor's integration history and the number of deployments it has with the vendor you are seeking to integrate with.

Write This Down: Just 28 percent of email marketers cite the ability for an ESP to have out-of-the-box integration capabilities to other applications as an important aspect of the vendor selection process. (Source: JupiterResearch)

Data Storage Although all vendors offer the ability to store your data and marketing results, many of them purge this data at preset intervals. Ensure that your data is available for trending and that the time period is married to your sales process or the type of historical analysis that your organization typically does.

Bounce Handling No mailing will reach everyone on your list. There might be a *soft bounce* when an inbox is full or a *hard bounce*, indicating that the address is no longer valid. You will have to determine, with the guidance of your ESP, how many times and at what interval to retry soft bounces until they become hard bounces. This element of consideration will vary greatly between business-to-business and business-to-consumer marketing, and it also depends on the domain composition of your list and the frequency of your mailings.

   In the coming chapters, as we guide you through the first several months of your email deployment, we will explore the actionable tactical portions of these technology design concepts.

Key Driver 6: Reporting/Analytics

Reporting and analytics are the lifeblood of email marketing. The discovery of what is working and what is not working, and the subsequent optimization, are made possible by your reporting and analytics capabilities. Reporting is often complicated by the lack of integrated data from other reporting systems, which is why designing your multi-channel data and integration strategies is imperative.

Early on in evaluating a potential email marketing technology provider, you should not only understand its analytical capabilities and tools but also investigate its metrics methodology. It seems that each ESP has a different approach for calculating email delivery and all of the metrics that follow, such as open rate, click-through rate, and so on. This makes comparing your mailing performance to industry benchmarks impossible, because any reported industry benchmarks collected across marketers that use different vendors is a muddied apples-and-oranges exercise. This is one of the industry issues that we have both identified, and it's why we are working to develop a standard metric framework for every vendor to use. Such a standard may take years for the industry to adopt. Until that happens, it is best to benchmark your metrics only against your own previous marketing performance and not concern yourself with the open and click rates of others, because they are directional indicators of your performance at best. Regardless, it is important for you to understand how your vendor or technology is calculating your performance, and you can do so by investigating your vendor's metrics methodology.

 Write This Down: In 2007, more than one-third (37 percent) of marketers said they were very satisfied or satisfied with drill-down analysis capabilities for cross-comparing mailing data points. (Source: JupiterResearch)

Beyond understanding the metric methodology, consider the following data analysis elements when you are designing your email marketing program:

- **Ensure that you have the ability to drill down into your data.** Most email marketing applications simply offer reporting, which is a static view of what happened, identifying common metrics such as delivered, clicked, and converted. Fewer email marketing applications have true analysis capabilities, that is, the ability to drill down into the data and understand patterns that are distinct to subsets of subscribers—women, men living in Chicago, and so on. At the very least, your email marketing application should report and display not only the subscribers who did what you wanted them to do (click, convert, and so on), but also those who did not perform those actions. The ability to easily access those subscribers is even more important so that you can remarket to them the same message or identify them over time as a group that is not engaged.

- **Identify your key performance indicators.** Create KPIs that detail performance across three distinct categories: barometer measures, engagement measures, and infrastructure/list measures. Barometer measures are those metrics that show in great detail the performance of a mailing and include the following:
  - Aggregate open rate (total number of times the message was opened)
  - Aggregate click-through rate
  - Revenue generated per subscriber
  - Average order value
  - Click-to-conversion rate
  - Profit margin per mailing

  Engagement measures are those more specific to subscribers and include the following:
  - Unique open rate (a subscriber-oriented view of the open rate)
  - Unique click-through rate
  - Unique conversion rate
  - Unsubscribe rate
  - Forward rate

  Infrastructure/list measures detail the operational performance of your list:
  - Opt-in rate
  - Value of email subscriber or address over time
  - Address churn rate
  - Complaint rate
  - Delivery rate
  - Bounce rate
  - Unknown user rate

  Combining these measures into one macro engagement-key-performance indicator can be helpful in trending the performance or mailing over time. As you saw in Chapter 3, where we showed one way to calculate such an indicator, an engagement metric or KPI is designed to be a simple number that goes up or down based on the indexing of the aforementioned metrics.

- **Use domain-level reporting.** This is a critical report because it will identify delivery issues with specific ISPs or domains. For example, if you see your open rate fall off drastically, it is probably an indicator that a significant portion of your mailing failed to be delivered. This report, which should highlight the top 20 or so domains on your list, will provide the necessary insight to pinpoint the problem domains.

As we roll you into action in the coming chapters, we will provide additional guidance about which reports and data will be essential to analyze.

Key Driver 7: Privacy/Governmental Control

For email marketing, the most important legislation that you need to concern yourself with is the federal CAN-SPAM Act of 2003, amended in 2008. (CAN-SPAM stands for "Controlling the Assault of Non-Solicited Pornography and Marketing.") As noted in Chapter 2, this law was enacted in response to a rise in spam, and it defines how unsolicited emails may function. You can find the complete text of the law at www.ftc. gov/bcp/conline/pubs/buspubs/canspam.shtm, and we recommend you read it all. Also, we are not lawyers, and we emphasize that the following discussion should not be taken as legal advice.

The law first bans fraudulent email by prohibiting false header information and misleading subject information. No one is likely to fall afoul of those requirements by mistake, but legitimate marketers need to understand two other key provisions:

- You must give recipients an opt-out mechanism that works for at least 30 days.
- Every commercial email message must identify itself as an advertisement and include the sender's valid physical postal address.

Again, you'll find more details on these provisions, and penalties for failing to meet them, on the FTC website for the legislation.

Additional rule making by the FTC provided two very important points of clarification, which began to be enforced on July 7, 2008. The first is that the sender must be identified in a mailing (such as a newsletter) that may contain multiple advertisers. The advertiser identified as the sender in the From address is the sender responsible for complete compliance with the act. The second point clarified the opt-out process, which requires a working opt-out mechanism, either a link or a reply-to email address, and that these unsubscribes must be removed from the list within ten days. The additional clarity that the FTC provided in 2008 was that this unsubscribe process must be "easy." This means that password-protected or multistep authentication subscriber preference centers are no longer valid in meeting this element of the requirement. So, think of easy as one click. We recommend that you, along with your corporate counsel and email marketing vendor, visit www.ftc.gov/spam for updates to the CAN-SPAM Act and to ensure that your interpretation of the law satisfies your internal legal counsel. (You'll also find further discussion of how the CAN-SPAM provisions are being interpreted as industry best practices in this and subsequent chapters.)

Additional regulations to be aware of include laws that are specific to other countries and the European Union, which operates on an opt-in basis and not an opt-out basis. The U.S. CAN-SPAM provision does not require subscribers to opt in; however, that is a best practice we suggest you utilize. Laws in other countries generally are based on opt-in, meaning you must have the user's consent before you begin mailing to them. For up-to-date details on the laws in foreign nations, consult www.spamlaws.com, which is a fantastic resource for staying abreast of the legal requirements of various foreign countries.

State Registries

The states of Utah and Michigan also operate registries that are designed to protect the welfare of minors. If you are marketing a product that is illegal for minors to consume, such as alcohol or tobacco, then you must, when marketing to recipients in these states, scrub your list against this registry. These registries have been very controversial, and there are continued legal challenges to the validly of their existence, but for now marketers must meet those states' requirements.

Privacy Policy Best Practices

To provide you with the best insight on privacy, we sat down with Alan Chappell of Chappell and Associates, a well-known strategic consulting firm that specializes in privacy and marketing. Alan is a lawyer who has been working in the direct marketing industry since the mid-1990s.

> Jeanniey Mullen and David Daniels: *Alan, what are the biggest privacy concerns that marketers should be familiar with?*
>
> Alan Chappell: *The first area to look at if you're an email marketer is the CAN-SPAM Act. Given that CAN-SPAM is almost five years old, many of the standards outlined in the law should be old hat to most email marketers. For example, I think most people reading this book will know not to send marketing emails with false and deceptive header information or deceptive subject lines (although I've certainly seen my fair share of subject lines that come awfully close to deceptive). Similarly, most email marketers know to place a working opt-out mechanism and a postal address within each message.*
>
> *In May 2008, the Federal Trade Commission issued some additional guidance on CAN-SPAM. The guidance focused on four specific rules:*
>
> *"(1) an e-mail recipient cannot be required to pay a fee, provide information other than his or her e-mail address and opt-out preferences, or take any steps other than sending a reply e-mail message or visiting a single Internet Web page to opt out of receiving future e-mail from a sender;"*
>
> *In other words, the FTC wanted to clarify that email marketers are not only required to offer an opt-out within each email but that any opt-out process offered should be relatively easy for consumers to use and must be free of charge. For many email marketers, this guidance should not be problematic. However, email marketers that require a consumer to log on to an email marketer's website in order to unsubscribe may need to make wholesale changes to their unsubscribe process in order to be in compliance.*

The second set of guidance focused on the definition of sender: *"(2) the definition of 'sender' was modified to make it easier to determine which of multiple parties advertising in a single e-mail message is responsible for complying with the Act's opt-out requirements;"*

Here, in situations where an email marketing message is coming from multiple senders, the guidance allows a single company to be designated as the sole sender for purposes of CAN-SPAM. The good news is that the sole sender, and not the other senders, would be solely responsible for compliance with CAN-SPAM. The bad news is that if the sole sender is deemed by the FTC as not qualifying to be the sole sender, then all other advertisers would be expected to comply with CAN-SPAM. This may be a case where the commission's guidance has created as many questions as it has answered. And if you're advertising in an email marketing message with multiple other advertisers, you should be extremely careful before assuming that the sole sender option is viable for those email marketing messages.

The third set of guidance addresses the oft-asked question regarding whether a P.O. box is a valid postal physical address for purposes of CAN-SPAM:

"(3) a 'sender' of commercial e-mail can include an accurately-registered post office box or private mailbox established under United States Postal Service regulations to satisfy the Act's requirement that a commercial e-mail display a 'valid physical postal address';"

The answer here, per the guidance, is an emphatic yes. So long as you include a functioning P.O. box (or a similar mail box from a private sector provider such as the UPS store) in the email, you're compliant with CAN-SPAM. A street address is no longer necessary.

Lastly, the FTC guidance addresses the definition of the term person *as it pertains to CAN-SPAM: "(4) a definition of the term 'person' was added to clarify that CAN-SPAM's obligations are not limited to natural persons."*

In other words, this makes it clear that business entities (corporations and general partnerships) or groups (for example, unincorporated associations) as well as individual persons are responsible for complying with CAN-SPAM. Many of the shadier email marketers often try to avoid liability under the act (not to mention making it much harder to find them) by setting up multiple divisions, affiliates, and subsidiaries. This provision seeks to make setting up such divisions less effective.

Those, in a nutshell, are the new changes to CAN-SPAM. It's unclear at this time if and when the FTC will issue additional guidance.

Jeanniey Mullen and David Daniels: *Beyond the federal CAN-SPAM requirements and state registries in Utah and Michigan, are there other regulations that email marketers should be familiar with?*

Alan Chappell: *I think it would behoove any email marketer to understand the Network Advertising Initiative (NAI) Principles for Online Preference Marketing. Among other things, the NAI principles provide standards around the merger of personally identifiable information with non-personally identifiable information collected as people navigate online.*

Many email marketers work with website analytics companies. And any company collecting information about consumer visits to their own and/ or other websites and linking it to an email address or other personally identifiable information such as street address or phone number should take heed. I recommend any company engaging in these practices to work with a privacy attorney to understand the NAI principles and ensure that such consumers are provided with the right type of notice of such practices and have the opportunity to consent to them.

Jeanniey Mullen and David Daniels: *Alan, in your opinion, what are the best resources that marketers should seek out to stay abreast of the latest updates on privacy as it relates to email marketing?*

Alan Chappell: *The best resource for privacy is the International Association of Privacy Professionals (IAPP). The IAPP has conferences, workshops, webinars, and newsletters covering all issues of consumer privacy. Other resources include the Email Sender and Provider Coalition (ESPC), the Internet Advertising Bureau (IAB), the Direct Marketing Association, and of course, the Email Experience Council.*

Jeanniey Mullen and David Daniels: *How much of a monetary impact does implementing a good privacy policy have, and is there such a thing as ROI on privacy policies?*

Alan Chappell: *A privacy policy is a component of a privacy program. There are too many marketers who view the privacy policy as the beginning and end of their privacy programs. Customers often trust companies that dedicate the time and resources to have a robust privacy program more. And recent studies have demonstrated an ROI for companies that execute robust privacy and permission programs.*

Key Driver 8: Reactivation

There is one thing we can guarantee that will happen to your email list: some portion of the addresses on your list are going to go bad—they will no longer be valid at some point in the future.

Considerations for reactivation include the following:

Deliverability Many Internet service providers are now using dormant email accounts as spam traps. If marketers hit enough dormant accounts, they will likely be branded spammers. List health is typically the primary attribute that mires marketers in deliverability issues.

Business Purpose Even facing such deliverability issues, publishers often dislike the notion of removing subscribers from their mailings because it would diminish cost per thousand (CPM). Publishers that monetize their lists in this number-of-eyeballs manner must be mindful of shifting interest to emerging action- and performance-based models.

Email Address Value Understanding the value of email subscribers is necessary before contemplating reactivation tactics such as offline mailings and contact center use. Earlier we spoke of using a contact center and offline store personnel in this manner to recapture email addresses, underscoring the importance of determining your email address value. Once address value has been established, email change-of-address services from FreshAddress and Return Path should also be explored.

A mistake frequently made by marketers is to continue mailing to their lists over and over again without removing inactive addresses or taking any substantial action to reactivate these addresses. Since it can be costly to acquire addresses, you must have your reactivation strategy and tactics well laid out to ensure that at worst you are simply backfilling dormant addresses on your list and at best are doing such a good job at this that your list continues to grow even with this churn in mind. Use the following tactics to spur dormant subscribers into action:

- **Monitor subscriber behavior.** Understand the unique click rate of your subscribers so that over time you can monitor whether your list is becoming more or less engaged.

- **Target subscribers who are failing to click.** Use discounts, surveys, and sweepstakes if it is appropriate for your brand to drive dormant subscribers to take some action.

- **Use other channels.** As discussed earlier, a call center and other in-person interactions can be a valid means of re-engaging your dormant subscribers, but also consider postal mail. Many retailers mail letters or postcards to subscribers asking them to reconfirm or update their email address.

- **Purge addresses.** Although this might seem like a nonsensical thing to do, given the delivery effects that hitting a massive number of inactive subscribers can have, you must at some point shed those addresses from your list. After you have tried these reactivation tactics and the address shows no interaction for ten to twelve months, you should consider removing them from your list altogether.

Now with these key drivers in hand, you are ready to move on to your first week and begin actually deploying your email. The coming chapters will take you through the necessary steps in great detail.

Test Your Knowledge

Do you know the answers to these three questions pertaining to content from this chapter? A score of 3 out of 3 will ensure you are on your way to email marketing success.

- What is COPPA, and what does it require you to do as a marketer?
- To accommodate the majority of email readers, what width should your email template be?
- True or false? CAN-SPAM requires that all your subscribers opt in to receive messages.

Preparing Your Email Marketing Strategy

6

Now is the time to kick off the most fun, frustrating, and rewarding experience you can have: creating your email campaign. This chapter and the next three form a calendar, guiding you through the details that will make you the best at your newfound craft. In this first month, you will lay the foundation for your campaign efforts. These are the most critical areas to build in the right way, because they will drive the success of anything else you do in your email campaign.

Chapter Contents

Week 1: Preparing Your Resource Arsenal

Week 2: Building the Blueprint for Success

Week 3: Counting Down to "Go Time"

Week 4: Testing Your Way to the First
  Campaign

Week 1: Preparing Your Resource Arsenal

An email campaign, like anything you do in life, is much easier when you are prepared. To begin building your email campaign, you want to have at hand all the resources and ingredients you will need. You should have a number of items ready to access as you dive into the strategy and content creation.

Over the years, the best way we have found to manage this process effectively is to create a comprehensive resource arsenal, which includes at a minimum the following items:

Checklists Many kinds of checklists exist: general, strategic, creative, technical, and assessment. See Appendix B for some of our favorite checklists created by the Email Experience Council.

Technology These include the hardware and software (onsite or via an ESP) for delivery, database, analysis, and best practice validation. See Chapter 5 for details.

Research Make sure you are armed with historical and benchmarking statistics, trends, compliance-related information and insights, and even competitive knowledge.

Creative Creative checklists include lists of what your competitors are doing, including sending frequency, their creative design, best practices for templates (which are covered in Chapter 7), and the best strategies for designing for people who are reading emails on the go (these are discussed in Chapter 8).

Strategy Resource Sites and Blogs These can keep you up-to-date on the latest research, give you fodder regarding a best practices debate, or even give you an outlet to ask an expert a question or two. See Appendix A for some of our favorite sites.

Case Studies Throughout the book you'll find case studies that enable you to learn first-hand from the experience of others about what works and what could be done better.

The focus of this week is to gather all the elements needed for your resource arsenal and then build the argument to get those elements funded that have an associated cost. Each day, you can spend one hour on a critical initiative that will send you on a trip to the bank Friday afternoon with that signed check:

Monday: Getting smart

Tuesday: Evaluating tools and resources

Wednesday: Budgeting

Thursday: Related marketing initiatives

Friday: Getting the boss to sign the check

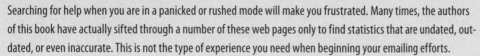

Write This Down: It is estimated that more than 500,000 individuals per week access "self-help" websites and online resources relating to email campaign design, development, and execution.

Googling *email marketing help* generates hundreds of results pertaining to where people can piece together guidance. The challenge with this is, Who has time to sort through all those entries?

Searching for help when you are in a panicked or rushed mode will make you frustrated. Many times, the authors of this book have actually sifted through a number of these web pages only to find statistics that are undated, outdated, or even inaccurate. This is not the type of experience you need when beginning your emailing efforts.

Monday: Getting Smart (the Seven Essential Truths About Email Marketing)

Getting smart about email marketing doesn't mean knowing all the answers. It means knowing what makes email marketing work and what type of resources you need to build something effective. A rule known as the *chunking principle* states that the mind can retain no more than seven items of information without memory loss. Because we want you to retain most of what you read, we have decided to condense what you need to know about email marketing into seven key truths. These are facts you should post on a wall somewhere. As you delve into email marketing, you will be challenged to remember these truths. So please, use today's hour wisely and keep this section handy.

Truth 1: Email Has Evolved into a Cornerstone of Our Lives

Omniture reports that more than 21 trillion emails were sent in the United States in 2007. These were, by no means, all marketing-based messages. One of the key truths about email you need to retain is that email marketing is just one small facet of a standard person's "email life". People use email today for many purposes, both personal and business. In many cases, the use of email is less about reading marketing messages and more about the improved facilitation of life.

And let's just put the argument to bed right now that only people of a certain age use email—it is just not true. In 2007, eMarketer surveyed the use of online access by various age ranges, and Table 6.1 shows the results.

▶ **Table 6.1** Selected Weekly Online Activities of U.S. Internet Users, by Age

	Millennials (13–24)	Generation X (25–41)	Baby Boomers (42–60)	Matures (61–75)
Watching and reading personal content created by others	71%	56%	40%	36%
Reading and posting on message boards	51%	43%	29%	22%
Socializing	62%	41%	25%	18%
Participating in a discussion forum	34%	33%	24%	19%

Source: eMarketer

Although this table doesn't specifically isolate email usage, it does demonstrate that people, of any age, go online to communicate and connect about personal elements of their lives.

So when you think about email, you must not think about it in the context of a campaign or a single effort, or even as marketing. You must think about it as an extension of personal and life-related communications. This will ensure that your design efforts consistently create a strong brand impact and a sense of personalized loyalty and interest among your readers.

Truth 2: Email Marketing Best Practices Change, *All the Time*

This is one truth that will help you maintain an edge over your competition. Think about it: When email marketing first started, the world was a different place. Email marketing was new, list growth was simple, spam was a type of meat, and the best practices written at the time did a great job of covering what to do in that environment. By about four years ago, the volume of spam changed best practices in our industry, and the CAN-SPAM legislation discussed in Chapter 5 was enacted in response to email's evolution. Best practices changed for creative, list growth, and delivery. Even as recently as early 2008, changes in the way that email unsubscribes are handled were introduced to ensure that the perception of email marketing remains positive.

What this means to you is that you must always look at the dates of research, case studies, and best practices and hold them up to the standards of the current day's trends.

Truth 3: *Any* Type of Messaging Done Electronically *Is* Email Marketing

Even today, there is still a perception that email marketing is one channel, mobile marketing a second, RSS a third, and even social networking a fourth. In these instances, many companies treat these as separate marketing channels. In today's online world, it is becoming increasingly difficult to keep these channels separate because they each act as drivers to the other.

Well, we have news for you! Any message sent electronically is considered email marketing.

Why is this a truth you need to know? It's because the lines among these types of messaging channels will continue to blur as time goes on, and soon the world will rely on "personal messaging" regardless of the location or the device. These media are all driven through Internet channels and require permission and selection of message interests/types. This means everything you are thinking about for email will also become critical to future messaging strategies for your company. As the famous philosopher Yoda once said, "Choose wisely you must."

Truth 4: Email Addresses Mean Money; Don't Ignore Your Non-responders

We recently heard a speaker at an email conference ask the audience this question: "Who here invests in increasing the delivery rate of their emails?" Almost 90 percent of the hands went up. He then asked another question: "Who here spends money to acquire new customers?" Again, 90 percent of the hands went up. And then he asked this: "Who here builds programs to monitor and target those people who provide you their email address but never respond to an email you send versus just removing them from your list after a certain time?"

After the crickets stopped chirping, he went on to explain that his company's research has indicated that less than 50 percent of a list will *ever* respond to email campaigns. And research that Jeanniey has done shows that even if someone on your list is not responsive, once they have provided an email address, they will purchase 150 percent more than those who shop at your company but do not opt in.

This means your list value has expanded. It is worth more than just the opens and clicks it drives. You should always plan to evaluate the purchase or response power that people on your list provide through all channels to identify their value.

Truth 5: This Is Not "The Farmer in the Dell"

Remember that grade-school song? The last line is, "The cheese stands alone." That's not a smart attitude for email marketing. Many people in marketing assume that email marketing is similar to the "cheese" in this song—a stand-alone messaging channel that drives revenue and strengthens relationships. The truth is, elements of email marketing live in every aspect of our messaging world. Forms sit on websites, capture points happen both online and offline, banners drive to landing pages with forms, and searches drive to deep pages that encourage engagement.

If email stood alone, none of these would be relevant. But for successful email marketing, you cannot afford *not* to think about all the touch points of your email marketing campaign.

Truth 6: Technology Partners Often Act Like Military Members

In the Chapter 3 analysis of email marketing technology, you saw that vendors can be tremendously helpful partners. That said, it has often been our experience that technology partners can easily slip into a "don't ask, don't tell" mentality. Many times, these partners wait for you to ask for a service, feature, or support effort before they provide it to you. The problem with that is that if you don't know what you are missing, you don't know what to request. It is for this reason that we encourage you to read the case studies on technology partners' sites—not just your own technology partner but the top ten technology partners. By doing so, you will be able to see, in context, what types of services and features you should and could be getting out of your partner.

Don't allow the money you spend in this area to provide you with just the basics. Push for ultimate service and support.

Truth 7: Ignore the Rules (Except the Law)

Someone once told us that you learn more from your mistakes in email than you do from your successes. In most cases, the best mistakes you make are not planned. When you don't have productive mistakes to learn from, ignoring the rules and trying something crazy to see how it flies can work pretty well, too. We certainly don't mean to imply that you should ignore the law. You definitely shouldn't. But, you should think of new ways to share emails and try them with a sample of your database. Some of the most successful "rule-breaking campaigns" of the past have included the following:

- Creating an email that scrolls sideways
- Sharing an "unsubscribe" confirmation landing page that offers ways to opt back in
- Posting a call to opt in at the end of a video on YouTube
- Sending an email with a blank subject line

Now that you know the seven truths of email, you can use them to evaluate your tools and resources.

Tuesday: Evaluating Tools and Resources

On this second day, we are going to continue having fun by getting all our tools and resources together. Whether this is your first time creating an email marketing plan or you are a veteran, you have our guarantee that you will take away something useful from this section.

A sound email strategy presents new opportunities for overall business improvement by putting into place tools and processes that can solve current performance problems and open new avenues to bolster sales and customer satisfaction.

Before selecting or even evaluating new technology solutions, an organization should start by determining the overall objective and scope of their email program, then identifying current problems and obstacles to meeting this objective, and finally creating an inventory of current resources. Once a company has a clear understanding of what it wants to achieve, what's keeping it from getting there, and what is already in place, then it can develop an evaluation and selection plan to find the solution and define the processes to fulfill its email strategy. You can use our handy quiz to help determine what your areas of focus should be.

The Naked Truth About Email

This is a true story. For privacy reasons (and other reasons you will read about), the names have all been left out or changed.

Company A called its email marketing vendor and requested that its account manager help them create a very special video email. The video would be coming from the CEO of the global organization and share critical news and insights about recent changes.

Everything was moving along just fine. The CEO's video was shot, edited, and uploaded into the email shell. A subject line was suggested: "An Important Video Message from the CEO: Recent Changes." Both the vendor and Company A understood that this was a long subject line but thought it would increase the open and viewership rates of the message.

Unfortunately, while the production of the email was happening, changes were taking place at the vendor. One of the video producers had to be let go from his job.

Now, normally that wouldn't be a big deal—but in this case, you won't believe what happened.

The morning the CEO's video email was being sent, the recently unemployed video producer hacked into the web server and switched out the video that was supposed to play, replacing it with a video of a naked, alternative lifestyle fashion show.

For the first ten minutes of the launch, whenever an employee clicked the "important video from the CEO regarding recent changes," they saw *quite* a show. The issue was corrected ten minutes after launch, but it left a lasting impression.

Besides being a funny story for anyone in email (except the CEO), this error created something else within the company: curiosity and an ongoing interest in seeing what was in every email sent from the CEO.

For the next twelve months, every email sent from the CEO received almost 100 percent open rates within two minutes of receiving the message. Everyone looked for the next mistake. Even the company's CEO learned how to use this mistake as a way to improve response and included random video clips that looked like they would turn into something scandalous.

It was an awful mistake, it was a great response, and it was a new way to market inside a company that no one had thought of before.

Quiz: What the H^&* Am I Trying to Do with My Emails?

Understanding what to do with your emails can be challenging. You will find that by answering a few questions and thinking through a strategy, you can move light-years ahead. This quiz should take only a few minutes of your time:

1. My job is solely email marketing to an existing house list.

   a) Yes

   b) No

   c) I don't know

2. I work for a company that has:

   a) More than 100 employees

   b) 15–99 employees

   c) Fewer than 14 employees

3. The role of the emails I send needs to be:

   a) To drive high open and click rates, and possibly purchases or leads.

   b) Multipurpose: sell, retain, provide service, and more.

   c) Every email I send needs to make money for my company.

4. I can build specific landing pages to support email or email address capture.

   a) No, my company uses one landing page for all media.

   b) Yep, sure—the more, the better.

   c) If they are premade, or free, yes; otherwise, no.

5. My email database *is* the company database.

   a) No, we have a CRM solution.

   b) Yes.

   c) You mean my email service provider can be my database?

6. How much of a budget do you have to invest in email technology or resources?

   a) More than $100,000 annually (or $.01 per email sent on average)

   b) $25,000–$100,000 (or $.005 per email sent on average)

   c) As little as possible, but as much as is needed to make emails work

Answer key:

Give yourself 5 points for every "a" answer you selected.

Give yourself 2 points for every "b" answer you selected.

Give yourself 0 points for every "c" answer you selected.

0–11 points: "Down and Dirty": You are a marketer with one focus: get it done profitably or else. In the list in the next section, you should look for technologies or services with one asterisk (*) next to them.

12–20 points: "Workin' It": With some investment dollars, you are a shrewd marketer who has many priorities and who needs technology that supports a multichannel mix with minimal excess expense. In the list in the next section, look for technologies or services with one or two asterisks (**) next to them.

20 points or more: "Fit and Fabulous": Your high-visibility company requires that each role in your organization remain focused on key aspects of communication that create the ultimate experience. That said, you need to remain within the boundaries of your group's efforts when implementing programs to ensure a common voice and brand is maintained. In the list in the next section, look for technologies or services with one (*), two (**), or three asterisks (***) next to them.

Knowing What Technologies or Services You May Need

Once you have determined the focus you have for your email programs and the goals you want to accomplish, you can effectively begin to evaluate which technology will best support your efforts.

Now would be a good time to revisit Chapter 2 to gain some key insights on email delivery providers. Keep in mind, though, that delivery services are not the only technology out there. Listed next are the different types of email resources (outside of email service providers) you will want to review. You'll find contact information for all the vendors in each category in Appendix A.

Statistics and best practices:

Email Experience Council's Whitepaper Room**

Center for Media Research*

MarketingCharts*

EmailStatCenter*

MarketingSherpa**

JupiterResearch***

Forrester Research***

eMarketer***

Email-specific design or design analysis:

Smith-Harmon**

MailChimp*

Bunnyfoot**

Eyetools*

Deliverability:

> Goodmail**
>
> Iconix*
>
> Habeas**
>
> Return Path**
>
> Pivotal Veracity**
>
> Lyris*

Analytics and testing:

> Omniture
>
> WebTrends
>
> Coremetrics

Email list growth:

> Datran Media**
>
> Yesmail**

For each of these areas, you will need to begin doing research to see which vendors to review. We suggest you keep them all in your back pocket. You will be surprised to see how they will come in handy down the road.

Wednesday: Budgeting

Drafting an email marketing budget can be a daunting task. It seems oddly simple in the beginning, but it quickly becomes riddled with complexities and challenges.

To begin with, you should make a list of every type of expense you think you may need. (Yes, if you haven't noticed already, planning for email marketing requires lots of lists.) There is a lot of research out there that will help you justify the budget you're proposing for email, including the recent survey results from Datran Media, as illustrated in Figure 6.1.

Once you've demonstrated to management the benefits of email marketing, what you need to focus on is making sure you have the money to account for all the email costs. In Chapter 4, we listed all the types of costs you should consider, including the following:

- List replacement fees
- Design
- Testing
- Data support
- Mad money

1. Compared to 2007, in 2008, your company is likely to?

Increase its use of email marketing	82.4%
Same →(15.3%)	
→ (Decrease its use of email marketing, 2.4%)	

2. In 2008, do you expect your company's email marketing ROI to be?

Higher than other channels	55.3%
→ (Roughly equal to the other channels, 25.9%)	
→ (Lower than the other channels, 18.8%)	

3. Which advertising media buys perform strongly for your company? (select all that apply)

Email	80%
Display	37.6%
Search	70.6%
Print →(16.5%)	
→ (Broadcast, 10.6%)	
→ (Cable, 7.1%)	
→ (Mobile, 1.2%)	
→ (RSS, 2.4%)	
Ad Network	34.1%
→ (Uncertain, 8.2%)	

4. Which media channels do you think complement the email media channel? (select all that apply)

Display	51.8%
Search	71.8%
Mobile	24.7%
→ (Broadcast, 17.6%)	
Direct	41.2%
→ (Cable, 10.6%)	
→ (None of the above, 9.4%)	

5. Has or does your company plan to employ email to do any of the following? (select all that apply)

Send newsletter	80%
Drive sales	78.8%
Increase up-sell or cross-sell opportunities	67.1%
Send transactional message	50.6%
Reactive dormant customers	52.9%
Enhance customer relationships	70.6%
Increase brand awareness and/or lift	64.7%

6. Do you currently send targeted email campaigns?

Yes	81.2%
No 18.8%	

7. If your company currently sends targeted email campaigns, which if any of the following applies? (select all that apply)

We target based on actions	56.5%
We target based on demographics and/or geography → 63.5%	
→ (We target based on psychographics or interests, 42.1%)	
→ (We don't send targeted campaigns, 20%)	

8. Does your company currently or plan to do any of the following?

Conduct A/B/C content or creative split testing	74.1%
→ (Test creative rendering across "inbox" devices, 36.5%)	
→ (Pay for email marketing based on a CPM model, 29.4%)	
Pay for email marketing based on a CPC or CPA model, 58.8%	
→ (Serve banner ads within newsletters or other email campaigns, 36.5%)	
→ (Measure email marketing's effect on brand lift, 25.9%)	
→ (Measure email marketing's effect on customer satisfaction and/or loyalty rates, 36.5%)	
Measure email marketing's effect on sales	64.7%
→ (None of the above, 4.7%)	

9. Do you believe email has helped boost sales through other channels?

Yes	67.1%
→ (No, 2.4%)	
Not sure	30.6%

10. Do you plan on integrating marketing messages in your transactional emails in 2008?

Yes	63.5%
No 23.5%	
→ (Unaware that this was possible, 12.9%)	

11. Do you currently use and/or plan on using an outside vendor for email marketing?

Yes	69.4%
No 20%	
→ (Not sure, 10.6%)	

Figure 6.1 Datran 2008 annual marketing and media survey results

To take these costs one step further, we recommend building a cohesive email marketing plan that also takes these factors into consideration:

- **Training costs, conference fees, and more.** It is always a wise investment to earmark some funds (no more than $2,500 per year) to attend conferences or purchase email intelligence. If you are a small company, this may seem like a large investment, but the dividends are phenomenal. The networking alone at email-specific events will provide months and years of higher return on investment.

- **Technical design resources.** In an earlier section, we mentioned including funds for technical support with your email vendor, but sometimes you will need to pay an outside company to design and test Flash, animation, video, or other new components.

- **Mobile messaging and RSS integration tests.** Although these may appear to fall outside your budget or realm of responsibility, they really don't. Planning for a mobile test with email is going to be the cornerstone to future email marketing strategies.

- **Preference center design.** This was introduced briefly in Chapter 2 and will be covered in more detail later in this chapter and in Chapter 8 (which looks at preference centers for the mobile channel). But for now, what you need to know is that designing a preference center can become a costly initiative and will need its own budget line.

Budget Timing and Assessment

Once you have your line items listed and associated costs of doing business identified, the next step to take today is to build an ROI calculator. Using this tool, you can calculate the expected response rate for each email sent and how many emails need to be sent in order to drive the return on investment. Some people choose to build these to determine what type of response rates they need to justify the cost. Others build them to determine how much they can spend based on the projected ROI. Either case is fine. Just make sure you build one. It should look something like the example shown in Figure 6.2. (The data were created for presentation purposes only and do not reflect any company's actual budget or business plan.) It should be a living document that you update and manipulate weekly at a minimum.

 Note: You can download a copy of the SampleROI.xls calculator from this book's web page at www.sybex.com/go/emailmarketinghouraday.

	March	April	May	June	July	August	September	October	November	December	Total
Acquisition Inputs:											
New email registrants	100,000	150,000	200,000	200,000	200,000	200,000	200,000	250,000	250,000	250,000	2,000,000
New subscription customers - direct from site	15,000	20,000	25,000	30,000	35,000	40,000	60,000	70,000	80,000	90,000	465,000
Retention Inputs:											
new subscription average order value (aov)	$ 19.00	$ 19.00	$ 19.00	$ 19.00	$ 19.00	$ 19.00	$ 19.00	$ 19.00	$ 19.00	$ 19.00	
activation rate - email reg to subscription	20%	20%	20%	20%	20%	20%	20%	20%	20%	20%	
upsell success rate -	30%	30%	30%	30%	30%	30%	30%	30%	30%	30%	
cross-sell success rate - new subscribers	1%	5%	5%	5%	10%	10%	10%	15%	15%	15%	
number of expiring subscriptions	10,000	10,000	10,000	10,000	10,000	10,000	10,000	10,000	10,000	10,000	100,000
renewal rate	25%	27%	29%	31%	33%	35%	37%	39%	41%	43%	
average renewal value	$ 15.00	$ 15.00	$ 15.00	$ 15.00	$ 15.00	$ 15.00	$ 15.00	$ 15.00	$ 15.00	$ 15.00	

Figure 6.2 An ROI calculator implemented in Excel

Thursday: Related Marketing Initiatives

You are now locked and loaded with knowledge about the email marketing space. You have a list of the types of services and technologies you can leverage and will need a budget (including an ROI forecasting document) in place as well as. What's next?

Remember the third truth from Monday's focus: Anything you do in the world of marketing has an email component. Regardless of whether you work for a large or small company, and whether your job is focused only on email or includes broader efforts, email will impact almost everything your company does. Today, your job is to review every aspect of marketing or advertising that your company may be doing and to see where and how email could or should be making an impact.

This is probably one of email marketing's most fun activities because it is very visual. By creating an email "look book," you will be able to effectively determine whether you need to make any changes to your budget to support other programs, design additional creative, or develop tests to supplement what you have noted.

You will also be surprised by your findings. Recent studies have shown that branding in email creative is consistent across all communications for only about 5 percent of companies. This is natural for large companies that work with multiple agencies. It is also expected for very small companies that implement efforts over time, as their services grow, often leaving older branding elements in play because of lack of resources or a volume demand to change it. So, where should you start?

The first place to look is at your print advertising. If your company is doing a print campaign, your creative may look something like the Sephora ad shown in Figure 6.3.

the popular click
beauty's gold standard
www.sephora.com

Golden Opportunity!
Sign up for sephora emails
to score:
· deluxe sample offers
· a first look at new beauty
· seasonal beauty trends

SEPHORA
THE BEAUTY AUTHORITY

Figure 6.3 A print ad for an email opt-in

This print campaign is built specifically to ask people to opt in to an email effort. If your advertising group is doing something like this, good for them! But, do you know what type of email is being sent once someone opts in? Or even what is happening to the name once it is in your database? If not, you should definitely find out. Also note that addresses coming in from a print experience deserve an email welcome message that references the source.

The second element to check is your customer service center. Once someone is live on the phone, is your representative asking for email address permission? Is there a workflow built to drive these customers to receive the right follow-up email or send them the most appropriate branding information? In Figure 6.4, American Express integrates the right brand with dynamic messaging, which is passed along to the email team to continue the messaging appropriately.

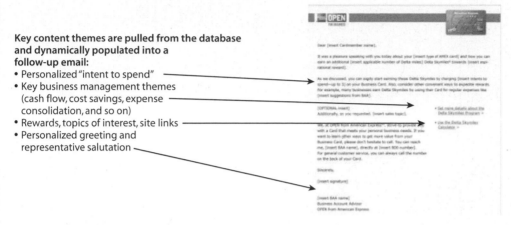

Key content themes are pulled from the database and dynamically populated into a follow-up email:
• Personalized "intent to spend"
• Key business management themes (cash flow, cost savings, expense consolidation, and so on)
• Rewards, topics of interest, site links
• Personalized greeting and representative salutation

Figure 6.4 An American Express dynamic email

If advertising and customer service have matters under control, move along to examine your corporate site. These sites often post research, press releases, and news coverage, which a visitor can share with a friend or colleague. That is fantastic news, as long as it is consistent with your efforts. Many companies fall short in this area because their pages ask to capture email addresses but then do nothing with them.

Figure 6.5 is an example from Nestle that shows the investor relations opt-in box. It does a good job of capturing profile information, but is it linked to other types of emails, or even using space inside the emails to promote the benefits of opt-in with other Nestle products? It is not.

Finally, the last large area you will want to review is your online media planning efforts. If you are a business-to-business company, your focus is on driving leads. Here is a great example of a banner that offers a free trial:

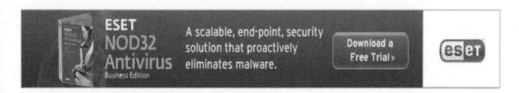

Once again, it is your job to determine what happens to the email address once someone provides it for the download.

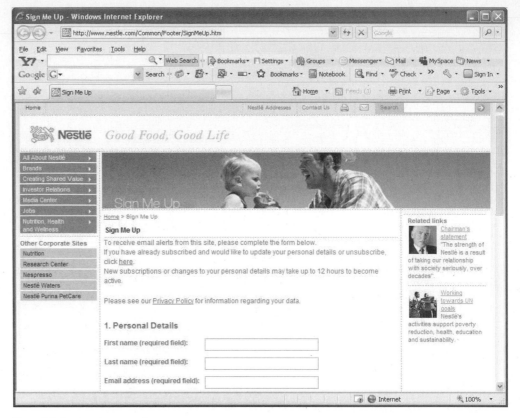

Figure 6.5 Nestle corporate opt-in

The impact of other marketing efforts on email grows constantly. Your job as an email marketer is twofold: to create the best email programs you can and to optimize them as you go. But it's also to ensure that any email marketing opportunities that arise thanks to your company's efforts are managed and effectively utilized in a way that creates the most positive brand experience around.

For each of these areas, ask yourself these questions:

- Is there a chance an email address can be collected?

- Is there a chance an email message will be sent?

- Where does this data go?

- What kind of messaging is sent?

- Can I use this person's data in the future for my program, and if so, how?

These questions will help you build a valuable resource for collecting new and highly active email addresses when you are looking for ways to increase your database size.

Friday: Getting the Boss to Sign the Check

It's D-day. You have spent the week researching what you need to know about email and what technologies and services you think will be of the most help to you. You've estimated the costs associated with your intended efforts, and you have identified areas of your website that will add value to your current programs. The meeting with the boss is set, and all you need to do is get the check signed.

Whether you are asking for $50 or $5,000 or $500,000, asking your boss for money to support your email marketing programs is going to require some discussion about the value of the email program to the company overall. We hope that by now you have picked up a few of the key highlights from earlier chapters in this book. These include the following:

- Email is more valuable to you than just one-time sales; email address opt-in is an indicator of high-value customers.

- Email marketing happens in every area of the company; it is a critical branding element.

- Email marketing saves significant dollars; sending an email saves more than 90 percent compared to postal mail.

To help support these facts and enable C-level executives to understand the value of supporting email marketing, the Email Experience Council created a report outlining the value of email addresses to a company, shown in Figure 6.6. Use these elements to help develop your plan of attack when you speak with your boss.

Note: You can download a copy of the ValueofEmailAddress.xls calculator from this book's web page at www.sybex.com/go/emailmarketinghouraday.

Your goal in this communication is to demonstrate the holistic power of email in the areas listed earlier. We urge you to stay away from tactical elements such as open rates and even click-through rates.

Write This Down: Nearly three-quarters of email marketers said in a recent survey that they plan to spend either the same amount or more on email marketing in 2008 as they did last year, according to the 2008 "E-Mail 2008: Top 10 Research Findings and Practical Ways to Increase E-Mail Performance" report. (Source: MarketingSherpa)

Costs				
Message copy/creative		$ 3,500		
List rental = # records		250,000	List Price CPM	$55.00 Per Thousand
List Rental = $$		$ 13,750	Effective CPA	$2.59 Per Visitor
List Rental = Fees		$ 250		
Landing page design		$ 1,500		
Incentive (tied to offer)	$ 3.00	$ 1,928	(assume that 55% of new subscribers use the incentive)	
Total campaign cost:		$ 19,000		

Response Metrics (Offer is to Subscribe to Email Program)				
Mailed universe	250,000		$0.08	Cost per name mailed
Delivered universe	212,500	85% Deliverability rate	$0.09	Cost per name delivered
Opens	31,875	15.0% Open rate	$0.60	Cost per open
Clickthroughs	5,313	2.5% Clickthrough rate	$3.58	Cost per clickthrough
		16.7% Click to Open rate		
Conversions	1,169	22.0% Conv rate (to subscriber)	$16.26	Cost per conversion
Cost per Email Record Acquired	$ 16.26			

Value of Email Address - Retailer Worksheet - ROI for Acquired Records
ROI Calculation

Value of an Email Address	$ 118.09
	minus
Cost Per Email Record Acquired	$ 16.26
	=
Acquired Email Address Value	$ 101.83

Figure 6.6 Calculating the value to a company of an email address

Week 2: Building the Blueprint for Success

Once the ink on the check for your email marketing program dries, it is time to get down to business. During the second week, your focus will be on designing the core plans and validating the destinations for your efforts. This can be either data related or creative driven. Skipping any section in this week can set your program efforts back significantly, and as you will see, there are many examples of ways you can approach these topics. Of course, the examples are being shown to illustrate concepts and will need to be customized to your company's specific needs and goals. There is no one-size-fits-all in email. So if you are ready, get your pen and paper, and get ready for this week's events.

Monday: Evaluating your current house file and file size needs

Tuesday: Creating the acquisition plans

Wednesday: Focusing on the opt-in process and customer preference centers

Thursday: Reviewing the opt-out process

Friday: Making sure your landing pages are a good place to land

Monday: Evaluating Your Current House File and File Size Needs

We have a friend who works at the Heinz factory in Pittsburgh, Pennsylvania. Her job is to schedule the delivery of Heinz products to grocery stores in the Midwest. It is a really challenging job because it has to take into consideration all of the following factors:

- Based on sales of products and prior-year trends, when is the current shipment expected to run out?

- How much does the new shipment need to contain in order to maximize pricing and delivery timing?

- What will the contingency plan be if/when a grocer calls with an emergency order they need filled within 12 hours (especially if the truck needs to get to a dock and be loaded)?

- What is the plan if the store is unable to sell the items because of a drastic change in the weather, the economy, or other uncontrollable occurrences?

How is she able to organize and manage all these elements dynamically and ensure there is no excess or lack of product? Somehow she is able to effectively create a process and workflow that allows her to forecast and manage to change.

When you think about it, we have the same need in our profession. Somehow, you need to effectively forecast the amount of interaction and turnover the names in your email databases will generate so that you can budget and plan for list growth initiatives at the right times and achieve optimal results. You have to do this without going over budget or losing valuable ground.

In 2006, Silverpop conducted a list growth survey of 321 marketers. As reported by *Direct* magazine, it found that when asked to name their list growth tactics, almost two-thirds of the email marketers surveyed cited offline advertising and direct marketing. More than half mentioned trade shows or online marketing and web searches. Viral marketing was third. The study also revealed a gap between planned list-building tactics and those seen as successful. For example, 24 percent intend to use viral marketing, but only 10 percent see it as successful.

These are interesting insights, but before you can get into worrying about how to grow you list, you need to evaluate how effective your list is.

> **Write This Down:** The average size of an email marketing database ranges from 20 to 60 percent of the total marketing database. (Source: Email Experience Council)

- **How big is your file compared to your company's total marketing database?** Knowing this will help determine the total impact your current file can ultimately have. For example, if your file size is less than 20 percent of your entire marketing database, you will need to ensure that it is the most responsive list ever or build in some serious plans to grow the file. In this case, growth through service emails or call centers would be the likely starting ground.

- **How old is the data on your database?** It's sad to say that even with the most responsive lists, email addresses that have been on your file for more than three years tend to not respond nearly as well as newly acquired email addresses. If you have an old file, you may very well want your starting technique to be in the areas on your website where you can attract some "fresh blood."

- **What is the average annual purchase of a person on your email list compared to names not on your list?** Although Forrester data indicates that the average person who opts in to your emails will purchase 138 percent more than someone who does not provide you with an opt-in email address, you should check the validity of this with your list. If your list of email opt-ins is not performing at the same rate as your offline list, your starting point may need to be the source of your email opt-in capture.

These three elements will get you well on your way to answering some critical questions not only about how large your list is but also about its effectiveness. Once you have this information, you will be in a good position to compare the size and response to your budget numbers, discussed in the previous section. This exercise will give you a clear indicator of how much you need to grow and what the starting points should be.

Staying on track with list growth is an important factor to focus on. Many times, we have seen people put the best plans into place and then have them fall through as soon as THEY LOSE THEIR FOCUS. Without your list, you will not be able to market. Don't lose sight of that.

Tuesday: Creating the Acquisition Plans

Now that you know how much you need to grow and have some indication of where you may need to start, it is time to put together the plan for growing your acquisition efforts. You will have a number of choices to make. Based on your budget and your time, and results of tests, your plan can be expected to change and develop over time. We strongly encourage you to launch your acquisition plans slowly over time. Test not only for the effectiveness of meeting name-capturing goals but also for the results these new names have for your company. Do they perform in the first 30 days? Are they still effective 90 days after adding them to the list? Are there high spam or complaint rates? All these elements are factors in determining what type of list growth efforts and acquisition plans will work best for you.

An Intelliseek survey by Forrester Research on U.S. consumers' trust or distrust by type of advertising found that roughly two-thirds of respondents said they trusted emails they signed up for. This confirms what many industry experts have known all along. Email marketing is a powerful relationship-building tool. So, how does an organization implement a successful email loyalty program?

According to a study on worldwide email messaging by the market research firm IDC, daily email traffic is now estimated at message sent after 60 billion. Without question, the easiest way to find relevant email addresses is to ask every consumer who visits your website for theirs. It's simple enough, but most sites do not generate enough online traffic to drive a high volume of opt-ins. And without a sufficient volume of site traffic to capture elusive opt-in addresses to drive strong relationships between buyer and seller; business owners will lose valuable market share faster than it takes the deliverability status on an unsolicited email to bounce. So, what can you do to generate site traffic?

The answer: channel surf. Start by using as many channels as possible to drive online interests and grow a company database. A marketer's push and pull tactics can range from one, many, or all of the following channels to help create a steady flow of site traffic:

- Keyword buys
- In-store point-of-sale displays
- Trade shows
- List rental
- Viral and cross promotion
- Co-registration
- Call center
- Direct mail
- Customer care
- Product warranty registration
- Co-marketing
- Partnership/third-party channels

The data in Figure 6.7 illustrate different inbound channels available to online marketers and how effective each channel is at generating opt-ins.

List acquisition doesn't need to be expensive. It can work very effectively given the right focus. However, we do recommend you never put more than 15 percent of your list growth strategy into one effort. This could cause serious issues and repercussions should something go wrong.

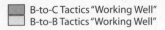

■ B-to-C Tactics "Working Well"
□ B-to-B Tactics "Working Well"

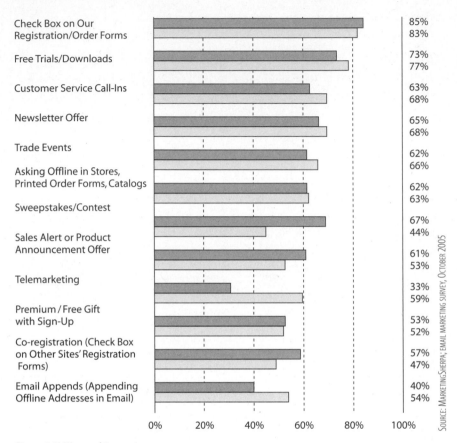

Check Box on Our Registration/Order Forms	85% 83%
Free Trials/Downloads	73% 77%
Customer Service Call-Ins	63% 68%
Newsletter Offer	65% 68%
Trade Events	62% 66%
Asking Offline in Stores, Printed Order Forms, Catalogs	62% 63%
Sweepstakes/Contest	67% 44%
Sales Alert or Product Announcement Offer	61% 53%
Telemarketing	33% 59%
Premium / Free Gift with Sign-Up	53% 52%
Co-registration (Check Box on Other Sites' Registration Forms)	57% 47%
Email Appends (Appending Offline Addresses in Email)	40% 54%

0%   20%   40%   60%   80%   100%

SOURCE: MARKETINGSHERPA; EMAIL MARKETING SURVEY, OCTOBER 2005

Figure 6.7 Ways to drive opt-ins

Wednesday: Focusing on the Opt-In Process and Customer Preference Centers

Assuming your strategy of "reaching out" to use as many channels as possible to generate a steady flow of site traffic is successful, what next? The next step, and probably the most important in your effort, is to generate responsive and long-term opt-in permission approval.

This requires a focus on the best practices of *today* (remember, we said you need to watch these all of the time) to develop the best customer experience.

To make it easy on you, we asked Cliff Seltzer of PureSend to craft the following list of the current best practices in opt-in and preference centers; Cliff also provided the phenomenal creative examples. Use this as a "tear me out" checklist to keep next to the email marketing truths, and you will always have something you will find useful in design and strategy meetings:

- **A prominent call to opt-in on all home and landing pages.** A survey by JupiterResearch on how U.S. marketing executives capture consumer addresses found that 60 percent of all opt-ins came from the online registration process.

- **Non-obtrusive link to all policies.** Links that enable readers to access the "about us" section and terms and conditions often engender a sense of trust.

- **Frequency options.** Giving your readers the ability to receive information more or less frequently can reduce unsubscribes up to 25 percent.

- **Sample content.** Sharing an example of what your email will look like helps set expectations.

- **Multichannel options (SMS, print, PDA).** Offering readers the ability to sign up for your information through a variety of ways gives readers a sense of control.

- **Content-type format (HTML/text/PDA).** This is a new trend, which you will read more about in Chapter 8.

- **Lots of content customization options.** The most successful email programs offer the ability to personalize messages (see the Petco example in Chapter 2).

- **Easy unsubscribe.** Based on updated CAN-SPAM laws, a one-click opt-out is critical.

- **Short and long registration options.** The email address is the only item that is truly required; many users will start at this level until you've earned their trust.

  In fact, a recent MarketingSherpa study on how to get more opt-ins found that 88 percent of users say they are willing to spend time answering questions about their tastes and interests online, and 25 percent said they would spend more than six minutes filling out an online registration form.

- **Clear expectations.** Set expectations on what will be delivered.

- **Reasons for subscribing.** Spell out the reasons the person should be subscribing.

- **Trust certificates.** Provide trust certificates somewhere on the page.

- **Delivery times.** Request specific delivery time, with time zones. This is a tough one for many ESPs who can't get email out fast enough to promise a specific time, so you may think of it as a future goal.

Opt-in Examples

Figures 6.8 and 6.9 illustrate opt-in interfaces from Olympus and Saks Fifth Avenue.

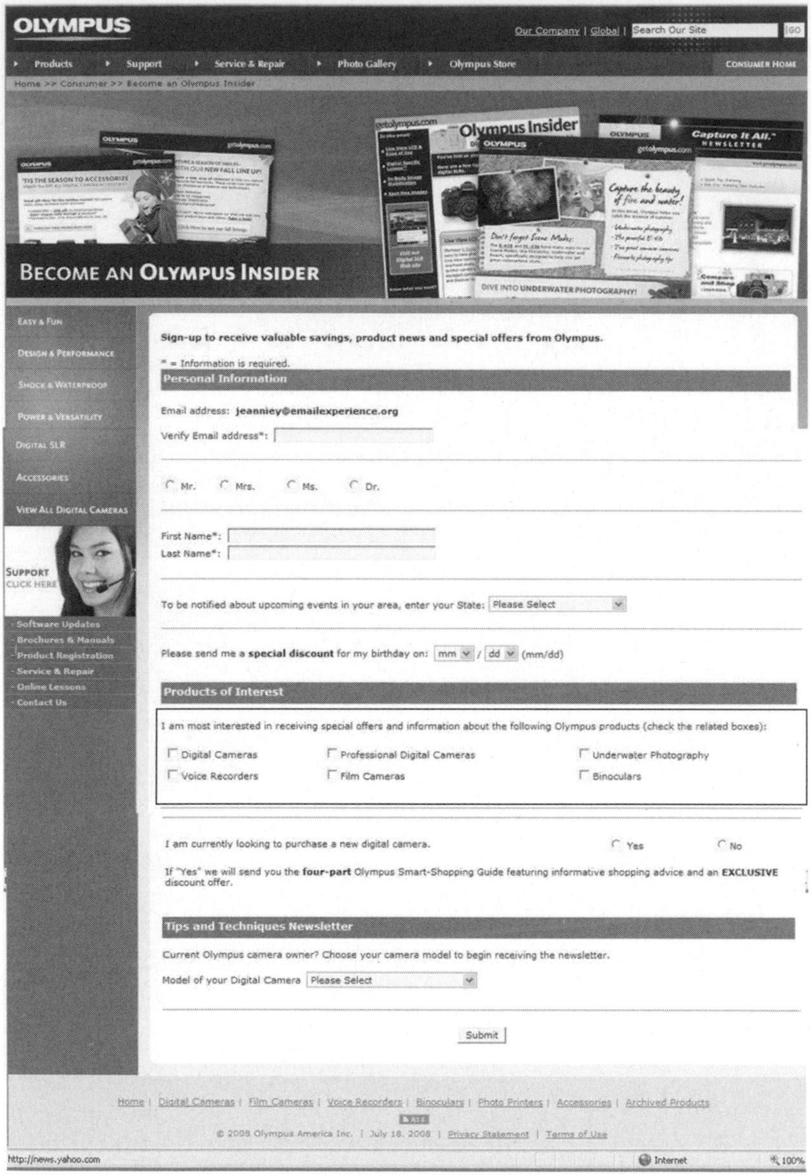

Figure 6.8 Olympus email opt-in page

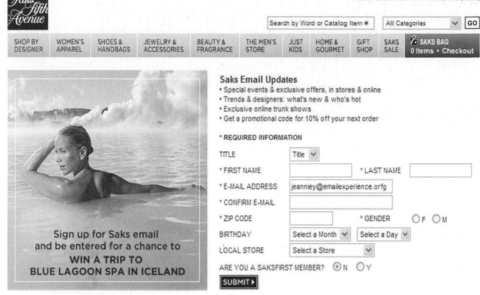

Figure 6.9 Saks Fifth Avenue email opt-in page

Another example is from Continental Airlines, which has always followed best practices in its opt-in strategy. Here are Continental's most important advantages:

- **It has preference centers.** Early on, Continental established best practices in preference centers. Figure 6.10 shows an example.

- **It takes chances.** Continental was an early adopter of RSS and mobile messaging. We had the chance to work with Continental a few years ago and were impressed by its willingness to look toward the future.

- **Its welcome messages speak to the consumer.** Many of Continental's frequent flyers have been impressed with the way the airline creates messaging that will help make flight planning and execution easier. Continental was among the first airlines to use email to alert customers to check in online and provide service updates via email mobile messaging. These transactional messages aren't viewed as interruptive at all. They're appreciated.

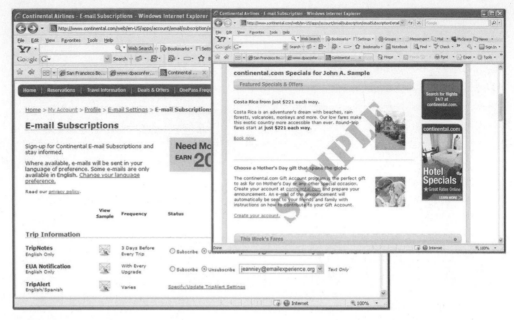

Figure 6.10 The Continental Airlines preference center

Thursday: Reviewing the Opt-Out Process

Setting up a plan for email acquisition, although it's essential, is only as effective as the opt-in methodology that is used. Once someone opts in, both best practices and CAN-SPAM say you must provide a simple, clear, one-click way to opt out. In reviewing your company's opt-out process, the first question you want to ask yourself is, "How well are we currently handling opt-outs?" As with the exercise to determine which elements of your advertising marketing program/website currently support an email conversation, this is also a good place to start gauging the effectiveness of your opt-out process.

In 2008, eROI, an integrated marketing service company, conducted an analysis of how companies are enabling people to opt in and opt out. Their findings contain insights you need to know when beginning to design your opt-out strategy.

A summary of their findings indicates that less than half of marketers used a confirmation process to validate opt-in requests. The difference between getting an opt-in approval and getting a confirmed opt-in can create significant differences in response rates for future emails.

To entice subscribers, 88 percent of companies reported offering a newsletter subscription, and 29 percent reported offering access to preferred content. Rewards came in second, with 24 percent offering discounts and coupons and 22 percent presenting a contest of some sort. When you are designing your opt-in strategy, these statistics and numbers can assist you in knowing what the rest of the market is offering.

Although people are looking for an exchange of value in order to provide their email address, they do not always need to be given gifts or larger rewards in exchange.

An additional set of findings from this same report indicated that most marketers provide a "thank you" page as the landing page. Yet most marketers don't take advantage of it, because only 29 percent of email marketers reiterate the benefits of subscribing. Data management was another area where companies were not up to speed. According to eROI, 65 percent of email marketers don't pass content on to another system. Although this could be acceptable for some companies, it could be an issue with CAN-SPAM compliance for others. So please, take note of the way your data flows moving forward.

Another insight is that after opting out, 90 percent of email marketers do not follow up with subscribers, leaving a huge opportunity for additional channel communication. Just because they don't want to receive email does not necessarily mean they don't want to hear from you in the future through a different channel. Of those that do follow up, 5 percent use direct mail, and 4 percent follow up via telephone.

Friday: Making Sure Your Landing Pages Are a Good Place to Land

This week has been pretty intense. You've looked at some crucial topics: driving traffic to your site, driving opt-ins to your database, securing preferences, and even managing opt-outs. There is only one item missing for the week, and that is the need to review every landing page on your website.

Landing pages are tricky, because there may be policies or guidelines that generate restrictions. Some companies have policies that require only one version of a landing page to be used regardless of the media entry point. Other companies do not allow certain types of cookies to be put in place, so content users' clickstreams cannot be tracked. In same cases, this makes it difficult to validate the impact that the landing page content or design has on conversion. In any case, there is one consistent truth: If you send an email with a link in it, the respondent who clicks, it has to land somewhere. Even if you are not responsible for the website strategy, you are responsible for making sure the email marketing experience remains on-brand and consistent and that it creates a positive outcome.

The Recipe for Successful Landing Pages

Just as you would with any other recipe, the first step in creating a successful landing page experience is to take a look around the kitchen (your company) and determine the resources you have available. Cooking up a successful landing page strategy will require you to have the following:

- **Your landing page policy.** Is it one-size-fits-all, or can it be customized by media type?

- **Your landing page template.** It should include an email address capture even if the visitor is coming here from an email.
- **Your landing page rollout time frame.** Does it take three days or three weeks to move a landing page from design to production?
- **Your landing page analytics capabilities.** Suppose you've driven 5,000 people to the page. How will you know what happened to them after that?

Event Challenge: Cisco and the Wordy Event Effort vs. AAAA and the Visual Invite

Cisco sent out an email to promote a webinar. It also presented online banners and other media. All efforts drove to the same landing page (which required lots of explanation since banner ads can't contain it all). This was a pretty poor experience for the readers. Those who made it through the text of the email were presented with the same information on the landing page. It was tough to find a link to register.

Event Challenge: Cisco and the Wordy Event Effort vs. AAAA and the Visual Invite *(Continued)*

AAAA was promoting an event at the same time. It, too, had a one-stop-landing-page rule. The difference with its email was that AAAA knew it. Instead of making the email do all the hard work, AAAA chose a more visual and high-level style of messaging that drove people to a fact-filled destination where they could continue learning and searching.

Continues

**Event Challenge: Cisco and the Wordy Event Effort vs.
AAAA and the Visual Invite** *(Continued)*

Dear Jeanniey,

The **AAAA Digital Conference** is just two weeks away, so you'll want to Register Now and join us on Wednesday, May 28, at TheTimesCenter, conveniently located in mid-town Manhattan. For everybody who cares about the ever-changing digital world, the AAAA Digital Conference is a MUST ATTEND.

Our conference agenda includes presentations and panel topics on every major area of interest in the digital realm. Featured speakers include:

- **Matt Bromberg**, President and CEO, Major League Gaming. Sports is an American passion; Major League Gaming allows sports passionistas to work hard at playing hard.
- **Joe Celia**, Chairman and CEO, G2. G2 is the highly successful activation arm of Grey Global Group. Joe Celia is the No. 1 activator.
- **Mark Kvamme**, Venture Capitalist, Sequoia Capital Partners. Mark has made a seamless transition from his early days as CEO of CKS to mover and shaker at deep-pocketed Sequoia Capital Partners.
- **Pippa Seichrist**, President and Co-Founder, Miami Ad School. The Miami Ad School is not just about training students for traditional advertising. Pippa will tell us how she is training for digital applications.

Add to these topics a panel of some of the best practitioners in developing digital talent, and you have a seriously kick-ass conference.

>> **View complete conference agenda**
>> **Register online now**

Cordially,

Nancy Hill

Nancy Hill
President-CEO
AAAA

The AAAA thanks the sponsors of the 2008 Digital Conference:

Google, Microsoft and Yahoo!

The path was integrated for the AAAA respondents. This is a key element to consider when creating any email campaign.

The next step is to build your landing page strategy. Define what needs to happen when someone clicks your email. This is important, because it will enable you to make sure the copy and layout of your email are appropriate based on the destination.

If your landing page is a one-stop shop, then your email should focus on getting people to click through to read more. Conversely, if the point of the landing page is data capture, your email marketing message has to work harder.

The third and fourth steps in your landing page strategy should be to drive the visitor to the appropriate destination and do some type of data capture. This doesn't mean you need to make it mandatory to provide an email address or other information in order to access landing page content. It does mean landing pages are no longer hidden from view, and many people will access these pages without ever having received your email. Giving someone the opportunity to engage with you is critical.

How to Determine the Appropriate Destination for Your Email Links

This is a tough one. Many companies make the mistake of sending people to the home page or an ordering page as a destination from an email. Home pages are too broad, and ordering pages are too narrow. You will need to assess the purpose of your email to determine the best destination to send someone to. Wherever that is, your visitor will expect a "helpful" push to the next location. For instance, suppose you send someone an email about ordering cable TV services. The best landing page will be a deep-link order form. That makes sense, but what happens if they are not ready to order yet? Does your landing page have ways for them to learn more, explore the site, or even push them to other valuable content? Most likely no one has thought past getting the order. This is now your job.

Why Data Capture on Any Landing Page Makes Sense

People who come to your landing page from an email may not be ready to do what you want. Or they might not be the right person. For example, if you are selling football tickets to your reader and they click through to check out the deal but they are hockey fans, they won't convert. However, if someone else in the house *is* a football fan, that email or landing page link will most likely be shared with someone not on your list. Having a section of your landing page that enables people to opt in can help grow your list and improve response rates.

Now that you know what the tools are, what the destination experience should be, and how to manage THE USER FLOW, you absolutely need to include one step to wrap up this week of learning: analysis.

Most email marketers look at top-level metrics: opens, clicks, and conversions. With a landing page, though, there is tremendous value in understanding what happens between the email click to the landing page and the conversion. It can often educate you about your email creative and even about the offer.

Figure 6.11 shows a landing page from IBM.

Figure 6.11 IBM Multichannel landing page

This page offers a number of places to click. You can explore content, reach a representative, navigate off the page, and more. If an email was sent to drive traffic to one of these specific areas to convert visitors and the conversion was low, it would be a huge help to be able to see where people *are* clicking on this page. You could then either change this page layout to make it more focused, change the destination link, or potentially even just gather clickstream data to create a very personal email follow-up. For more advanced email marketers, your landing page is a great place to try multivariate testing. We will speak about that in more detail in Chapter 7.

Knowing how your landing pages work is a key element of creating a big splash with your email marketing efforts. And as you move forward into week 3, you will need to remember all of these cornerstone elements so you can apply them appropriately to build the blueprint for success.

Week 3: Counting Down to "Go Time"

Now that you have filled your head with many different best practices and strategies, it is quickly coming down to the time to send your email campaign. This week focuses on helping you make sure you have thought through all the key elements you will need to have in place in both the short-term and the long-term to ensure success. In this week, there is a good bit of information to absorb. One caution: Even if you think you can cut corners here, you can't. Keep this section in front of you as you begin to design your campaign, even if you don't activate it for a few months.

Monday: Mapping out a realistic strategy

Tuesday: Defining your data transfer process

Wednesday: Making sure tracking and links will work

Thursday: Checking for the deliverability "basics"

Friday: Testing for actionability

Monday: Mapping Out a Realistic Strategy

For our purposes, strategy is the reason you are creating your email program. There can be many reasons to send an email to people: acquisition, conversion, loyalty, retention, up-sell, cross-sell, viral, service, transactional, invites, and more. All of these fit within the larger umbrella of a program. Maybe your emails are part of a multichannel program, maybe they are the only marketing elements you use, or maybe they are meant to drive to a larger effort. In any event, your program is meant to help achieve some presumably monetary goal for your company: sell more, or get more X. And using email has become one of the most effective ways to make that happen. That ultimate company goal is 100 percent the guiding principle of your email strategy.

Although creating a strategy from company goals seems easy, it can very quickly become overwhelming and unproductive if you are not careful. Why? Because email offers so many opportunities to personalize, customize, and build individual messaging, that one simple email, intended to be targeted for different types of response or data, can turn into 100 messages. So to keep you on track, we have built the following ten-question strategy/workflow organizer for your strategy design. This is another section you may find useful to bookmark, rip out, or highlight like crazy.

The Strategy/Workflow Organizer for Email

1. List three company goals that are measurable. Example: increase sales by 5 percent.

    a)

    b)

    c)

2. List all the types of email messages you have thought of sending. Examples: newsletter, stand-alone, direct email.

    a)

b)

c)

d)

e)

3.   Now, prioritize the top two types of email from the previous answer:

a)

b)

4.   Which is *the* most important to you? Pick one.

a) New sales on a continual basis

b) Existing customer up-sell

c) Supporting longer customer life cycles through thought leadership or news

d) Notifying customers of product- or service-related updates

5.   What is your average unit sale price?

6.   What is your average sales cycle? Examples: immediate, three months.

7.   Does any other group, person, or department need to be involved in making a sale/transaction happen? (For example, do your emails drive leads that salespeople need to close?)

8.   How many different demographic data elements do you have available on your list?

9.   Do you have any past email response data?

10. Will your campaign be an email-only effort, or are other channels promoting the same efforts as well? (For example, if you don't have an email address, will a direct-mail campaign be utilized?)

Once you have answered all these questions, you are ready to build your realistic email strategy. To make your efforts as successful as possible, we suggest you start small and add on. This means you need to build a messaging and data flow capability (discussed further in tomorrow's section) that will allow you to expand as your knowledge does. Don't try to segment and send and make messages to every person on your list in the beginning. To get the best return, follow these rules:

- **Determine how the access to email assets you have can best support your company goal.** Pick the most impactful effort, and begin your strategy there. Sure, it is fun to create a birthday email campaign with a special offer. But if the goal of your company is to decrease the cost of sales by migrating away from print messaging, that campaign strategy won't help you, because it is reaching only those who have already migrated.

- **Choose a demographic-driven segmentation strategy, or response-driven strategy, but not both.** If you try to map out a contact strategy for welcome emails that is driven 100 percent by responsiveness to prior messages, you will see that it gets pretty complex pretty quickly. If you try to add demographics on top, it will ruin the program. Determining whether response or demographics makes more sense for you is going to be based on your line of business. If your company is selling lawn care products, for example, beginning with demographics to enable messages by geography would make much more sense.

- **Before you finalize your strategy, vet it against your data.** This is an area where many marketers fall short. One of us witnessed a $100,000 consulting project in which an advertising agency created a very comprehensive, best-in-class contact strategy for a client. When the advertisers went to implement the personalized and segmented messages, they found that the cell sizes were, in many cases, zero—no one fit into the ideal groups. So, the strategy had to be thrown away. Once you think you have a strategy outlined, stop and think for a minute about how many email addresses you will have to send the message to. It is OK to begin broad and become more personal from there.

- **Keep the next step in mind.** Your email campaign strategy is most likely part of a larger strategy. If you are a retailer, the ultimate strategy goal may be to drive to an online purchase or into a store. If you are a B2B company, your strategy might be to drive to a validated lead, which can be picked up by a salesperson. If you are a health-care provider, your ultimate strategy may be to get the reader to ask their doctor for more information about a product or drug. Whatever the case, it is important to think about, and be aware of, how your email message will need to be used.

Here's an example: Your reader has allergies. They did some research on the Internet and came to your site. They opted in for allergy-related emails. Your company sells allergy relief products. The goal of your email campaigns is to educate readers about allergy management and prevention and drive them to trial/purchase. Ultimately, your reader will need to go to a pharmacy to make a larger purchase.

The end step here is to drive them to a pharmacy. This means at some point you will need to create a secondary email campaign, which is focused on trial, usage, and community around the use of the product, to maintain their loyalty.

Knowing this ahead of time is critical. It enables you to create an email strategy that will support polls or questions that trigger this switch from a prospect to a consumer. Maybe at this point you offer the ability to switch to a different type of email, to participate in a community group, or to receive coupons for people connecting through mobile devices.

If you go into the development of an email campaign without thinking through all the "next steps" and determining what will need to happen, you will end up with a great but short-lived and only partially successful effort.

We suggest you stop now for a bit and actually sketch out your strategy. Even if it is just a bunch of boxes and arrows, it will be an important reference for the next section.

Tuesday: Defining Your Data Transfer Process

Now that you have a map for your email strategy, you can build your data transfer process. Depending on the size of your company database, this can be a simple task or the most horrible experience you have ever had. For that reason, the following sections are going to be split based on complexity levels of the databases inside your company. Feel free to skip the other sections, or read them all and have pity on the people whose company has a multidepartmental CRM solution.

A Few Basics About Your Data Strategy

Email relies on the access to, and usage of, email addresses. In most cases, those are stored in a database somewhere. For your strategy to work, you will need to have access to these addresses, in some cases in real time. Sadly, many large companies, or companies whose databases were built more than ten years ago, don't have the ability to capture an email address as a field or store responses to emails. This can significantly limit your ability to message dynamically or even employ some of your great strategic ideas.

At this point, we recommend you take the time to use our database needs assessment checklist as a reference point and then build your own. (Figure 6.12 shows the opening screen; you'll find the complete `Databaseanalysis.xls` checklist at www.sybex .com/go/emailmarketinghouraday.) Knowing what your needs are going to be will be critical for knowing how to manage and build data flows.

Once you've done this assessment, you'll have a very good understanding of your needs for data management, transfer, and support. You can then consider your options based on company database size.

Small Companies, or Companies with Limited Database Ability

Believe it or not, these types of organizations have the easiest path to starting email marketing because they can leverage the power of the email provider's database. Most email marketing providers have database capabilities that store hundreds of fields about your customer. Because this information is stored inside their database,s the ability to create dynamic, rules-based messaging is simple.

If this is your scenario, the only two elements you need to worry about are the flow to get data into the database and the ability to extract it for reporting or analysis purposes when you need it. You can refer to Chapter 7 for more information about how to utilize reports and analytics to optimize your efforts.

List all of the requirements for your efforts in each of these areas. Put a star next to those that will require some sort of data storage or transfer

Email delivery

1. Email delivery that determines automatic select of format (text, html and rich text) based on browser's acceptance level
2. Content and code analysis to avoid spam filters and blocking
3. Record accurate bounce-backs by reason codes, and deliver status to CRM solution
4. Retry non-fatal bounce-backs (soft bounces) automatically a specified number of times.
5. Ability to support rich media, video or flash
6. Ability to... determine if the contact status is opt in - opt out and manage accordingly
7. Ability to...trigger time activated Emails, and activity driven messages
8. Easy to use interface and tool
9. Ability to send faster than 50K per hour
10. Ability to vary delivery based on customers preference (ex. Weekly, monthly)
11. Ability to...build complex logic message streams using business rules
12. Ability to personalize web page experience
13. Ability to...support viral functionality which includes tracking and reporting
14. Ability to...manage co-marketing efforts (e.g. dynamically generate BP logo on landing page)
15. Provide automatic e-fulfillment capability (ex. Auto reply with link or attachments)
16. Ability to...track responses from the Email through the site (ex. Client 1 opened the email, clicked on the link, and registered for my offer)
17. Ability to...leverage transactions to trigger marketing emails - ex: sw renewals, orders, enotifications etc must be able to access data from multiple data sources to accomplish this
18. Ability to designate Sender name, From Address, Reply address either for entire campaign as a dynamic field in the Email

Email assembly

1. Email contains personal, trackable urls for each recipient
2. Ability to hard code, by country, the privacy and legal statements in footer or other areas
3. Ability to include seed list with mailings
4. Supports double byte character sets
5. Ability to merge personalization from any field in the database into the Email content

Figure 6.12 Database assessment checklist

Midsize Companies, or Companies with Moderate Database Abilities

Things get a little complex if your company has a database that is able to store email address records and a few other fields but not all response data. Many companies in this situation unintentionally make it impossible to do multi-touch messaging because they use the "batch and blast" method for messaging. This means pulling a list from the central database and uploading it into the email system for mailing.

This form of email marketing is very poor because it does not allow you to create a history of responsiveness by reader. That insight is critical to determining the average life span of an email opt-in or what points or types of messages cause the most significant drop-off.

If this is your scenario, you will need to bring your email strategy list to the database team and enlist the help of your ESP. Most likely, your ESP has dealt with this challenge before and can work with your data team to do the heavy lifting. This means your ESP can store your data and response elements in their database to enable you to do triggered messaging and create daily or weekly feeds of new email addresses and opt-outs to keep your main database up to date.

Large Companies or Large CRM Databases

If you work for a global entity that has a large customer relationship management (CRM) solution in place (like those provided by Siebel or Ephiphany), your email marketing data transfer efforts are going to be tricky. In many cases, your large CRM solution is a powerhouse of insights. Multichannel purchase behaviors are integrated from all channels: the Web, in-store call center, and email.

Just because a person doesn't purchase from an email does not mean they are not one of the best customers in the collective database.

In these cases, the email messaging strategy you wrote will need to be bounced off the CRM strategy already in place. This means you will need to adapt your email strategy to consider all the larger impacts occurring through other channels. It also means your email capture strategy may be constrained by some data flow. For example, suppose you are a consumer packaged goods company and have 40 products. Each one of those products has its own website and email program. Behind the scenes, your CRM solution and analytics team have built predictive models that say if a person buys product 1, they are very likely to buy product 4 within 60 days.

If you are the email manager for product 4, you won't want to build a campaign that speaks just to new opt-ins. You will want a program that speaks to opt-ins, with the caveat that if they have bought product 1 recently, they get a different message. This will require that the data you receive not only be uploaded into the database for messaging but also be compared to other product databases.

In these cases, our best advice is to start your efforts by sitting down with the technical team to understand the timing of data flows and then rethink your email strategies to work within the constraints. It is difficult to turn the *Titanic* with a spoon. Once your programs have garnered high response rates and insights that may support changing the timing or way data flows, you can revisit the conversation.

Regardless of your company size, understanding and organizing your data flow can make or break your campaign efforts.

Wednesday: Making Sure Your Tracking Links Will Work

The focus of today's efforts is ensuring that your tracking links will work. This suggestion might seem kind of silly, especially since we spoke quite a bit about creative design elements in the previous chapter, but it is important.

These days, successful deliverability is contingent upon the perceived security of the content of an email. This means every image and link inside an email is subject to automated validation by ISPs.

There is a real threat we need to be aware of as email marketers: the misuse of links for phishing scams. Craig Spiezle, the director of security for Internet Explorer, is a leading email deliverability authority and offers these insights to share with you on the topic:

- Leading brands have found that upwards of 80 percent of emails purportedly sent from them are actually spoofed messages.

- In December 2007, there were more than 25,000 phishing sites, a tenfold increase since January 2005.

- Sixty-one percent of consumers are concerned about becoming victims of online fraud.

- In 2007, U.S. citizens lost more than $120 million in fake foreign lottery scams plus more than $100 million from the notorious Nigerian offers, both of which originated from forged and deceptive email.

- Among the most common types of spoof messages are the following:

  - IRS tax filing and refunds
  - Social greetings
  - Valentine's Day offers (roses to diamonds)
  - Campaign contributions
  - 401K contributions
  - Lottery scams
  - Viagra offers
  - PayPal scams

Table 6.2 shows the February 2008 percentage of messages appearing to be from legitimate domains that are actually spoofed.

▶ **Table 6.2** The Most Commonly Spoofed Email Domains

Domain	Email Spoof Rate
bankofamerica.com	87.10%
yahoo.com	87.00%
paypal.com	45.60%
irs.gov	41.20%
telefonica.net	40.40%
comcast.net	33.00%
hotmail.com	24.60%
amazon.com	10.40%

And the examples in Figures 6.13 and 6.14 will show you that a spoofed email doesn't necessarily look like spam.

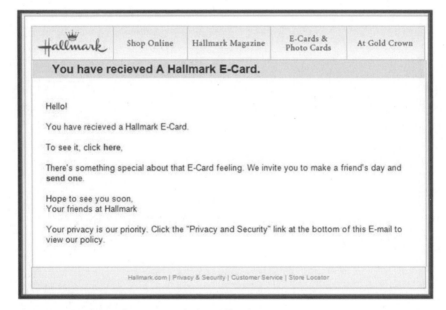

Figure 6.13   Spoofed email purporting to be from CitiBusiness

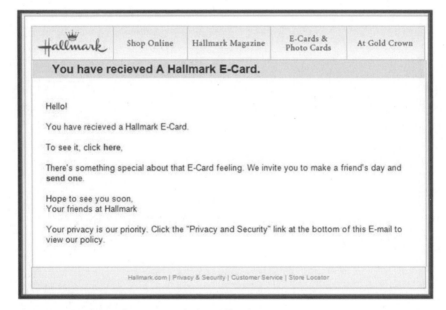

Figure 6.14   Spoofed email purporting to be from Hallmark

So, why should readers trust your email? We know you are not a spammer or spoofing domains, but what would be worse than spending all this time building an email campaign and having it blocked because the tracking links you have in it are highly spoofed or flagged as "non-reputable."

Now is the time to ensure that your email links are using domains and IP addresses that are appropriately registered and established and will successfully track and resolve appropriately to your database. Registering these links and IP addresses with the right monitoring and reputation system will be one of the only ways you can ensure you are not being spoofed.

Thursday: Checking for the Deliverability Basics

By most estimates, spam accounts for more than 50 percent of all email communications. But just because it may look like spam and may act like spam doesn't mean it is spam. Spam filters don't really care if your message is legitimate and valued. To get some expert advice on the deliverability basics, we interviewed two top email marketing deliverability experts, Ray Everett-Church, the chief privacy officer for Habeas, and Erick Mott, the director of marketing for Habeas. Today's lesson is based on what they had to say.

Most ISPs now use spam filters to cull undesirable email to protect their subscribers and cut down on the amount of email traffic that can potentially bog down the network and slow down service. The more emails their customers get, the more it consumes expensive bandwidth.

To combat this waste of resources, ISPs, corporations, and institutions of all sizes have deployed antivirus software and other security solutions. In doing so, they have set policies about what is considered undesirable content. More often than not, the IT department is responsible for developing and enforcing policies that may not necessarily be in line with legitimate business priorities or the needs of individual users. So, sometimes valuable information is intercepted and thrown into the spam heap inadvertently.

And last, but hardly least, are the consumers who implement desktop applications that automatically delete messages that qualify as spam. Many consumers may never even see messages that might be of interest to them.

Spam filters are becoming an obstacle for legitimate e-newsletter publishers and email marketers. To get your mail into the inbox, consider implementing these four basic strategies.

Step 1: Check Your Content for Spam Triggers

Spam filters scan headers, the subject line, the content, and the format of every email message. Do you monitor your messaging for words and punctuation that set off spam triggers? Most spam filters look at word choices, punctuation, and case usage. For example, liberally sprinkling your text with exclamation marks and inserting shrill sales language that screams out in capital letters is a surefire way to get blocked:

- **Keep your subject lines relevant, and edit them for trigger words.** Your subject lines should never include words such as *free*, *special offer*, *extra income*, *money-back guarantee*, and other language associated with promotions for medications, pornography, mortgages, or software. Also, keep subject lines to 50 characters, including the spaces between words so that they show up in their entireties in inboxes. You may want to send test emails to selected subscriber groups with different subject lines for each group. That way, you can determine which ones will bypass filters.

- **Craft your message carefully in your own voice.** Use plain English—common, everyday language. The same rules that apply to subject lines apply to your body copy. Stay away from words and phrases that make your email sound too much like a sales pitch. If you have advertisers, you might want to rewrite their ads to align with your style. Use a thesaurus or a skilled writer to assist you with editing out offensive language.

- **Target your message.** If you have a good database with information on your subscriber's demographics and preferences, you'll be able to segment your audience and tailor your campaigns and communications. You might also consider inserting the names of each subscriber in your greeting. Messages that are personalized will result in fewer unsubscribes and are more likely to be opened.

Step 2: Consider Plain Text for Your Message Format

Spam filters have biases against particular email formats. Although HTML offers many creative options for expressing your message, it is also quite often sniffed out by spam filters. HTML emails may be blocked because the format is widely used by spammers and because their large file size may cause ISPs to strip them out. Plain-text messages are more likely to circumvent filters.

If you still want to send emails in HTML format, send a text version as well. In the text version, you'll want to embed a link to your website where recipients can conveniently view the HTML version to get the full impact of your message:

- **Go easy on graphics.** Too many images in an email will also send out a red alert.

- **Practice basic list hygiene.** One of the best ways to ensure that your emails find their way to their destinations is to make sure you are emailing only real email addresses and responsive people. Purge your lists of old, invalid, and non-performing addresses.

- **Get permission.** Use confirmed opt-in, which sends a unique link to the subscriber when they request information to make sure they really and truly want to be included in your mailings. Also be sure to provide clear instructions on how to unsubscribe or opt out.

- **Try to get subscriber email addresses from ISPs other than Yahoo or Hotmail.** These casual accounts may not be reviewed very often by recipients, so your valuable message may sit unopened indefinitely.

- **Remove bounce-backs and unsubscribes immediately.** ISPs may block your emails to all recipients if you continue to send communications to invalid email addresses. Many major ISPs provide useful codes in their bounce messages in order to help senders determine whether an address should be removed.

- **Encourage your subscribers to put you on their whitelists.** After someone has registered, you might consider sending them a welcome email letting them know what the sender header for your communications will look like, for example, `newsletter@corporation.com`. Then you can suggest they place you on their whitelists. It's best to send out the welcome letter fairly soon after a subscriber has registered so they don't forget they have done so.

Step 3: Let Everyone Know You're a Good Internet Citizen

Many ISPs block email before the filter even scans the subject line for spam trigger words. The reason for this is that they can't be sure you are who you say you are. Deliverability is significantly higher for legitimate senders, with a reputation that can be verified. You can let ISPs know you are a trusted sender in several ways:

- **Have a static IP address.** Every Domain Name System (DNS) has a corresponding IP address, which is the numerical identifier assigned to computers for that domain. It's best to consistently use the same IP address for your email server(s) so that the ISP knows you are an established sender and can build a reputation profile about your IPs/domains. Dynamic IP addresses change every time the computer connects to the network or Internet. ISPs are leery of messages sent from dynamic IP addresses because many spammers constantly change their sending IP addresses to avoid detection. Email filters will consequently look upon dynamic IPs as indicative of fly-by-night spam operations.

- **Make sure that both forward and reverse DNS are set up for your domain.** Spammers and spoofers forge domain names or IP addresses to hide the actual address. To detect these, spam filters do a reverse DNS lookup. A forward lookup checks to see which IP addresses are associated with a domain name. A reverse lookup checks to see which domains are associated with an IP address.

- **Set up a sender-permitted framework (SPF) or sender ID framework (SIDF) record for your domain, and consider other authentication.** SPF and SIDF are authentication initiatives launched by Microsoft and utilized by major ISPs such as AOL, Earthlink, and others. They were developed to make it easy to distinguish reputable organizations and businesses from DNS forgers. SPF and SIDF allow recipients to see which IP addresses have been approved to send mail from your domain. If email comes in from a rogue IP address, it can be automatically blocked. Some ISPs, most notably Yahoo, are experimenting with a new form of authentication called Domain Keys Identified Mail (DKIM). With DKIM, each email contains a small digital signature, embedded in the headers, which helps guarantee the legitimacy of the sending domain. To combat "phishing"-related identity theft, PayPal is one of the earliest adopters of DKIM and is already digitally signing most of their outbound email.

- **Get your business certified by an online reputation management services firm.** When it comes to email deliverability, reputation matters. Enlist a credible service to vouch for your name, integrity, and best practices. Working with an online reputation management (ORM) services firm can help you see where deliverability problems may arise and minimize the likelihood of being filtered out by ISPs. Third-party whitelists are widely used by ISPs and receivers of all sizes.

Definition of ORM

To stand out from the flood of spam and other illegitimate online activities and build trust with consumers and email receivers such as ISPs and antispam systems, legitimate businesses must apply the tenets and practices of online reputation management (ORM) to maintain positive online brand equity and trust.

ORM is a necessary best practice for any organization using email and the Web to conduct business. It encompasses the areas of online identity, compliance, infrastructure, consumer assessment, feedback processes, and third-party certification.

ORM ensures that an entity will maintain a positive online reputation, which will improve a business' email inbox delivery rates, email response rates, website traffic volume and response rates, and their ability to partner with other organizations online.

• **Get on the whitelists of all the major ISPs.** Major ISPs 'such as Yahoo and AOL have reputation-based programs that invite legitimate businesses to put themselves on the ISP's internal whitelist. This ensures that your emails are delivered to recipients as long as you follow their rules. Having a good reputation increases the probability of a successful e-marketing program.

Step 4: Follow the Letter of the Law

Make it a regular practice to study the latest news about antispam legislation. Sending spam is a serious crime and can result in irreparable damage to your reputation and your business, not to mention heavy fines and imprisonment.

• **Educate yourself about CAN-SPAM compliance.** Learn everything you can about the CAN-SPAM Act of 2003, as we discussed in Chapter 5.

• **Include a physical address and simple unsubscribe process for all your commercial email communications.** The law requires that the "sender" of a commercial email provider include identifying information, including a valid physical postal address, and that the emails include a simple unsubscribe method. The FTC's definition of "sender" is complicated, so you will need to understand what the law expects of you if you are considered a sender under the law.

- **Develop a privacy policy and stick to it.** Make sure all the details are readily available on your website. Your subscribers will appreciate that you value their confidential information and respect their wishes. They want to be assured you won't sell their names or send them unsolicited email.

- **Keep accurate records of subscribers and unsubscribe requests.** If you are accused of spamming, you'll have all the evidence you need to prove that you have conducted business lawfully and have acted on the requests of your subscribers.

Why These Steps Are Important

It sounds like a great deal of work, and it is. But if your business has a loyal subscriber base and email communication is an integral part of your business, monitoring and maintaining a good reputation is worth all the effort. Although there's no absolute guarantee that your email won't be filtered out, these strategies will increase the likelihood of delivery significantly, leading to better response, reduced costs and ultimately, improved profitability.

Tap into www.reputationwiki.org, a collaboration and educational resource on the Web for business professionals in marketing, sales, and brand stewardship roles.

Friday: Testing for Actionability

Hooray! You've made it through week 3. With a strong strategy in place, a data flow process, and assurance that your messages are going to be delivered, you are down to the wire. It's time to test one more aspect of your campaign: the ability for someone to take action with it.

The first rule to keep in mind here is that the definition of "action" does not mean a click-through, because, in reality, emails never die. It's true—once an email is delivered, even if it is put in the trash folder, unread, it has a chance of being referenced at a future date.

Write This Down: Twenty-one percent of all emails are accessed and read up to three months after they are received. (Source: Zinio)

To determine whether your email is actionable, you can use the following checklist as a starting point:

- **The From name.** Does the From name present the brand strength, even if it is the *only* thing read? (For example, imagine a recipient saying "Yes, I do recall an email from Williams-Sonoma.")

- **The subject line.** Does the subject line tell you what is inside the email without having to open it?

- **The header information.** Do you have a way to get to the HTML version *and* a mobile version of the email for ease of reading on the run? (It is often the person standing in the store who wants to access your email on their BlackBerry to get the coupon code.)
- **The copy.** Does it paint a clear message about *what* you want the reader to do?
- **The landing page.** Does the landing page continue the conversation and set the reader up for the next steps?

Once you feel comfortable your emails can induce or support action, either now or later, give yourself a pat on the back. You've come a long way, and now it is time to get ready to put all your hard work into motion. It is time to get ready to send!

Week 4: Testing Your Way to the First Campaign

The last two weeks have focused on getting your house in order, and this is the final week of preparation. The most difficult part of being an email marketer is getting a campaign and process established for the first time. As you have read, this takes weeks of planning. In the end, though, every second you spend will pay off in dividends with the successes you create. Canadian entrepreneur David Gilmour has a phrase: "Two gets you twenty." It means that if you take your eye off the ball for even 2 percent of the time, you lose 20 percent of the resulting effects. This analogy is certainly true in email.

For that reason, we are going to make you spend one more week getting ready to prepare your campaign for launch. Our final week will pull together what you have learned in order to create a strategy and then make sure you have all the cogs working together like a well-oiled machine. In month 2 (Chapter 7), you will be able to send your first campaign and test your way to success. Ready for this final week? Let's go!

Monday: Choosing a From address and subject line strategy

Tuesday: Making sure your templates can be read

Wednesday: Ensuring personalization is accurate

Thursday: Remembering that emails get forwarded and saved

Friday: Going through the success checklist one more time

Monday: Choosing the Subject Line Strategy

As you were growing up, your mother may have told you, "You are what you eat." The same is true in email. Your email messages are only as good as the content inside. The trick is, how do you get people to look inside? In today's effort we will take a deep dive into the ways that the "actionability" of your email can be impacted.

Chapter 5 does a thorough job of providing you with tactics that will help you create your own From address and subject line strategy. In this chapter, we thought it would be beneficial for you to see how your subject line strategy can actually impact results and the kind of impact it will have on results.

In 2008, U.K. advertising agency Alchemy Worx produced a very compelling report on the correlation of subject lines and response rates. Its report showed that a shorter subject line will positively impact open rates. Specifically, 11–20 words drive the highest open rates for emails. (The testing looked at subject lines that ranged from 11–140 words). This is a fairly widely held belief. Shorter subject lines can be read in more email clients and can be read on handheld devices. For years, the standard has been to try to keep the total number of characters to less than 50 to ensure most email clients will render all the words in the preview pane.

Although this information is consistent with most historical recommendations, the information the report provides immediately following this is new, exciting, and a bit different from any information that has ever been shared before. The report indicated that although shorter subject lines drive the highest open rates, it is the longer subject lines that drive the highest click-to-open rates. This is new information, and when you think about it, it makes quite a bit of sense. Longer subject lines act as content filters for what is in the email. Subject lines like "Get 50% now" is great, but you need to open the email to see what you are saving money on. Longer subject lines like "Get 50% off on your new iPhone 3G" provide much more specific insight. These subject lines will drive lower but more qualified open rates and click rates.

Deciding between volume and quality has long been a heated debate among marketers. Which one you make your focus for subject lines will ultimately be a decision only you can make based on company goals. To make the most informed decision, review the elements of Chapter 5, and then test both strategies before making a final decision.

Tuesday: Making Sure Your Content Can Be Seen

It is crucial that recipients can see everything in the emails you send. Yet this is often an area where marketers drop the ball. In the previous chapter, we covered creative design and best practices. But as you get ready to kick off your first campaign, after someone opens your message, you want them to be able to get all your content, even if images are blocked or turned off.

Some of the most up-to-date results focusing on the reality of the state of rendering come from the Email Experience Council. A report released in June 2008 examined the email design practices of 104 top online retailers and their performance in an images-off email environment. It also includes the results of a survey of 472 marketers regarding rendering issues, conducted in conjunction with SubscriberMail.

Increasingly, images are being blocked by default by email and webmail clients, changing the game for B2C marketers, many of whom have become accustomed to designing emails that are composed mostly of images. "The results of this study underscore the importance of proactively designing email to compensate for image suppression," said Jordan Ayan, CEO of SubscriberMail.

She continues, "Specifically, email marketers must design emails to work with and without images present and test to ensure optimal image rendering. Marketers whose design accounted for image suppression reported impressive lifts in key performance areas. Still, a significant percent of email marketers realize this issue, yet fail to take action to address it."

Here's a summary of the results of the Email Experience Council rendering study:

- Twenty-three percent of retailers send emails that are completely unintelligible when images are blocked. Of the 77 percent that sent intelligible emails, there were significant variations in clarity based on their use of HTML text and alt tags.

- Fourteen percent of retailers compose their navigation bars with HTML text rather than images.

- Three percent of retailers used HTML call-to-action buttons rather than images.

- Eighty-eight percent of retailers include a "click to view" link in their pre-header text.

- Sixty-three percent of retailers include whitelisting instructions in their pre-header text.

Based on the importance of image rendering and the need to quickly read the copy in an email, many marketers take precautionary steps. These include the actions shown in Figure 6.15.

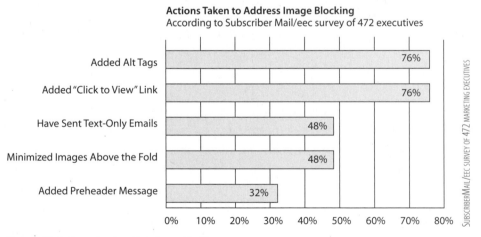

Figure 6.15 Actions taken to address image blocking

Whitelisting

Figure 6.16 shows an example of how an email message can look when sent to someone who is very cautious about what they receive or doesn't know that their images are turned off in their email client.

Figure 6.16 Email with images blocked

To avoid having your emails look like this, you should encourage people to whitelist or safelist your messages. Figure 6.17 shows current actions taken by marketers ranked by usage frequency.

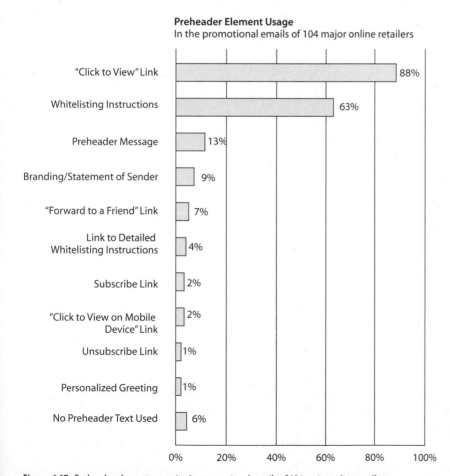

Preheader Element Usage
In the promotional emails of 104 major online retailers

- "Click to View" Link — 88%
- Whitelisting Instructions — 63%
- Preheader Message — 13%
- Branding/Statement of Sender — 9%
- "Forward to a Friend" Link — 7%
- Link to Detailed Whitelisting Instructions — 4%
- Subscribe Link — 2%
- "Click to View on Mobile Device" Link — 2%
- Unsubscribe Link — 1%
- Personalized Greeting — 1%
- No Preheader Text Used — 6%

Figure 6.17 Preheader element usage in the promotional emails of 104 major online retailers

Forms Rendering

In addition to image rendering, there is often a question about using forms in email. Although there is still much debate about forms in email, the handy checklist shown in Table 6.3, provided by Pivotal Veracity, can be a huge help with rendering and the ability to interact with a form for your campaigns. And we believe that even on platforms where the forms are not operable, their appearance alone can create a perception of value that generates higher response rates than without.

▶ **Table 6.3** Forms rendering by ISPs

ISP/Desktop/Mobile	Rendered?	Operable?
AOL.com	Yes	No
AOL 9	Yes	Yes
AT&T	Yes	No
Comcast	Yes	N/A
Cox	Yes	No
Earthlink	Yes	Yes
Gmail	Yes	Yes*
Hotmail/WLM	Yes	No
Lotus	Yes	Yes
MAC	Yes	No
Netzero/Juno	Yes	Yes
Outlook 2003	Yes	Yes
Outlook 2007	No	No
Outlook Express	Yes	Yes
Outlook XP	Yes	Yes*
Road Runner	Yes	N/A
Thunderbird	Yes	Yes
Verizon	Yes	Yes
Yahoo! Beta	Yes	Yes
Yahoo! Classic	Yes	Yes

Wednesday: Ensuring Personalization Is Accurate

It's the middle of the last week before you send your campaign, and you are working hard to make sure everything is checked and a contingency plan is in place. Personalization is one of the tactics many marketers use to make sure emails are recognized and opened. Today's focus is making sure your data feeds and dynamic content strategies are set up correctly to avoid embarrassing personalization errors.

Of course, you should test every new campaign you set up. However, when it comes to personalization of data inside an email, you will want to employ a few additional best practices:

- Establish consistent data entry capture fields for each field on your database. For example, you may want a rule that the first name must have at least two letters; for the state entry, you'll need to decide whether to allow the entire state name or require a two-digit abbreviation.

- Ensure that all data capture points/forms on your website and in email are capturing consistent data.

- Create some rules for using personalization inside an email. For example, no one wants to see a first name that is one letter: "Dear, G." To avoid this type of issue, create a rule to use the default personalization when a first name has less than three characters.

- Determine what your default personalization strategy will be regardless of what the data entered is. Figure 6.18 shows an email one of the authors received from JetBlue. It is a perfect example of a well-intended personalization strategy gone wrong.

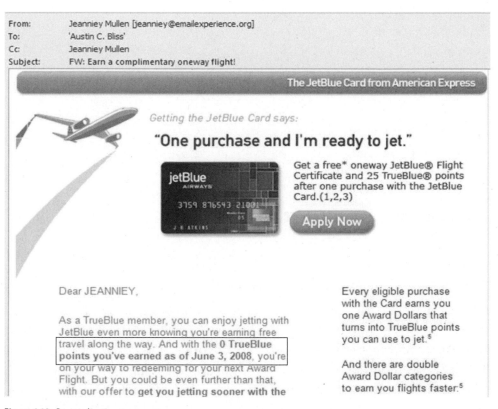

Figure 6.18 Personalization gone wrong

Notice the copy: "And with the 0 TrueBlue points you've earned as of June 3, 2008, you're on your way..." Really? With 0 points, Jeanniey won't get very far. A more appropriate personalized message would have been to send people with 0 points the same email with a statement like this replacing the one I received: "We noticed you don't have any points yet, so now is a great time to take advantage of this offer." You see, personalization does matter to the reader.

Personalization may seem simple at first, but please begin using it in smaller chunks and with great caution to ensure you get the hang of it before you go full stream ahead.

Thursday: Remembering That Emails Get Forwarded and Saved

We have spoken about this concept a number of times throughout the book already. Email is unique. Unlike paper, even when you throw it away, you can still dig it out of the trash folder a week later. Unlike a phone call, when are you done with it, it is still there. Once you send an email to someone, it lives forever. This means your messages, your brand, and your offer all need to maintain the highest level of quality they can.

When we are speaking with people about email marketing, we often conduct a quiz called "What Kind of Emailer Are You?" In this quiz, we tell people to imagine they receive an email about a sale on flowers. We then ask people to imagine what they would do with the email, and it always ends up that their actions fall into one of five possibilities:

- They see the subject line or from address and delete the email.
- They see the subject line or from address and save the email in a folder to read later.
- They read the email and click it.
- They read the email and delete it.
- They read the email and file it away.

We then ask people to imagine that three weeks later their best friend calls in a panic that she forgot her mother's birthday and is desperate to send flowers and is looking for a recommendation.

At this point, regardless of which of the five types of readers we have in the room, every single person says they would remember the email received weeks ago (admitting that they might not remember the details of the content) and will go as far as digging into their trash folder to find it and send to their friend.

You can try this email life-span test with any type of content, and it is always the same reaction. Emails live forever.

This is something you need to know and understand before your first campaign goes out. Why? Because this means your branding, your offers, and your editorial content will be read and referenced not just for days or weeks but potentially for months and, in the business world, even for years.

Understanding that email lives forever can give you a leg up as you think of copy. Referencing previous emails special offers or upcoming content keeps people engaged well beyond the one-email-readership trend that many new emailers fall into.

Use this information wisely.

Friday: Going Through the Success Checklist One More Time

A funny thing happens when you are the person who actually clicks the button to send an email campaign. Even if you are 100 percent sure your email campaign is set up perfectly, when it comes time to click the Send button, your heart begins to race, and you start questioning everything you have done up to this point.

This is not something that goes away quickly. It lives for each new send you do. In the email world, we call this *sender's remorse*.

For that reason, on the day before you send, we recommend you take the time to review all the elements of this chapter and go through the success list one more time. We also recommend sending a final test to both yourself and someone who's not involved with the campaign at all. Having a fresh set of eyes never hurts.

Your success checklist should include the following:

- Verifying your data source and data flow
- Making sure your messaging strategy matches your customer profile
- Following best practices on creative design, which includes deliverability
- Knowing that the reporting and tracking you need will be there
- Following the user experience through to the landing pages and website
- And last but not least, having a backup plan in place in case something goes wrong

We recommend you go through this chapter in detail one last time, because next week is your big chance to click that Send button and drive some revenue and results.

Test Your Knowledge

This chapter was filled with information. See how much you retained. A score of 5 out of 5 will ensure you are on your way to email marketing success.

- What are the six elements you need to have in your intelligence arsenal to get ready to build your strategy?
- How is email being used as a media channel by marketers?
- Why do you need to be concerned with your deliverability and reputation score?
- What is the main opportunity area for marketers when it comes to confirming opt-in?
- Name three basics of deliverability you need to know.

Month 2: Ensuring Success as You Launch Your Campaign

7

During this month, you will learn quite a lot about how your entire marketing plan is executed and how to continually optimize in accordance that plan. We'll take you through the components to launch your campaign, measure your progress, and manage your reputation.

Chapter Contents

Week 1: Sending Your First Campaign

Reporting and measurement are going to be a central part of your first week of sending email messages. Your primary task this week is going to be focusing on reporting data that will highlight challenges, such as email deliverability issues, as well as data that will pinpoint opportunities, such as identifying subscribers who appear to be engaged and profitable. Marketers often gravitate to the success metrics, focusing only on the positive results, and do not take the time to dive into the data to understand what is causing the list to perform or underperform. Month 2 is all about monitoring your data and responding to what you find. Here we will provide you with the necessary tactics to ensure you are making appropriate use of the data available to you.

Monday: What to do once you hit Send

Tuesday: Reading reports

Wednesday: Managing customer service replies

Thursday: Matching your response rates to your forecast and plan

Friday: Keeping your database clean and your reputation strong

Monday: What to Do Once You Hit Send

Congratulations, you have sent your first email message to start your first campaign. Multiple studies show that the first 48 hours after sending your mailing produce 80 percent of the response behavior. With so much of your list response at stake, you need to focus on the most important tasks after you click the Send button.

You must take two steps immediately. The first is to monitor your *seed list*—that portion of your list that contains addresses for mailboxes you monitor. Your seed list should contain the following types of addresses:

- **Your work email address.** This will ensure you are getting a copy of the mailing.
- **Company employees involved in the marketing campaign.** You need to know those individuals within your department who worked on the email campaign.
- **Customer service management.** It is also important your counterparts in your call center or customer service departments have a copy of each email campaign on file that they can refer to, should customers have any questions.
- **Store managers, sales, and field staff.** An internal distribution list of employees who work in the field, such as store managers, should also keep a copy of each mailing on file.
- **Dummy email addresses to which you have access.** Create a handful of email accounts at the top domains on your list, such as Yahoo, AOL, Gmail, Hotmail, and AIM, that you can access so you can quickly verify that your email actually reached these top-tier domains.

- **Deliverability services seed list.** As discussed in previous chapters, you will want to work with a delivery services provider such as Return Path, Pivotal Veracity, Habeas, or Lyris that can provide delivery seeding capabilities across hundreds of domains and can report on the delivery disposition—inbox, bulk (spam) box, missing, and so on—of your messages. Appendix A lists these and other service providers.

The second step is to watch the initial results come in via your application's reporting dashboard. This reporting will provide insight into how much mail is being delivered as well as aggregate open and click rates.

In addition, you will want to work with your ESP to understand how it is handling bounced messages. There are two primary types of bounces. *Hard bounces* are those that are dead on arrival, such as "mailbox does not exist at that domain" or a malformed email address; these should be less than 10 percent of bounces. *Soft bounces* are emails that did not reach the intended inbox for one of a host of reasons, including that the mailbox was full or there was a connection issue with the ISP. Your ESP can provide you with the details of how it treats these soft bounces and at what rate and interval it retries them. For example, these soft bounces may be re-sent as many as five times over a period of days until the messages are either delivered or moved into the failure or hard bounce category. Typically these addresses are not removed from a list unless they soft bounce five or more times within the retry pattern on a single mailing. Understand how your ESP treats these failures and messages as well as how they are calculated into your overall email delivery rate. The Email Measurement Accuracy Roundtable at the Email Experience Council suggests that email delivery rates should include all hard bounces and failures so that the delivery rate is representative of the messages that could not be delivered.

> **Write This Down:** Eighty percent of marketing emails that were opened were opened within 48 hours after delivery. By the sixth day, 95 percent of the people who opened had now done so, according to the 2005 "Email Marketing: The First 48 Hours Are Critical" report. (Source: MarketingProfs)

Tuesday: Reading Reports

Your email results are going to come in very quickly, typically within the first 24 to 48 hours after you hit Send. Here are some critical reports and metrics you must use to gauge the effectiveness of your mailing:

Domain Delivery Report This report (Figure 7.1 shows an example) will allow to you understand how much of your email was delivered at all the top domains that make up your email list. This report can quickly pinpoint whether one ISP dropped a significant portion of your email or whether you are having potential reputation-based issues at a particular ISP. If you notice that your open rate is below its historical average, this is usually a telltale sign that you have a delivery issue at one of the ISPs that makes up a significant portion of your list. The domain delivery report can further validate this suspicion, or it can confirm that all your email was delivered and that your low open rate is being driven by another reason, such as a poor subject line that is not relevant to a portion of subscribers or a sending frequency that is too high.

Additional Metrics	
Opened HTML Email more than once	7185
Aggregate Clickthroughs	9280
Clicked on more than one link	819
Clicked on one link multiple times	496

Domain Deliverability						
Domain	Sent	Bounced	Read	Clicked	Total Unsubscribed	Unsubscribe - Spam Complaints
@aol.com	351461	207 (0.1%)	7684 (2.2%)	1563 (0.4%)	332 (0.1%)	203 (0.1%)
@yahoo.com	328952	125 (0.0%)	10284 (3.1%)	1335 (0.4%)	260 (0.1%)	84 (0.0%)
@hotmail.com	179755	117 (0.1%)	6955 (3.9%)	730 (0.4%)	147 (0.1%)	83 (0.0%)
@msn.com	69592	46 (0.1%)	3687 (5.3%)	380 (0.5%)	58 (0.1%)	24 (0.0%)
@sbcglobal.net	49009	109 (0.2%)	3701 (7.6%)	367 (0.7%)	47 (0.1%)	12 (0.0%)
.rr.com	45188	90 (0.2%)	5927 (13.1%)	378 (0.8%)	39 (0.1%)	1 (0.0%)
@verizon.net	34972	24 (0.1%)	4047 (11.6%)	288 (0.8%)	34 (0.1%)	3 (0.0%)
@gmail.com	28283	2 (0.0%)	1419 (5.0%)	246 (0.9%)	51 (0.2%)	0 (0.0%)
@earthlink.com	25539	218 (0.9%)	2849 (11.2%)	145 (0.6%)	21 (0.1%)	0 (0.0%)
@comcast.net	15416	14064 (91.2%)	194 (1.3%)	20 (0.1%)	7 (0.0%)	0 (0.0%)
@charter.net	14897	3358 (22.5%)	1817 (12.2%)	109 (0.7%)	13 (0.1%)	0 (0.0%)

Figure 7.1 A domain delivery report

Open Rate This is the number of HTML message recipients who opened your email, usually stated as a percentage of the total number of emails sent. The open rate is considered a key metric for judging an email campaign's success, but it has several limitations. For example, notice in Figure 7.1 the column labeled "Read." Well, that is a misnomer—just because an email has registered as open does not necessarily mean it was actually read by a person. The email could have been registered as read just by the user previewing it in the preview pane of an email client application, such as Microsoft Outlook. The second problem with the accuracy of the open rate is that it measures the number of emails opened out of the total number sent, not just out of those that were actually delivered. Recall that the open rate is calculated by placing an invisible 1-pixel GIF (known as a *beacon*) in your email; this means that when images are blocked, so is this beacon image. And since this metric relies on images, it means that opens also can't be calculated on text emails.

The open rate can be directionally useful, as we mentioned, for its ability to spot potential delivery issues. Understand when you are reading your report whether the open rate is an aggregate open rate or a unique open rate. Unique open rates are more useful to the marketer because they show the actual number of individual subscribers who opened the email; by contrast, aggregate open rates can be flawed by preview panes and users who may open the message multiple times. Because opens cannot be calculated on text emails, some ESPs add opens for those text emails that registered a click because it is safe to assume that if the user clicked it, the user would have had to open it. Speak with your ESP to understand how it is calculating the open metric.

Opens Over Time This is typically a unique subscriber-oriented view into open rates to detail which subscribers are opening your email repeatedly on which days and what time of day. This metric can be meaningful if you are doing advertising-supported email, because this data may be valuable to get the sponsor to pay more for its email placement if it is in a mailing that has a high percentage of subscribers who tend to view their messages multiple times. On average, an email is opened one and a half to two times. However, most marketers should focus instead on click behavior and conversion data within their reports.

Total Time Email Was Open This metric, which some ESPs offer, is essentially a timer that shows the average amount of time a consumer had your email open. Although this might be an interesting factoid, many variables can skew it, such as preview panes, and it is not something you are ever likely to use as a segmentation attribute. Additionally, since it is based on the open beacon, it is subject to all the flaws and misinformation that we've noted for open rates.

Total Clicks This is a great stat to bring to your boss to demonstrate how many clicks—visits to your website—your email program delivered. It is a directional metric and, as we discussed in Chapter 5, something that could be incorporated into an engagement metric.

Unique Clicks Also referred to as the *unique click-through rate*, this details the unique number of times each subscriber clicked an individual link. For example, if you have two links in your email and the user clicked the first one just once and the second link three times, the unique calculation would register as two clicks.

Clicks by URL This will tell you exactly which URLs in your email were clicked and how many times. This data helps you understand the kind of content your subscribers prefer. For instance, do they respond better to white papers and research articles or to special offers and promotions?

Conversion Rate This will show the number of people who made it through the entire shopping cart process or landed on a registration page—whichever page you decided to tag in order to measure that the desired task had been completed. Tagging a page requires a web beacon and typically dropping a cookie. Nearly every ESP has this capability to tag and beacon pages.

Unsubscribe Rate This is the rate at which people unsubscribe from your list. It is typically half of 1 percent or less.

Abuse Complaint Rate This is the number of subscribers who report your email as spam. Increasingly, ESPs are adding this statistic to their email reporting. It is one more measurement that you should watch carefully.

Revenue per Mailing This metric can be displayed a number of ways in aggregate, detailing both the total amount of revenue that was delivered in a mailing and the average order size, which divides the number of orders into the total revenue. This is another great metric to show your co-workers and boss in order to "Hollywood" the results from your email marketing program. Imagine showing a graph like Figure 7.2 at the big project meeting.

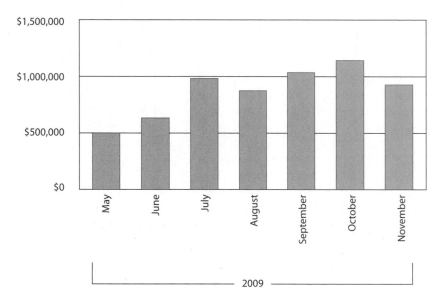

Figure 7.2 A graph of email revenue by month

These metrics can begin to inform your segmentation strategy, such as focusing on identifying individuals who are and are not clicking or those who purchased and those who did not. Additionally, enlisting website traffic behavior from web analytics solutions can provide a richer set of data to make your segments even more granular. We will cover some of these additional segmentation strategies later in this chapter.

Wednesday: Managing Customer Service Replies

Your outbound email will produce a number of inbound replies, some of which may be out-of-office messages that can be quickly categorized and deleted. Other messages will require a bit more work. For example, you will likely get some unsubscribe requests from clients who did not want to use the Unsubscribe link in your email. These people need to be identified, suppressed from any future mailings, and sent a confirmation message that they were removed from the email list. Other inbound emails may need to be routed to customer service or sales, such as from those who may have general questions about items in your promotion or customer service concerns, perhaps from previous orders with your organization.

Your inbound email inbox must be monitored for such customer service messages, and it is important to resolve those questions quickly and respond to the subscriber in a timely manner. Most consumers expect a response within one business day, so after a send on a Monday, by Wednesday you should have all your service-related replies handled.

> **Write This Down:** A 2007 JupiterResearch "Customer Service & Support Metrics" report found, via a dummy customer service email sent to hundreds of online businesses, that only 50 percent resolved email inquiries within 24 hours and that 31 percent of sites took three days or longer to respond or were completely unresponsive. (Source: JupiterResearch)

Use customer service data as a segmentation attribute. If your subscribers are emailing you service-related queries, whether they are generated from your outbound email or from your website, this data should be used as a segmentation point to pull out from mailings those subscribers who might be potentially upset with you. Additionally, you can focus on these service-oriented subscribers, sending them offers with deeper discounts in order to win them back, sending them surveys to better capture their attitudes, or potentially mailing to the problem subscribers less frequently.

To ensure that these addresses are monitored in a timely fashion, use a unique reply-to address that can be pushed into its own mailbox. This will make it easier to identify your marketing-related inbound mail and assign the proper priority to answering the messages quickly.

Thursday: Matching Your Response Rates to Your Forecast and Plan

There is a classic saying in sales: "Plan your work, and work your plan." This encapsulates what you must adhere to in every mailing; do not become complacent with your results, and test every variable that may be driving your results lower.

To ensure you are comparing apples to apples, you must first understand what your ESP or email application is reporting and how those metrics are calculated. This will ensure that your goals are reasonable and your planned metrics are being reported as you imagined they would be.

However, even with such an understanding, you may still find that your results are not what you had initially planned. In week 2 we will offer detailed tactics to employ specific metrics when your results are far off your plan.

First map out the deviation between your plan and the results, whether that is positive or negative, and track that in a spreadsheet or a custom-built report within your email marketing application. Do this on each mailing to develop a historical perspective of your mailing's performance. A funnel report like the one in Figure 7.3 shows how well your email list is performing as a whole, or it can be run for individual campaigns.

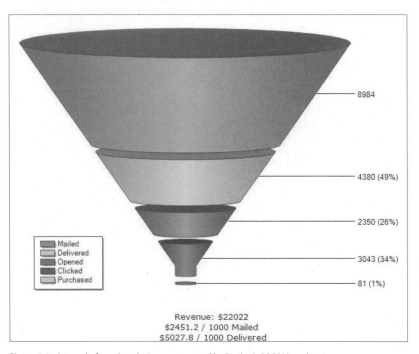

Figure 7.3 A sample funnel analysis report created by Epsilon's DREAM application

Next, begin to highlight the largest deviations and think of the variables that could be causing such great fluctuations, such as content and timing. Although we suggest specific tests that you can conduct to zero in on the variables that are causing such deviations, at this point you should have enough knowledge to begin to apply some of the lessons from earlier chapters to identify what you may want to test in future mailings. However, if your results are far below what you had expected, this could point to issues of data hygiene and delivery. Figure 7.4 illustrates what this dashboard may look like. The Friday after your first mailing is a good opportunity to spend some time investigating these issues.

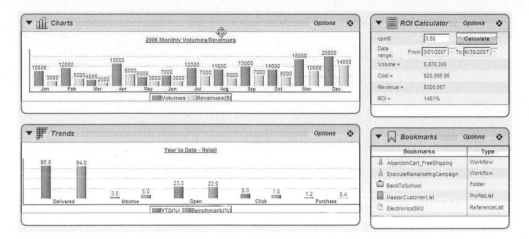

Figure 7.4 A sample email dashboard and ROI calculator

Friday: Keeping Your Database Clean and Your Reputation Strong

Earlier in this chapter we discussed the issues that affect deliverability and bounce handling. Make sure you have the following pieces in place for your ongoing email marketing program to keep your list clean and your reputation strong:

Unsubscribe Suppression Scheme Ensure that all unsubscribes are suppressed immediately and that any customer service replies to outbound mailings are also removed quickly. If you are working as a publisher with other advertisers, or vice versa, it is required under the CAN-SPAM law that you have identified yourself as the sender. If you are using names from other lists—either other sponsors or advertisers—you must also ensure that any names that have unsubscribed from your house list are also removed from the advertiser's or sponsor's list. Datran Media's UnsubCentral offering allows such a mechanism to securely compare and contrast lists to build one master, mailable file.

Authentication Scheme It is necessary for your mailing infrastructure to incorporate SPF, Sender ID, and DKIM. These are the message authentication standards used at MSN, Hotmail, Yahoo, and AOL. Email without these pieces in the header may be blocked, or at the very least get a "spammier" disposition when the ISP looks at the email. Your ESP should be using all these standards, at the very least SPF and DKIM.

Feedback Loops (FBLs) ISPs including Microsoft, AOL, Yahoo, and Comcast provide data, known as *feedback loops*, on which subscribers are marking your email as spam. Of course, you want to remove these subscribers from your list immediately, but you also want to understand your overall IP score at these various ISPs, of which the FBLs are a part. Each ISP has its own approach for setting a threshold that will block your email, but deliverability service providers such as Return Path and others will assist in navigating the ISP relationships for you. To keep your reputation strong, it is critical to subscribe to FBLs, suppress those former subscribers, and understand your disposition with each of the major ISPs.

IP Throttling Ask your ESP whether it is doing domain-level IP throttling. Although the term might sound like technical gobbledygook, it means that if you exceed the domain's ability to take messages from you, then you will get blocked, and your reputation will be tainted. For example, Comcast limits senders to two simultaneous connections per IP address and 1,000 messages per connection. This varies from ISP to ISP, and often the ISP will reset and change its rules. Although it is important how fast an ESP or piece of email marketing technology can send, it is more important to send email smartly where the rules are different at each different door. Your ESP should be familiar with these throttling limits and manage your email send stream accordingly, because delivery rates can change throughout the day in the middle of the mailing. Figure 7.5 illustrates such a pattern.

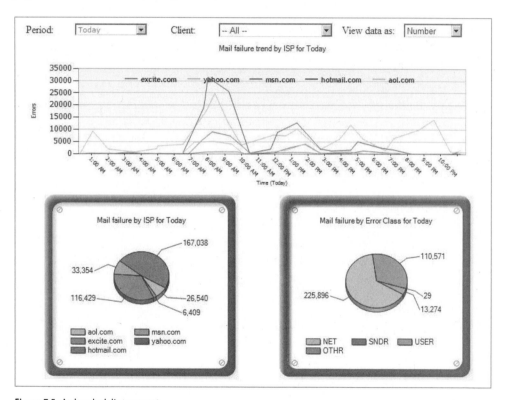

Figure 7.5 An hourly delivery report

Nonresponsive Subscriber Suppression If you have email addresses you have mailed to for eight to ten months at a time and there is no response from those subscribers, they may resolve to dormant accounts. It is important to remove non-responders from your email list, because those dormant email boxes can also impact your reputation. Keep those bad and nonresponsive email addresses off your list.

Welcome Campaigns In earlier chapters, we discussed the benefits of using welcome campaigns. One good reason to use such a campaign, or at least an autoresponder that confirms the email address is valid, is because bogus email addresses will not make your list. It is not uncommon for spam vigilantes to purposely add spam-trap addresses or bad addresses to marketers' lists just to cause them havoc.

Common Email Address Suppression Work with your ESP; most have a common suppression scheme that blocks addresses that are known problems such as `info@` or `abuse@`. Suppressing these addresses will allow you to further keep your list and reputation clean.

Week 2: Creating a Plan to Optimize Your Results

Now that you have your first mailing underway, it is time to recalibrate your expectations and use the data from your first mailing for further optimization. Week 2 is all about selling your mailing success to your co-workers and boss, as well as incorporating their feedback and your subscribers' behavior to enhance your future mailings.

> Monday: What your reports are really saying
> Tuesday: Analyzing the effectiveness of your creative
> Wednesday: Pulling together the comprehensive report
> Thursday: Optimizing the opt-in points on your website
> Friday: Creating your test

Monday: What Your Reports Are Really Saying

What we offered as a guide to your reporting in the previous week will be utilized thoroughly in this section. So, let's consider two of the primary measures that marketers use to judge their mailing effectiveness: opens and clicks. The following are several scenarios that may stump you after your first mailing and even after our suggestions about how to react to this data:

- **Many unique opens but not as many unique clicks.** It is common to see more unique opens than unique clicks. There are two primary reasons your unique open rate will typically be higher than your unique click rate. The first is that the human subscriber really never opened it or at least never intended to open and look at it for very long. This is the flaw we discussed earlier, in which clicking preview panes registers as opens in clients such as Microsoft Outlook and Outlook Express. There isn't much you can do about this.

  The second reason, however, is something over which you have more control. People actually did open your email, perhaps even clicking the button in their email client for the images to render, but after looking at your email, they were not interested enough to click. If the difference between your unique open rate and unique click-thorough rate is more than 25 points, the data suggests a disconnect between the expectations you set and the content in the body of the email. Simply put, if this trend continues over time, it means your email is not relevant to that group of subscribers, or it means you are hitting them at the wrong time. The "A Tactic to Apply: A/B Split-Path Testing" sidebar describes *A/B split-path testing*, one of the most important tactics you can employ to further improve your open-to-click ratio.

A Tactic to Apply: A/B Split-Path Testing

Use A/B split-path testing to reduce the amount of content offered in your email copy. On your next send, create two versions of your mailing to send to a representative portion of the group of subscribers who opened but did not click. In the A version, repeat the approach you used in the previous mailing—likely one subject line that communicates the value or content of multiple content assets and promotions in the email body copy.

Now create a new, B version. In that version, use a subject line that speaks to only two options that will be put forth in the email body copy. Those two options could be something such as two different types of promotions. For example, the subject line could be, "David, Choose Your Own Discount." The body copy could suggest that the subscriber has been selected to "Be Part of Customer Choice Week." Then create two distinct offers with two separate links. One will be discount-oriented, such as 10 percent off their order, while the second link would offer free shipping.

Although this is a retail-oriented example, you can apply the concept to a variety of industries. In airline travel, for example, the offer could begin as, "Fly like one of our elite passengers, book your next flight, and reap the rewards of our in-flight Elite Passenger benefits." The second offer could be, "Take advantage of preflight Elite Passenger benefits such as free entry into our Presidents Club room." You get the idea. Limiting the customer choice in this test will likely drive higher click-through rates as well as identify for which type of offer the subscriber has an affinity. Once that data is collected, it should be noted in the subscriber data table, so you can further target subscribers later based on their stated preferences. This test will also help you determine whether your email body is cluttered with too many offers, as well as which offers are best for which subscribers.

- **Click-through rates that are higher than your open rate.** This would indicate that a significant portion of the images in your email creative are not rendering or that a significant portion of your email is being delivered in a text format. If you are using a multipart/MIME format for your creative, as we suggested in Chapter 5, this could mean that many of your subscribers are opening your email on mobile devices, which could impact your open rate and show higher click-through rates. However, this group will likely show lower conversion rates since marketers frequently do not have their landing pages enabled for mobile and portable devices (that is, they don't use Wireless Application Protocol–formatted landing pages, discussed in Chapter 8). Tactics to remedy this issue include using fewer images. We will give you some more pointers on optimizing your creative in the next section.

- **Open and click performance that is lower than your historical benchmarks or your plan.** As discussed in the previous section, this could suggest that your email did not get delivered to one or more domains or ISPs that represent 10 percent or more of your list. Utilize your domain delivery report to see whether this is the problem. If delivery to a particular set of domains is not a problem, then it could be the timing or frequency of your mailing. Over time if this problem persists, it could mean you have a larger number of inactive email addresses or simply subscribers who are no longer engaged with your mailings. Previously mentioned tactics such as deploying surveys or sweepstakes offers can be a remedy to check this. However, if this is a one-time anomaly and delivery is not an issue, it could point to a timing issue. Be sure to take holidays into account as well as certain days, such as Thursdays, when there tends to be more email in the consumer's inbox. Thursday is an important day of the week for advertisers, as it allows brands to tell consumers what movies to see on Friday, what sales to go to on Saturday, last minute travel deals, and what cars to test drive. Television programming is very important on Thursday nights, because it is necessary for advertisers to have a large audience for them to deliver their message to. Email marketing is no different, which is why on Thursdays there tends to be more email in the consumer's inbox.

- **Adjusting and testing your mailing frequency, time of day, or day of week are all areas to explore to validate the casaul variables.** Doing an A/B test to split the email to the nonresponsive subscribers, and sending either on two different days or at two different times the same day is the first step in analyzing the effectiveness of your email.

The next step to building the road to optimization is to analyze the effectiveness of your creative. We suggest dedicating the next day to this task.

Tuesday: Analyzing the Effectiveness of Your Creative

Analyzing the effectiveness of your creative is where art intersects science. Here you will be guided by the science of the empirical behavioral data from your mailing and by the emotional constructs of your perceptions of beauty and aesthetics. Judging the effectiveness of your email creative is often complicated by a set of loosely defined criteria, steeped in perceptions of your corporate brand image, personal preferences, design best practices, and your vision of what is appealing and potentially effective. Leaving this up to a committee process often will further complicate the issue—as often found in consumer-based focus groups, where the results usually create more questions than a common set of answers. Over time, you will have a history of mailing performance to further guide your judgment about the effectiveness of your email creative, but for now we offer the following set of criteria to help you begin to assess and optimize your creative. Keep in mind that you can apply this process to all your creative endeavors, including landing pages. This hierarchy builds from the bottom up, and you can identify and isolate the variables that may be either causing you heartache or driving your co-workers to sing your praises.

Mass Convenience

Make sure you have followed the creative best practices we discussed in Chapter 5 regarding HTML table layout and template pixel width. It is necessary to adhere to these loosely defined standards, because all email client software is different. Given that, the first rule of creative optimization must be mass convenience. Can your email be rendered appropriately in one single version on a wide array of email and webmail clients? Is it viewable and accessible not only on those clients but also on a wide variety of mobile email devices? Is your template designed to meet those delivery-rendering best practices? These rules are fluid, which is why it is imperative to use an inbox-rendering tool from a delivery services provider (see Appendix A for a list of providers). Those rendering tools will give you a clear and ultimate picture of how your email appears to your subscriber.

Ease of Use

Get off the computer, and print your email on a color printer. Hand it out to your email team and a handful of co-workers along with three differently colored pencils. Instruct them to take the printout and with the first color pencil circle the first pass of their eye motion, circling the first three things they read in the email copy. In this exercise, remove the subject line—you want them to focus on the body. The next colored pencil is for the next three things they read, and the third and last color is for the last three things they read.

Take those results from your five to eight co-workers and put them in a spreadsheet, with each column being a piece of navigation, content, and links—group those header columns in that fashion. In the nine rows of the spreadsheet (three rows to each color), count the color ticks of each one of those co-workers. Does a pattern exist? If it does, then you are close to having some consensus about how easily your content can be scanned.

If the results vary greatly, then your layout is not well aligned with the expectations of your subscribers, who are meant to engage with these messages. Is there a high number of test subscribers who have the same eye path, and do those paths easily intersect with your calls to action? If not, go back to the drawing table and start the process again. Remember, if there are too many options or is too much clutter within your message, then the message is not efficient for your subscribers. This will lead most people to frustration, and they will simply give up, delete your message, and go on to the next ones in their inboxes.

Creative Efficiency

Creative efficiency means two different things. First, consider whether the creative elements, the template, and the content assets contained in the message are laid out to facilitate an efficient production process. Does the email creative leverage as much as it can from your content management design to afford quick tests, and is that design reusable in future mailings? Second, did your ease-of-use colored-pencil test prove to be an efficient experience for your test subscribers and co-workers? Did they do the things you wanted them to do first? Ensuring that your creative can both be rapidly deployed internally and be consumed rapidly externally will prove you are well on your way to creating a creative foundation that can be continually optimized.

Clarity

Did your colored-pencil test reveal confusion in your intent of tone and action, or did it reveal a common clarity that you were aiming for? Are your action anchors—your links, your calls to action—above the fold? Are the offers and their intent clear? If not, some creative or graphical redesign and wordsmithing may be in order.

Conciseness

This is another aspect of efficiency. Are you using links in the appropriate manner? In email, your goal should be not to tell a long story; it should be to sell a short one. Teasing subscribers with just enough information to lead them to your website or a dedicated landing page that provides further information should be the primary purpose of your links. There are a couple of exceptions. The first is when the purpose of your email is a newsletter where you are delivering one topical story or article to the subscriber. The second is when you are sending a branding-oriented email whose purpose is to introduce one brand concept or one product. For example, in a message where the creative is one large image, similar to a postcard, the email creative might be meant to deliver information on a single product or concept. In those cases, you can embellish your text a bit more, but even here the general rule still applies: Get them to click!

Consistency

Does your email creative week in and week out use the same layout, navigation, and colors? If it doesn't, it should. Create a standard level of consistency in your mailings so that your subscribers become familiar with your email layout and create a common expectation of how to interact with the message. Although colors can add flash and call out certain elements, such as promotions, it is critical that you do not make your email too "busy." Use consistent colors and standard fonts such as Arial and others that render on a wide variety of computers across operating systems.

Personalization

Are you using any personalization, such as the most basic form, which is your subscribers' names? Are you using personalization too much? You are if you keep reminding your subscriber that you are so tricky that you can use their name in every bit of the creative.

Are you using offers or content assets—news stories or items such as products—that are personalized or tailored to either the user's preference or their behavior? As discussed in previous sections, personalization, particularly tailoring that is driven by user behavior, is something that has proven to be more effective than sending the same message to every subscriber on your list.

Design Tips from the Pros

To add some perspective, we'd like to share a conversation we had with Aaron Smith and Lisa Harmon, principals of Smith-Harmon, a leading email marketing design shop:

David Daniels and Jeanniey Mullen: *To get the best work from your email designers and copywriters, how do you challenge them?*

Lisa Harmon: *The potential for economy, efficiency, even poetry is a virtue of email that makes it not only an effective communication channel but also an engaging form of creative work. I challenge email designers and copywriters to continually strive to find that just-right place where—ah!—form and function meet: where every image, every word, has meaning.*

David Daniels and Jeanniey Mullen: *What if an individual shows creative ability in other forms of marketing such as print? Can it be instantly transferred to email?*

Aaron Smith: *While it shares characteristics with both print and web, email creative is a distinct discipline that requires designers to address channel-specific issues. Good email designers must take a results-oriented approach and—just as importantly—have a thorough knowledge and understanding of the many platform combinations across which their designs are displayed.*

David Daniels and Jeanniey Mullen: *Can you put your finger on the one or two things that make good email creative?*

Lisa Harmon: *The success of an email design is dependent upon a unique intersection of considerations: your brand, your business objectives, your resources, the inbox environment, and—most importantly—your recipients. Understanding general email creative best practices is only the first step; the second is applying best practices appropriately based on the above factors. What works for Sears does not work for Saks.*

David Daniels and Jeanniey Mullen: *Testing is a big component to making email effective. Are there a few keys that you can share with our readers to what makes a successful test?*

Lisa Harmon: *The three keys to creative testing are (1) Build creative testing into your process. Ideally, you should be testing at least one creative element with every send. (2) Keep each test controlled and simple in order to easily identify which variables move the needle. (3) Archive and share metrics with your creative team so that they can "own the results" and leverage the data to inform their work.*

David Daniels and Jeanniey Mullen: *We are certainly not immune from making mistakes when creating an email. Are there things that you do to avoid the "gotcha headache" after you hit Send?*

Lisa Harmon: *For us it is the three-question check. Before you hit Send, give your message a two-second scan and ask yourself three simple questions: What is this email about? Why should my subscribers care? What should my subscribers do about it? Do not deploy unless the answers to these questions are immediately obvious.*

David Daniels and Jeanniey Mullen: *When it comes to laying out a reusable creative framework, is there one size or one rule that fits all? What is most important, the data or the creative elements?*

Aaron Smith *A flexible email creative framework becomes increasingly important as we leverage more dynamic data and as we increase segmentation.*

David Daniels and Jeanniey Mullen: *How much is too much? That is, should marketers attempt to jam an entire store in their email or simply be sending window dressing draped in HTML?*

Lisa Harmon: *An email is like a retail store window; it needs to reveal just enough to compel viewers to enter the store.*

Tomorrow, in your Wednesday hour, we will give you a few examples of reports that you can use to develop a comprehensive analysis of your mailings' performance.

Wednesday: Pulling Together the Comprehensive Report

Most ESPs offer a handy dashboard report that is comprehensive enough for most marketers. They all look a little different; Figure 7.4 earlier in the chapter showed one example, and Figure 7.6 shows another.

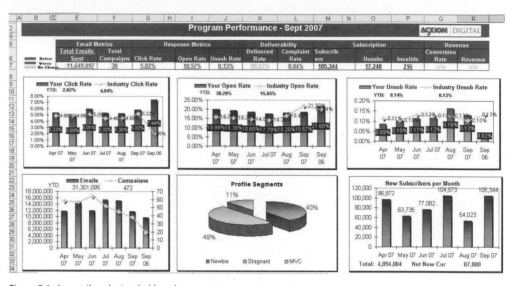

Figure 7.6 An email marketing dashboard

This report should display the following metrics: number of emails sent, total emails attempted (this could be higher than number of emails sent to account for retries because of soft bounces), total emails delivered, total emails missing (sometimes displayed as delivery rate), total conversions, and all of the aforementioned metrics in aggregate and displayed as unique including opens and clicks. Additionally, these metrics should be displayed as a percentage of all the email that was successfully delivered. Check with your ESP to determine whether it is calculating these percentages into the total email sent or into the total number that was delivered. Lastly, you will want to see the number of unsubscribes and spam complaints.

In a previous chapter, we also gave you a recipe for an engagement metric. This should also be included in your dashboard metric to understand the overall health and engagement of your list.

Additional metrics to report on include the following:

- **Click-to-open rate (CTOR).** This is simply the ratio of unique clicks as a percentage of unique opens. The CTOR measures how effective your email message was in motivating recipients who opened it to then click a link. In other words, the click-to-open rate expresses the measure of click-through rates as a percentage of messages opened, instead of messages delivered.

Loren McDonald is a seasoned email marketing professional at Silverpop and along with David serves as the co-chair of the Email Measurement Accuracy Roundtable of the Email Experience Council. Loren explains the benefits of the CTOR as follows:

"By removing unopened messages from the picture, the CTOR then becomes a better measure of the value and effectiveness of the actual email message content, messaging, and layout. Specifically, the CTOR measures:

- *Relevance of the message content*
- *Effectiveness of offers*
- *Effectiveness of the copy*
- *Effectiveness of the message design and layout*
- *Timeliness and immediacy of the content or offer*
- *Effectiveness of the number and location of text and image links*

"To some extent, it also measures the level of trust recipients place in your brand and it value proposition (the open rate is the better measure of trust, since if trust is lacking, the recipient will not even open the email)."

- **Forward rate.** This metric has become less meaningful over time because in order to understand how many people are actually forwarding your email, you need to include a Forward to a Friend option. Although all ESPs offer such a widget that can be placed in your email, David's work at JupiterResearch reveals that most individuals forward email to others using the Forward button in their email software clients, such as Outlook. It is impossible to measure forwarding behavior via the general Forward button.

- **Nonresponsive subscriber rate.** This is the number of subscribers who received your message but did not register any opens or clicks. This number should be expressed as a percentage of the total emails delivered. Monitoring this metric over time will indicate whether your subscribers are increasing or decreasing their engagement with your mailing. Remember, we provided a good deal of granular detail earlier related to domain delivery reporting to pinpoint whether your overall engagement is being impacted by undelivered emails to a set of domains.

- **Opt-in rate.** This metric is designed to illustrate the ongoing effectiveness of your opt-in process. The number should be displayed in the following ways. First, you should measure the percentage of unique opt-ins to unique visitors to your website. Next, you will want to measure the number of opt-ins coming from third-party locations such as co-registration and partner sites. After that column, you should report the number of opt-ins that are being gathered through your external channels, such as your call center, kiosks, or in-store efforts. Lastly, all those numbers should be combined and compared against your total list size and expressed as a percentage of weekly opt-ins or new subscribers.

- **Click-overlay-reporting.** Remember that colored-pencil test we had you do with your co-workers earlier in this chapter? Well, the good news is that many ESPs offer a report that shows a click map on top of your email creative. These reports are usually color-coded, with the number of clicks or click-through rate that the link achieved. This is a wonderful report to print and take to the boardroom to pore over with your co-workers. Although the colored-pencil test is still an accurate measure to create a visual heatmap of where people are looking first, the click overlay reports on the links that were clicked but not the order in which they were clicked. Both tools are valid and should be incorporated into your overall marketing plan.

Although all the previous metrics and reports should be built into your comprehensive weekly reporting, we recommend a third dashboard that takes your critical metrics and cuts them by primary segmentation attributes. This creates a dashboard view of all the metrics that are most important to your most important subscribers. For example, you'll see how different demographics responded—by gender, by age, and by spending history. This will allow you to gauge at a macro level the importance of the demographics and segments that are most important to you and your organization. The report would be laid out like a matrix, with all the aforementioned important metrics across the top and the demographic segments down the side. In this matrix, you should also list the previous mailing's performance so that each week you can gauge whether the needle is moving up or down.

Thursday: Optimizing the Opt-In Points on Your Website

Now that you have measured the performance of your opt-in sources, you can begin to think about how you might want to begin optimizing your opt-in points. Let's revisit a couple of key points to the opt-in process:

- **Promote your opt-in newsletter registration.** Place it above the fold on your website. Give it the space and attention it deserves.
- **Don't ask for too much information.** Keep it simple; gather only the information you are going to use to target your subscribers when communicating with them.
- **Communicate expectations.** Provide an example of your newsletter through a clickable thumbnail graphic that opens in a new window. Let the reader know how often you will be mailing them.

- **Sell the benefits.** Ask yourself why someone should opt in to your newsletter. What are the benefits they are going to receive? Discounts, breaking news, exclusive "member" benefits, and being the first to know about new products and offers—these are all appropriate benefit statements that should accompany your opt-in page.

- **Properly formed forms.** Let the subscribers know which fields are required. Use standard form field names so that the autocomplete functions in browsers and browser toolbars (for example, the Google Toolbar) match up and it is easy for subscribers to quickly complete your form.

- **Privacy policy.** What are you doing with the subscribers' data? Let them know in plain English on the opt-in page, and then provide a link to your full privacy policy that is full of all the legal terms and conditions.

- **Promote opt-in across channels.** Print ads, call centers, in-store signs, banners, and even TV commercials should highlight the benefits of joining your email list. In earlier chapters, you saw some unique examples, such as the airline that posts a banner at baggage claim areas telling passengers to send an SMS text message with their email address to get miles for their trips. This is a great vehicle to get subscribers to join your list. Can you leverage that tactic in your cross-channel marketing efforts?

Now let's move beyond those basics and focus on what you can do to harness more of your website traffic:

- **Use dynamic landing pages.** Do you use dynamic landing pages for when people click your search engine results listings? Congratulations! But you should also be promoting your newsletter registration. A study that David conducted at JupiterResearch found that most retailers using dynamic landing pages did not include any reference to their newsletters on that page. Most companies simply promote the newsletter in one or two places on their websites but hardly ever on these dynamically generated pages. As we showed in Chapter 5's discussion of using your website to build your email list, by using personalization technologies it is possible to not only include a reference link to your subscription page but also to use the client's own words from the Google search in that page. Specifically, Figure 5.3 used the example of leveraging the search string *Flat-Panel TV* as in Figure 5.3 and placing that dynamically into the section that promotes the newsletter subscription to make it more relevant for the subscriber. The next step would be to collect that *flat-panel* attribute as a segmentation attribute and send the subscriber a series of welcome messages that pertain to flat-panel TVs. Then, over time, you would move these subscribers into your normal set of weekly mailings. Although this concept does take some production effort, it is something you can begin to map out to improve the relevancy of not only your opt-in process but also the relevancy of the messages that those sub-scribers will receive. Additionally, we have found that it works particularly well for those companies that have a very broad product line.

- **Make web analytics your best friend.** That is right. Outside of all the tools that you will be using to optimize your mailing, web analytics tools are powerful tools to improve the effectiveness of your mailings. Applying your web analytics data to your opt-in process is an insightful way in which to optimize it. Do you know the top entry pages and the top exit pages to your website? If you don't you should; go ask your web analytics guru to share their wisdom with you. Now take those top entry and exit pages and make sure your email registration and opt-in offer are at the top of both pages, or at the very least well promoted. Also test opening a new window as subscribers exit the purchase process and ask them whether they would like to sign up for your email newsletter.

- **Make opt-in part of your purchase or download process.** Always include a check box for subscribers to tick off the option of opting into your newsletter on order and download confirmation pages. Make this easy, and, again, clearly set the expectation of what they will be receiving.

- **Include opt-ins on order confirmations.** If they didn't opt-in at check out, or even if they did, hit them again on the order confirmation or other service or transactional message. There are technically two approaches here. The first is harder, which is to present this option dynamically only for non-subscribers. The second and easier approach is to include the opt-in message on all outbound service related messages and simply suppress for duplicate addresses when you mail. The issue with this second, easier approach is that subscribers may think you are not in tune with them. When you present a generic offer to all transac-tional email recipients, they may not think you have your act together, or they may fear they will get even more email from you. Although it's more elaborate, the first option ensures your list will be free of duplicated addresses and removes the risk of suppressing addresses unnecessarily. Addresses that tie back to a profile might have richer demographic or behavioral information than purely an email address.

- **Include the Subscribe link in your email newsletters.** Do this especially if you are using the Forward to a Friend widget from your ESP. However, since most indi-viduals simply use the Forward button in their email clients, you should include a Subscribe link in your email, particularly if you offer a virally oriented news-letter (with words like *funny*, *newsworthy*, and *discount-laden*).

- **Are you on social networking sites?** Some of David's most interesting research recently at JupiterResearch details the shifting communication patterns of indi-viduals to social sites such as Facebook. Does your organization have a brand page or group on Facebook or MySpace? If not, you should. This should feature a link to your email subscription page so that this group of subscribers can easily opt in to your newsletter. Figure 7.7 shows this example in detail.

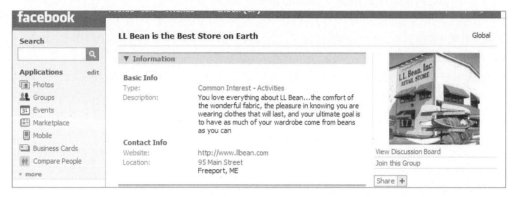

Figure 7.7 Fan of a product on Facebook

- **Provide an incentive.** This works well in B2B settings, for example, "Register for our mailing and get this free white paper." You may not want to use this tactic in a B2C setting, unless your company is known as a discount brand. The concept of providing an incentive to opt in is further complicated by the CAN-SPAM Act, particularly because it refers to the notion of "consideration." That is, if you promise something to someone, you have to deliver it. Moreover, this process can get complicated if you are using "consideration" to get other subscribers to act on your behalf by offering incentives to build your list. Since we are not lawyers, we urge you to look at the CAN-SPAM requirements with your legal counsel.

- **Footprint the opt-in.** Use a time and date stamp on the opt-in as well as the source. Keep this in your database in case you are ever asked to produce it as the CAN-SPAM regulation stipulates: "The recipient expressly consented to receive the message, either in response to a clear and conspicuous request for such consent or at the recipient's own initiative." This means that although the CAN-SPAM law is based on the notion of opt-out, it prohibits you from harvesting email addresses (for example, by copying them from a website using a dictionary attack). The burden of proof that the user "expressly consented" is on your shoulders. Document each opt-in. Some marketers even put this in the footer of each message, personalized to each subscriber: "You opted into receive this message on this date, at this time, and at this website." This approach can also help remind an individual that your message is not spam.

In Chapter 5, we provided a host of additional sources, such as co-registration and working with affiliates, to further build your list. Remember to always source those email addresses differently so you can always identify which sources are performing better than your house list.

One last thought on opt-in is your opt-out page: Although the newest CAN-SPAM requirements that took effect on July 7, 2008, require your opt-out process to be "easy" (meaning no passwords, roadblocks, or a ping-pong process that puts your subscriber through multiple steps), you are not prevented from asking the subscriber to *opt down*. The opt-down process is simply asking the subscriber whether they would like to stay on the list but receive fewer messages. This of course implies you will create a separate segment or list of subscribers that you will mail to at that longer intervals. This is something to experiment with.

A large financial provider reported that its new credit card offering was getting opt-out rates that were well above its historical benchmarks for its other email newsletters to its other credit card subscribers. So, why, the company asked us, might this be? How can a newer list have a higher opt-out rate than older lists?

The answer is that lists that have been in existence for five to ten years likely have scores of email subscribers who opted out using the "this is spam" button, which predated the ISP feedback loops that have been around since 2007 as formal mechanisms. So, keep in mind that improved feedback loops, the inclusion of Unsubscribe buttons in ISP clients, and "this is spam" buttons may result in higher unsubscribe rates than your peers may have seen in historical industry benchmarks. This is one case where such benchmarks will cause you nothing but heartache and problems. Remember our rule of thumb: All business is local. This means you should benchmark to your own historical performance and not those competitors or peer groups that likely have very different lists, email frequencies, and perhaps even metric methodologies. Until there is a consistent method that all email technology providers use to calculate email performance, such benchmarks must be taken with a cup of salt—these differences of variables are so great that a grain of salt won't even give you the proper adjustment or calibration.

With so many differences in performance across marketer types and categories, the best tool to optimize your mailings is testing, which is what you will focus on in Friday's lesson. Until then, highlight the top three opt-in optimization initiatives from this section that you will undertake and commit to them.

Friday: Creating Your Test

John Wanamaker, one of America's first department store owners, famously said, "Half the money I spend on advertising is wasted. The trouble is, I don't know which half." Thankfully, in today's world of email marketing, we have plenty of data that Wanamaker didn't have. We can make informed decisions based on determining just what parts of our marketing spend are falling on deaf ears and which parts are resonating in the triumphant sound of the cash register's ring. And it is no secret: Testing is the tactic to sway some of that silence into the harmonic bells of commerce. As a marker, testing will always be your primary instrument of optimization and your primary agent of change.

To be comfortable with the concept of testing, you must be comfortable with the notion of failure. That is right, failure! What we are talking about here is that if you are not testing, then you are not giving yourself the opportunity to succeed. And we all know that one cannot succeed all the time and that, through testing, we might fail sometimes; it is only then that we can see what actually is working. Such lessons will demonstrate what is actually moving the needle of effectiveness and optimization. As an email marketer, you must embrace the notion of failure and be comfortable with it, because it is the only road to success. So, with that framework in mind, what should you test to begin your optimization process? Well, only you have that answer; it is in the data you have already begun to scrutinize.

By the middle of your second week you should have analyzed enough data to have some questions that need answers. These questions—or, as we like to think of them, variables—are the levers you need to adjust so you can focus on what you are trying to optimize. Here are a bevy of tactics that will help you develop a proper test:

- **Create a control group.** First create a control group that doesn't get exposed to any of the tests. This group should get your standard mailing. The subscribers in this control group should stay in this segment for at least ten months. You can roll your control group over as your marketing program matures, but to maintain and understand the effects of your test, you must maintain a control group that does not get exposed to any of your optimization. This is difficult since a portion of your list may potentially underperform as your successful optimization tactics are employed across the broader list. This control should be statistically relevant, representative of your list as a whole, and representative of your different demographics, domains, and spending. Most email marketing applications will automatically build a statistically relevant random sample control group, but even with small lists, this group should contain at a minimum 1,000 subscribers.

- **Create random test groups.** In a typical A/B split-path test, you will test one permutation (the B version) against your A version, which would be your control subjects, or the "business as usual" group. Just as when selecting a control group, most email marketing applications easily allow you to develop test cells that are random and a statistically valid representation of your list.

- **Test one element at a time.** When you begin testing, you want to test only one variable at a time so that you measure what impact that part had on the performance of your mailing. Once you have tested that element and understand it, you can begin to incorporate additional variables into your test. For example, you may want to begin testing the day of week. After you have established the impact of that test, you could begin to test the subject line.

- **Conduct time-based tests.** One area to start testing is the day of week or the time of day. If you are testing the impact of the day of week, keep both test sends within the same week. This allows you to understand a send on Monday versus a send on Wednesday, without the fluctuations of what the next week may have in store. Additionally, you can experiment with testing sends at different times of the day, morning versus later in the evening, for example.

- **Conduct From line tests.** Although you must keep your actual email sender address (you@you.com) the same, the friendly From display name such as "Your Company" can be changed and tested over time. For example, some business-to-business marketers will experiment with placing a salesperson's name to achieve a "friendly" From field such as "Joe Doe of Your Company." This can be achieved through personalization merge fields, particularly if you have your salespeople's names associated with different clients in your database.

- **Conduct subject line tests.** This is a popular test where you are determining the impact of your subject line, and the primary measure of success here is open rate as well as the subsequent measures such as click-through. A common test is to try using personalization in the subject line of the test group and to do the control without any subject line personalization. In addition to personalization, newsletter publishers will often test the impact of placing an author's or story's name in the subject line.

- **Conduct multivariate testing.** In this test, you are running multiple permutations of your test element against your control group. This is also referred to as A/B/C/D (and so on) testing, where each letter represents a different element you are testing. In the previous subject line test, you could try one with personalization, one without personalization, one that mentions a dollar-off discount, and one that mentions free shipping. The power of multivariate testing comes from the ability to test many of these variables within one test. Setting up complex multivariate tests generally requires the help of an expert in the field.

- **Test email copy.** Testing offers, copy, and product assortment in the email body allows you to determine the appropriate number of products or offers in or the size of the assortment. In these tests, you will want to validate your test by reviewing the click-to-open rate (CTOR). A compelling or winning test should drive a higher CTOR. In copy tests, you can test promotional tone versus branding-oriented tone as well as compare both to general benefit statements. You can also test the length of the copy, comparing longer to shorter. Many marketers also use this tactic to test creative elements such as color or the greater or lesser use of graphics. As with subject line testing, you can also test price sensitivity, 10 percent discounts versus 15 percent discounts, and so on. When testing offers or copy-related elements, be sure to keep the other creative elements, such as the layout and colors, the same from version to version.

- **Test landing pages.** In this test, you will be evaluating the layout and clarity of the subscriber landing page. In this test, your click-to-conversion rate will be the metric to watch. A successful test will show higher conversion clicks than the number of aggregate clicks to the landing page.

- **Don't make snap judgments.** Give your test results some time to come in. Most marketers will wait at least 48 hours before acting on the test results in order to ensure that enough of the results have come in and the results are a statistically valid representation of the test groups.

- **Do automated testing.** One approach that David has long advocated and that a handful of ESPs can facilitate is to automatically send out the winning version of a test to the rest of the list. In this approach, your application essentially creates three versions: the A version (the control group), the B version (the version being tested), and a C version that, using personalization merge fields and/or dynamic content, is populated automatically with the winning version.

  To successfully pull this off, you will tell the application what you want the winning metric to be, for example, clicks, and the time duration you want the test period to run, for example, 48 hours. When using automatic testing, the application will tell you which version won, and you simply click to acknowledge the winner while the system does the rest. Over time, as you build further confidence in this approach, most systems can be configured to mail the rest of the list the winning version automatically.

- **Build time into your production process for testing.** Testing is such a critical part to becoming a successful marketer that you must account for the additional time it takes to build and deploy these tests.

- **Analyze test results.** Don't simply rely on those top-tier metrics to determine the winners. Instead, look behind that metric at the subscribers' long-term behavior, spending levels, and demographics to determine whether other patterns are emerging; for example, perhaps men respond more to free shipping offers and women to dollar-off discounts.

You've learned quite a lot this week. Now is the time to reflect on what you've absorbed and begin to plan for the week ahead, where we will discuss how other channels can impact your email marketing campaigns and how to measure them. For now take a break—you deserve it!

Week 3: Measuring Email's Impact on Other Channels

Email is not for just driving online purchases. As we discussed in Chapters 2 and 4, email plays a role at every part of the customer dialogue, across every channel. The better you become at measuring email's effectiveness throughout this process, the easier it will be to determine where the customer needs additional nudging to be pushed through the purchase process (or, if you are a publisher, to keep them engaged with your newsletter over time).

Monday: Measuring the role of email in a customer's purchase
Tuesday: Determining the value of your email addresses and campaigns
Wednesday: Increasing email-sending costs to improve top-line results
Thursday: Exploring web analytics and email integration
Friday: Finding and targeting your advocates

Monday: Measuring the Role of Email in a Customer's Purchase

For many marketers, email drives anywhere from 10 to 25 percent of their company's revenue. Let's take a look at how you use and measure email throughout the purchase process and customer life cycle.

 Write This Down: Fifty percent of consumers online in the United States report having made at least one offline purchase based upon a promotional email they received. (Source: JupiterResearch)

You have already designed your email strategy, and we would hope that if you are a multichannel business, your strategy includes using email to drive offline purchases. Measuring your email effectiveness across channels depends on your ability to source the effectiveness of the marketing offer across channels. You do this tracking using a unique code that in the direct marketing world is referred to as the *source code*.

Catalog marketers use a source code that is printed on the back of their catalogs to measure the effectiveness of the mailing, the list, and possibly even the segment. You can also apply this tactic to measure the effectiveness of your mailing when a click cannot be recorded in an offline setting such as a store. There are a variety of methods to do this:

- **Use a customer record identifier.** The type of customer record identifier that you use is in part based on your in-store point of sale's ability to capture, store, and report on this additional detail. Record keys that can be used include the following:

  - **Ask for an email address.** Some marketers will ask the customer for their email address at the point of sale so that they can either capture it for the first time or validate that the address on file is the correct address, as well as measure the customer's offline spending and attribute all of that spending, or a portion of it, to the email marketing campaign.

  - **Use loyalty cards and programs.** Using a loyalty card or program allows marketers to record with a high level of accuracy all of a customer's spending history. Research that David conducted for JupiterResearch found that consumers on average belong to seven loyalty programs. These programs are designed to give the customer something in return for joining the program, such as exclusive member events or sales, discounts, or points that can be redeemed. In most cases, the email address is a key part of these programs because it is often the primary point of communication that marketers use to drive customers through the buying and retention process.

- **Offer specific source codes.** Some marketers would rather have the customer take their email, print it, and bring it into the store for its redemption. In these instances, the offer is redeemable only offline and cannot be used online. Shoe retailer Nine West uses this tactic because it knows that on average its clients spend more in the Nine West offline stores than in the online store. With this insight, Nine West sends email to its subscribers with an offline-only coupon. When this coupon code is keyed in at the point of sale, the company knows and can attribute the sale to its email promotion.

- **Put source codes on direct mail.** Marketers that have integrated email into their cross-channel marketing strategies also will add digits or some identifier to the source code that is placed on their outbound postal mailings to categorize those customers as email subscribers. In this instance, the goal is to attribute some of that revenue to the effectiveness of the email program. This can also be used in print ads in magazines, as Sephora has done, or even in TV commercials, as General Motors has done.

Another consideration for using email to push the subscriber through the purchase process is to set up a series of messages. This concept is similar to what we laid out earlier when we discussed how you should be using welcome campaigns when a subscriber signs up for your email marketing program. For example, hotel and ski resort company Intrawest uses this approach after someone has booked a vacation at one of its resorts. Intrawest's experience demonstrates how you can set up a series of messages around the customer's purchase:

Message 1 This is a confirmation message that gives all the typical transactional details. In this example, Intrawest would include the price, the arrival and departure dates, and links to information about the resort, such as directions and a list of activities that can be enjoyed at the property.

Message 2 This message typically comes a week or two before the customer's planned stay. The goal of this message is to up-sell additional services, such as ski lessons, day-camp services for children, and information about nightlife at the resort, including links to restaurants and promotional information about entertainment, such as bands.

Message 3 This message is sent just prior to the client's stay. The purpose of this message is to tell the subscriber what to bring and what not to bring to the resort. For example, it promotes the pro shop, clothing stores, and other merchants at the location.

Additionally, it provides a weather forecast for the duration of the subscriber's stay at the resort. Finally, it reminds the customer to book those additional services, such as ski lessons, child-care services, and dinner reservations at the restaurants on the property.

Message 4 This is sent while the customer is at the resort to remind them of the activities and entertainment that are occurring at the resort during the week. Typically this message does not have a promotional element; it is simply an informational message.

Message 5 This is a post-stay message serving a dual purpose. The first is a survey for feedback about their experience, and the second and more important purpose is to have the subscriber book their vacation at the resort for the following season. They use a playful and fun tone in the message, such as, "Hope your vacation was a blast; book your next vacation now."

Message 6 There are several variations of this message that continue to be sent throughout the year to promote additional resorts owned by the marketer. This is a retention message that is aimed at subscribers who have already stayed at the resort, which results in a different message stream than those subscribers who have never stayed at the resort. Essentially, this becomes a twelve-month string of messages, meaning that this marketer has two primary campaigns they do in each mailing—one aimed at non-purchasers and one aimed at subscribers who have made a purchase.

Can you think of a way that such a message stream could be applied to your email program? Here are some suggestions for other retail categories:

- **General retail categories such as electronics and apparel.** Use a post-purchase message stream to cut down on support costs. For example, immediately after the customer's purchase, you can cross-sell them to accessories such as cables. More important, you can send two follow-up messages. The first has links to support information, such as FAQs, manuals, and a support forum. The other follow-up message can invite the customer to post a review of the product on your website. This will continue to keep the user engaged, and it is another point where you can measure engagement and participation, perhaps even acting as an advocate with your brand as a whole.

- **Service-related categories, such as financial services.** The same approach can be used as in the previous bullet, where the first follow-up message may ask the subscriber for feedback and the second one may begin to cross-sell or up-sell the subscriber to additional products or services, such as additional credit cards.

Segmenting your subscribers' engagement based on their behavior across this message stream will allow you to further craft messages that are personalized to their individual behavior. Here is a recipe to build the subscribers into distinct segments:

1. First place all your nonresponsive subscribers into one segment. As we discussed earlier, if this segment continues to be nonresponsive, you can employ a number of tactics (surveys, sweepstakes, and so on) to spur them into action.

2. Then create three additional groups. The first consists of those who have already purchased. The second two groups are based on click behavior. The first group is based on subscribers who have clicked one or more links in one or more emails (more engaged), and the second is a group of subscribers who have clicked only once. From this point on, you have four different groups: non-responders, purchasers, engaged, and less engaged. Enlist the following tactics to spur the last three groups into action:

   • **Purchasers.** This is a segment you can continue to mail without using too many promotional elements, unless you have decided to use discount-laden offers continually. This group has already self-selected themselves as individuals who have some affinity for your offers, brands, and products. Test using less of a discount, and test using different frequency intervals in the fold, particularly if your product offering is a considered purchase or one that happens only at a preset interval, such a cruises, automobiles, or large purchases such as home appliances.

   • **Engaged.** With this segment, you are very close to turning them into buyers. This is a segment where after analyzing the types of things they have clicked, you can employ dynamic content to make your mailings more relevant to them. For example, you could create one mailing to this segment but vary the first product offering by targeting them with the category of product they have already shown interest in.

     To make this process less complicated, create three to five offers that aggregate the click behavior of the top links that were clicked. In this message template, 90 percent of the content to these subscribers will be the same, but 10 percent will be a dynamic block of content that will change to meet the interests of those three to five distinct groups based on their click behavior. For an apparel retailer, this might represent three groups: those who clicked tops, those who clicked bottoms, and those who clicked accessories. This offer will represent a product or an offer that best meets each one of their interest areas.

     Dynamic content can be achieved through nearly every commercial email marketing application. It allows you to easily change one or more portions of your email template to meet the preferences or expressed interest areas of your different subscribers. When the email is sent, dynamic content changes that one portion of the email to render the offer that is best for the subscriber. See the previous section in this chapter for more information.

- **Less engaged.** With this segment, you may need to up the promotional ante to spur the behavior you want. This could involve basic subject line testing to spur a greater number of individuals to open and click the offers in the message. Measure the performance of this group by focusing on the CTOR we discussed previously in this chapter. Using promotional offers too frequently can create a habitual behavior where you are training the subscriber to react only when they are given promotions. However, for those in the less engaged segment, discounts can be used to spur behavior.

Effective Subject Lines

Subject lines can be an effective way to tune your campaigns to drive greater response.

Research from AlchemyWorx, a full-service email agency in London, and other ESPs indicate that shorter subject lines generate higher open rates, which is a measure of reader interest, but they indicate much lower click-to-open rates. Further, longer subject lines earn a much higher click-to-open rate, which indicates real relevance.

More customers open emails when subject lines are shorter—but are they the right customers? We asked this question of Della Quist, who is the principal at AlchemyWorx. This is what Della said of the research AlchemyWorx conducted after analyzing the subject lines of 205 million emails:

> *"A short subject line, such as 'Summer starts here,' containing an offer for discounted Nike trainers is likely to result in a high open rate but low click-through rate. Subscribers are likely to be opening because of their relationship with the brand and/or curiosity. Relevant customers may not realize that the email contains a proposition of interest to them and may not open it and therefore cannot click. A more specific subject line, containing more than one proposition, such as "50% off Nike trainers, the latest from Wimbledon, plus your chance to win a spa weekend," ensures that all the propositions contained in the email are communicated, maximizing the number of relevant customers who open.*

> *"Strong, valuable, single-proposition emails are the exception that proves the rule that longer is better. A subject line of "Nike trainers—50% off" conveys the entire content of an email, to as many people as it is relevant to, in a clear and concise way. Increasing the number of words or characters in this situation is unlikely to make the content of the email more obvious to relevant customers."*

As we discussed earlier in this chapter, testing is the most effective way to determine which subject lines are working, that is, which ones are driving the correct response. The general rule of thumb here is that shorter is better.

Tuesday: Determining the Value of Your Email Addresses and Campaigns

Now that you have sent some email and have seen some positive results from your marketing efforts, it is time to start placing a value on the success of that email. Here are a variety of attributes that you can begin to look at to determine the value of your email addresses and campaign.

> **Write This Down:** A study of retailers found that, as of 2008, email has an average marketing cost per order of $6.85 and an average dollar value of $120.27 per order. (Source: Shop.org Annual Retailer Survey)

Direct Transactions This is the easiest metric to use to calculate the effectiveness of your email marketing campaign. These are orders that were a direct result of clicks from the email. You should also break out what percentage of your overall email subscriber database and your overall client list direct transactions represent. More difficult is attributing the effect of the email campaign on revenue derived from other channels or subscribers who made multiple site visits before purchasing, even if that purchase was originally spurred by an email.

Attribution By using cookies, you should be able to determine how many ads, email clicks, and search engine searches your clients performed before making a purchase. Some marketers will take whatever the client did more of before that sale and attribute the entire amount of the revenue there. For example, if there were two clicks from an email mailing but only one from an ad they viewed on one of your affiliate sites, then the marketer would attribute the entire dollar amount from the sale to the email program. Others will equally break the transaction's revenue into the various advertising touch points; for example, one click for search, one for email, and one for a display ad would be broken into thirds and the dollars attributed in that manner.

Cost Savings If you are mailing fewer catalogs, postcards, or another traditional form of direct marketing with your email mailings, then you can attribute the cost savings from those print, paper, and production costs to email. To make this calculation easier, come up with the average fully loaded print costs (including production and postage), and apply that to the number of pieces by which you have reduced your print mailings.

Although the previous are methods of looking at the overall effectiveness of the campaign, research by the Email Experience Council indicates that many marketers have not begun to determine the value that their email subscribers represent. Here is Stephanie Miller, an executive at Return Path and co-chair of the EEC's List Growth and Engagement Roundtable, to further explain the findings:

> *"We conducted a survey late last year [2007] and found only two out of five marketers (41 percent) know the cost to acquire an email address,*

while 59 percent are either not sure (31 percent) or do not know (28 percent). Two-thirds (60 percent) of marketers are able to determine a monetary value for their entire email database, while 40 percent cannot. Not surprisingly, the most commonly used success metrics around the value of an email file are those that tend to be easy to track today—deliverability to the inbox (56 percent), revenue generated (52 percent), open rate (50 percent), total quantity of email addresses (48 percent), and click-through rate (47 percent). Significantly, 10 percent to 30 percent of marketers surveyed are not using these metrics at all in determining the value of their email file."

Clearly, your success in determining the value of your subscribers and mailings goes back to your ability to understand your email campaign metrics at a subscriber or segment level. Email addresses have a shelf life. Nearly a third of them go bad every year. Some email addresses are gold, others are duds, and some behave the way you want them to only at particular times of the year.

First, you must understand the customers and prospects these addresses represent. Analyze customer spending, customer behavior, and the acquisition source. Though most marketers associate an email address with an individual, far fewer associate a value with that email address. A JupiterResearch report that David wrote in 2004 found that 71 percent of email marketers surveyed didn't associate a value with their email addresses.

With so few adhering to this practice, email marketers can make decisions about their lists and email practices somewhat blindly. Tactics for high-value subscribers may not work or make financial sense when applied to lower-value subscribers. List churn management can be misinterpreted. You can't fully analyze the merits of email address reactivation tactics, such as sending a postcard or making an outbound call, if you don't know whether the tactics' costs are higher than the value of the addresses you're trying to reactivate. Analysis may reveal Hotmail addresses aren't as valuable as AOL addresses, so you shouldn't use the same reactivation tactics for both. Here are some additional approaches to use to determine the value of specific subscribers:

Customer Lifetime Value One of the more accurate but complicated ways to determine your addresses' value is to link them to your customers' lifetime value. Multiply a customer's average spending on a given transaction by the number of transactions in a year. Apply to this number a factor that represents the number of years the customer remains active and whether transaction frequency increases or declines over time. Subtract servicing costs, and apply other assumptions, such as crediting customers who act as advocates to recognize this goodwill. Though this approach is useful for transaction-oriented marketers such as retailers, it's harder to apply to a publishing model or lists largely comprising new clients or prospects.

Acquisition Source Another approach is to use email acquisition costs as an aggregate proxy for an address's value. Depending on your acquisition sources, you may want to apply a higher value to addresses acquired through partner co-registration agreements and a lower value to addresses acquired on your website.

Fuzzy Math Use a combination of sources. Publishers could assign aggregate sponsorship ad revenues across the active portion (openers and clickers) of their lists. Further refine with the response and delivery differences of the domains that make up the list's active portion. Associate a lower value with domains that are more expensive to deliver to.

Apply the Valuations

Once you have values for your email addresses, apply them to your segmentation scheme and targeting and testing tactics, such as message frequency. More important, use these values to determine which reactivation tactics are warranted.

Computing email address value is a necessary function for every email marketer. The methodology you use can be simple or incredibly complex. When in doubt, start with the simple, back-of-the-envelope acquisition cost approach. If you're a retailer, leverage your existing recency, frequency, and monetary (RFM) scores.

In general, we find a company's approach is largely tied to either how conservative the company is or how much strategic value it places on email as a marketing medium. In the end, you want to understand the value of your addresses and lists. Determining this can be as complicated or as simple as it needs to be for your organization.

One approach is to allocate a relative value for each name or by the acquisition source of the list and then factor in the cost of acquiring the name in the first place. This will give you a relative figure to compare how valuable names are for your organization. Finally, introduce the estimated "shelf life" of these email addresses (based on previous history), because this will greatly influence the overall value. This exercise can help you make more efficient marketing decisions. It can even highlight to the rest of your organization just how valuable your email programs are.

Adestra, a U.K.-based ESP, shares this example of determining whether a client's source for acquiring names is a profitable one. Its client broadcasts a regular email newsletter to 25,000 contacts. The average sale value from the email campaign is £32.68 (determined by the total value of total orders for the last three editions of the email newsletter). This means the following:

- For its 25,000 contacts that it has in the database, it delivers email to 24,550 (98.2 percent).

- Of those delivered, 184 convert into sales (a 0.75 percent conversion rate), each spending an average of £32.68.

- This makes a total revenue of £6,013.12 for each "average" campaign.

- This means each email address it holds is worth £0.24 (£6,013.12 divided by 25,000).
- Thus, if the cost of acquiring an extra email address is less than £0.24 per email, then it is a sensible acquisition route.

Another approach is simply to take the size of your list, apply the average number of converting email subscribers, and apply the average dollar value of orders driven by your email campaigns to those subscribers. Now take the percentage of inactive subscribers, or those who you expect to lapse each year, and apply that to your list size in order to understand how this number will be impacted in the second and third years of your email marketing campaigns.

This is yet another metric that you can build into your comprehensive weekly reporting to determine how this number is changing from week to week.

Such information, whether it is top-line growth or bottom-line cost savings, will provide you with a business case for further funding and respect for your email program within your organization.

Wednesday: Increasing Email Sending Costs to Improve Top-Line Results

In previous chapters, we took you through the basics of improving email deliverability as well as the tactics to use to maintain a good reputation with ISPs and adhere to federal regulations.

However, in recent years, third-party accreditation services have emerged that can help to not only improve your deliverability but also to ensure that your emails are delivered with all the graphics fully rendered. There are a few vendors in this space, with the primary players being Goodmail Systems, Return Path, and Habeas. Although these programs will increase your CPM (ranges vary based on volume), the return on investment for these programs can be measured by higher delivery and higher response/conversion rates. The challenge currently is that the aforementioned vendors do not work with every consumer ISP, so it is possible you will have to work with two of them to get coverage at all the top-tier ISPs. Goodmail, for example, has coverage at AOL and Yahoo. Return Path offers coverage at the Microsoft webmail portals. Determining which solution is right for you involves knowing the domain distribution of your list, for example, what percentage AOL versus Hotmail represents on your list. Additionally, the solution may only be warranted if you are having severe delivery issues at those particular domains.

For publishers, the ROI can simply be placed on higher delivery and the fact that all your images—or more likely, your advertisers' banners—will be rendered in every one of the emails. For transasctionally oriented marketers, the ROI obviously is going to be measured in conversion rates and average order value. Although these programs certainly offer all marketers an additional level of value, not all marketers can participate in them. That is, they all have strict barriers to participation, which include your complaint rate ratio and ensuring that your opt-in and mailing process are all above board. We will leave it up to you to contact those companies to learn their specifics, but let's take a look at some of their case studies to better understand the results that can be achieved through these programs.

StubHub, the ticket marketplace, uses Goodmail's CertifiedEmail to help increase its deliverability rate. StubHub sends a bi-weekly newsletter promoting entertainment events based on a subscriber's preference for events, concerts, and venues. Although StubHub has good mailing practices, it was having issues delivering to AOL, which represents about a quarter of its subscribers. In an interview with DM News, Albert Lee, StubHub's email marketing manager, explained, "We were having issues with spam complaints and bounces in deliverability, and we wanted to get through to our customers so we decided to test sending CertifiedMail against our regular mailing." With Goodmail's email delivery service, StubHub reported a 17 percent increase in the number of ticket orders, a 16 percent increase in click-through rates, and a 36 percent lift in ticket sales directly attributable to email.

Write This Down: In the 2006 report "The State of Deliverability," 69 percent of email marketers reported that they would be willing to pay to participate in accreditation programs to improve deliverability and email send results. (Source: JupiterResearch)

The use of systems such as Goodmail's has been increasing over the past several years. For example, it reported recently that it sent 1.3 billion messages in March 2008 and 1.6 billion messages in April 2008. Similarly, Return Path's Sender Score Reputation monitor is seeing increases in usage, because it now leverages feedback from more than 55 million email inboxes. Return Path's Sender Score senders have its email images and links turned on in Windows Live Hotmail, among other ISPs. Using Sender Score, CNET was able to increase its open rates to top-tier ISPs by 15 percent, which for the publisher meant that more users were viewing the ads placed in its newsletters.

Here are some of the ways you can approach valuing the impact of adding the cost of participating in an email accreditation program:

Higher Ad Revenues If you're a publisher, your ability to guarantee that the images, or in this case, the advertisements, will be rendered will allow you to garner higher CPMs from your advertisers. In this instance, you can begin to charge your publishers not for a flat CPM but for a CPA (cost per action, often referred to as the *effective* CPM) in which the price is based on an action, such as a sale or a subscriber registering on the site.

Higher Transaction Revenues For a promotional marketer, your additional spending on accreditation programs should be compensated by higher conversion rates as well as higher average order values. Overstock.com reported that when it tested Goodmail's certified email program, its revenue per email increased by 22 percent over the control group that was sent without Goodmail's certified email.

Reduced Deliverability Servicing Costs If fewer emails are getting blocked, it would likely mean you could spend less with delivery service providers or reduce the time your own production staff spends mitigating deliverability failures. To compute this, benchmark the amount of time you or your staff spends on deliverability issues, and compare that amount of time to mailings that are done with the accreditation piece in place.

Lower List Fatigue As discussed earlier in this chapter, you should be beginning the process of valuing your email addresses, if not simply what it costs to acquire an email address. If more of your email is getting delivered, rendered, and consumed (measured in your subscriber's behavior), then you can begin to realize the value that having more active addresses represents to your organization.

 Write This Down: Organizations believe the most significant impact on their business models between 2008 and 2013 will be as a result of technology-led operational changes. (Source: Habeas)

If you decide in 2008 and 2009 to participate in one or more of the accreditation programs, you will still be considered an early adopter. We imagine that in a few years these accreditation programs, particularly for large senders, will be standard. Your ability to push your competitors out of the way and be noticed in the inbox will determine the duration of your competitive advantage. Speed and time to market is everything, and this is one area where you can't rest on your laurels.

Thursday: Exploring Web Analytics and Email Integration

Are you ready to integrate and use website clickstream data with your email campaigns? To get started, this section highlights what you need.

First you need to already have a good understanding of the email metrics and reporting data contained within your email program. This would include all the comprehensive reporting that we discussed earlier in this chapter. Next you are going to need a web analytics solution. We would imagine that if you are operating a website online today, you already have one of those solutions in place. Vendors such as Omniture, Coremetrics, WebTrends, Google, Yahoo, Lyris, and Unica are all top providers in this category offering a range of solutions (see Appendix A for contact information). The web analytics solution you select should be one that can measure site traffic through page-tag analysis, which will be easier to understand and apply to individual subscribers.

Next you'll need a mechanism or point of integration between the analytics tool and your ESP. Most of the major ESPs offer quick integration to these solutions. If you opt not to utilize a standard integration, you can export data from the web analytics solution if you have a common customer key (record key) between the two solutions. However, we find that using web analytics is one of the more powerful segmentation and targeting attributes you can apply to email.

Write This Down: Only 15 percent of marketers actively use website clickstream behavior as an audience segmentation attribute. (Source: JupiterResearch)

The notion of using website clickstream data (which records customer behavior on your website) to create email segments and target email campaigns isn't new. The industry was littered with startups promising to leverage this data to drive truly targeted email communications based on site behavior. The idea was ahead of market demand, relegating many of these firms to the dot-com graveyard or mergers that basically shelved the technology. Until now.

Although adoption is still slow, it is higher now than it has been in the past several years. Still, data from research firms indicate that far fewer marketers actually implement this feature than say they are planning to do so.

Another major difference is that email marketing and web analytics technologies have matured. We've progressed from server-side web analytics (for example, log files) to client-side page tagging, which allows for more efficient and reliable site traffic analysis. The real progress, though, has been within 2008, when we've seen true packaged integration of these disparate disciplines.

Vendors Today Are Doing Real Integration

Here are just a few web analytic firms that have integrated offerings with email service providers (ESPs):

- WebTrends has integrated with ExactTarget. WebTrends' browser overlay functionality allows the user to see the web metrics on top of the email campaign performance. The user can drill into site click behavior to create segments.

- Coremetrics has seven ESPs partners, including Responsys, Yesmail, and CheetahMail. They've built connectors to the application so the data flow easily between the applications.

- Digital River acquired web analytic firm Fireclick and ESP BlueHornet. Though each has mutual clients, the integrated product offering will provide both firms with greater sales opportunities.

Small Doses of Relevancy

This tactic is ideal for improving a mailing's relevancy because it leverages a visitor's actual page-view behavior to craft highly targeted messages. Many companies, from banks to retailers, use this approach to improve campaign performance. One consistent challenge, however, is the relatively small portion of the email list that lends itself to clickstream targeting.

Clickstream data is collected from nearly all site visitors, but as an email marketer you will have email addresses for only some of them. Similarly, only a portion of subscribers will click through to the site, ultimately lowering the number of individuals who can be targeted with the website data.

Though this approach is effective, it should be used in tandem with existing campaign tactics. It's an iterative process; over time, more of your list can be moved into the clickstream segment. One retailer who uses this approach regards these opportunities as "seducible moments." You can easily identify pages visitors looked at and where they left the site and then use this information to craft a highly targeted mailing. As we discussed when we discussed welcome messages and other forms of triggered messages, this is where you can leverage the notion of continuity campaigns—those that are triggered by subscriber behavior to automate these tasks.

Clickstream Targeting Correlates with Improved Performance!

Years ago, David wrote for JupiterResearch a series of popular research papers demonstrating that marketers who use clickstream data create campaigns with higher ROI than those who don't. See the "A View into the ROI of Email Relevance" sidebar for more details on this research, which still applies to the market today.

A View into the ROI of Email Relevance

The landmark JupiterResearch report "The ROI of Email Relevance" published in May 2005 is still valid and useful today. The research studied the performance of marketers who use segmentation, particularly based on clickstream web analytics, and compared it to the performance of marketers who sent the same message to all subscribers. Although marketers using web analytics data had larger marketing departments and higher technology costs because of the integration of the email and analytics applications, the results even when figuring in those additional costs were very impressive. For example, the aggregate increase in net profits from these targeted campaigns (triggered through clickstream) was found to be 18 times more than that from broadcast messages, even when figuring in additional costs. These results show additional expenses are well worth the cost. The use of website clickstream as a targeting attribute is particularly beneficial for both top-line and bottom-line results—even after including additional web analytics spending.

Though this targeting approach isn't new, it's promising that easy-to-use, affordable tools are now available, which should encourage adoption. As with everything else, testing will really identify whether this tactic is right for your organization.

The following are several case studies that you can leverage to make clickstream data an important part of your email marketing effort.

Using Web Analytics to Optimize Opt-In Points of Interest

A home improvement and equipment retailer puts a simple opt-in form (email address and a Submit button) at the top of every one of its pages on its website. To better understand a subscriber's interest areas, the company looks at the three previous pages clicked to determine whether there is a common category of products that the subscriber seemed to be interested in, such as gardening, plumbing, or power tools. The company determines that there is a category preference if at least two of the three pages match one category.

This is an automated routine that is run, so beyond the initial setup of the rules, there is little or no human intervention. This organization automatically pulls the latest content set up in the company's merchandising solution that houses its weekly specials. However, for other marketers, it may require human intervention to maintain the set of merchandising rules and content assets.

This report then groups the subscribers into categories (gardening, for example) and formats and sends a series of messages that feature products from that category. The next message that the subscriber gets is purely informational, such as "Tips to Make Your Garden Grow," which includes a link to weekly specials for that product category but does not promote any one specific product over another. Since moving to this format, the retailer has discovered the following. Opt-in rates increased 60 percent over their previous one-page subscription layout, simply because the ability to opt in was on every page of its website. However, it has been the use of web analytics that has made its results really shine, with open, click, and conversion rates of 15 percent to 25 percent over the group in which no category preference could be discerned, because they get the general weekly offer.

Optimizing Site Drop-Off Points

One popular method of using web analytics is to determine which were the last pages or products that a customer viewed before exiting the site. This tactic can be used for publishers to see whether subscribers tend to read only one type or category of stories, such as entertainment over sports, which can help optimize future ad placement in newsletters aimed at these subscribers. Retailers can similarly use this tactic to see whether category patterns exist. A swimsuit retailer uses this approach to target its email subscribers into two segments, women interested in one-piece suits and those expressing interest in two-piece swimsuits, and adapts the offers and creative elements accordingly.

Using Web Analytics to Match Back to Demographic Targets

If you are a marketer who relies heavily on demographic segmentation—gender, age, income, and so on—then this web analytics approach may be for you. Most web analytics providers can provide not only site user behavior but also demographic details about those users. The source of the demographic data can vary, either in the form of panel data from third-party data providers such as Experian or Acxiom or from their ability to marry your web analytics data to data you already possess about your subscribers.

Automobile companies and banks often use this approach to group their subscribers into lifestyle segments, such as students, new parents, empty nesters, and so on. In these instances, the demographics are aligned with the product and category preferences that the marketer believes will match those segments. Home improvement wholesaler and retailer BuildDirect has used this approach with Google Analytics. In a Google Analytics case study, BuildDirect's director of operations, Dan Brodie, said that BuildDirect could see its email marketing channel was not converting as well as he would have liked. After implementing the marriage of website analytics to its subscriber demographic data, BuildDirect doubled its email marketing conversion rate. "Once we began using Google Analytics cross-segment performance analytic tools to identify our customer demographics, we were able to design specific creative tailored to our buyers," said Brodie.

You can see how these examples of using web analytics data can help make your email mailings more effective. However, two words of caution when using web analytics data: Start small! It is easy to get overwhelmed with the volume of data, and it is very important when harnessing this data to start with one goal in mind. For example, abandoned purchases and single underperforming products are both good places to start looking. Targeting subscribers who have demonstrated an interest or potentially an affinity to a product or category of products is the next approach you should take to working with web analytics data.

This will allow you to test the concept of integrating this data, and it will allow you to determine (using the aforementioned rules of testing) whether this data is having an impact on your top- and bottom-line performance. Remember when calculating this impact to document and calculate the additional employees necessary to use this data effectively as well as the additional costs related to the access and integration of this data.

Friday: Finding and Targeting Your Advocates

Your best customers are usually defined as those who show their love for your company with their pocketbook (or, if you are a content publisher, with their level of engagement). Although this is certainly true and a conventional way to measure customer performance, it may not give you a full picture of who your best customers actually are.

First, don't confuse evangelism with customer spending. Obviously, customers who spend more than average and do so quite often are demonstrating their advocacy with their wallets. However, another group of customers just beyond that group might be your biggest advocates even if their own spending doesn't indicate it. They may not be loyal, but they act as evangelists. So, how do you know who those individuals are? How can you possibly target them without the spending hook to hang the loyalty or evangelist hat on? Use these five sure-fire ways to identify and target these subscribers:

Forward Behavior While writing this book, we subscribed to hundreds of promotional offers and newsletters. We took a random sample of the top 35 household name brands across a variety of industries and found that only 46 percent of them included a Forward to a Friend option. We told you earlier that most consumers use the Forward button in their email clients, not the forward mechanism in the email. However, shouldn't you include this option to understand which portion of your list is acting as an advocate to others, even if it is the minority? Existing research and books from a variety of sources have long established that trendsetters—that viral group—are always a minority. We recommend you include a Forward to a Friend option not only to build your list but also to identify those subscribers who are acting as a valuable conduit to new customers and generally acting as an advocate for your company. Of course, unless the forwardee opts into your mailing, you cannot mail to them, but you can monitor and act on the behavior of subscribers who are promoting your email newsletter and marketing message to others. You can enlist a variety of tactics to recognize these subscribers:

- **Send more coupons and discounts to the advocate segment.** Ninety or ninety-five percent of a dollar captured is often better than not capturing a dollar at all.

- **Discounts may not be appropriate for every brand, but if they are for yours, this is a good way for your customer to share the message.** Additionally, you could send a campaign to this set of subscribers suggesting they take a survey or post product reviews on your website.

- **Recognize customer advocacy in the subscriber's profile.** You will want to be able to segment your subscribers by the forward behavior you can measure in your email marketing application. However, as we previously mentioned, these advocate subscribers may not appear to be your best customers if their own spending does not meet your definition of a "high-spending" customer that most of us label as "best." To combat this financial difference, we suggest you take your average customer acquisition cost and place it as a positive value on the customer's profile in order to recognize their goodwill. You could make this more complex by multiplying that average cost against their aggregate forward behavior.

Product Reviews It is no secret that consumers love product reviews, and increasingly more and more consumers are posting them on websites as well as using them to influence their product purchases. If you are using product reviews, you should require your customers to register on your website with their email address. This will allow you to identify those subscribers who are acting as advocates, as well as those potentially writing a series of negative reviews. Enlist the same tactics as mentioned previously, but be sure to include the Forward to a Friend option in those emails so that the consumer can further be your advocate.

Blogs Although generally less than a quarter of the online population reads blogs on a regular basis, they are a powerful group that can influence your search engine listings and even the news cycle (for example, think of CNN's use of blogger content in its news coverage). It is important you are at least listening to what the bloggers have to say about your brand and products. Services such as blog search engine Technorati and others allow you to measure in aggregate how often your product names are being mentioned in the "blogosphere." Often you may find that these sites are being used to "spam search engines" in order for them to compete with your own paid or organic search engine listings. You will be able to determine whether these bloggers are acting as advocates or detractors by listening to them. Again, comparing these individuals to your email subscriber file may lead you to insights that will result in suppressing subscribers or in mailing to them more frequently.

Social and Community Sites In the Web 1.0 world, we would refer to these purely as *community sites*, but the introduction of Facebook, MySpace, and the countless other social sites indicates that consumers generally are developing a new preference for communication and information discovery. Create an advocate or "become a friend of" page on Facebook or the other social sites to further fan the social fire, as well as create a new way to reach this audience in tandem with your email marketing efforts. It is also possible to gather data from these sites and compare it to your subscriber list to determine which subscribers continue to be loyal fans of your brand outside your website. Again, targeting these individuals with messages that recognize their allegiance can help further their behavior as advocates.

Customer Service and Support Although we talk quite a bit more in week 4 of this chapter on working with customer service and support, the first thing you must do to bridge your marketing and service gap is to understand the servicing behavior of your email subscribers. If it is positive, you may want to mail that segment more. If they are individuals who typically return everything they buy or run up costs of your service team, then you may want to mail to them less or suppress them altogether. Understanding the voice of the customer shows your constituents you are listening. Netflix recently suggested to its audience that it was going to do away with customer profiles—the information that shows what people have rented and reviewed. However, it received such negative feedback from their customers about removing this function that it sent a note to their subscribers saying, "We are keeping Netflix profiles." This stated, in effect, that "you spoke, and we heard you." Recognizing customer feedback in the context of marketing a brand or product is a powerful thing.

Central to leveraging all these viral tactics is using a Forward to a Friend link to further boost customer advocacy. Here are some Forward to a Friend best practices to keep in mind:

- **Focus on the forwarding experience.** No Forward to a Friend pages in our sample tests returned subscribers to offer pages after forward forms were submitted. That is, after we were sent to a web page where we entered our friend's email address, we got a page that said "thank you" or confirmed our simple form post. However, wouldn't it be better if you took that subscriber, along with that confirmation message, to an offer or perhaps even the main home page of the website? Current implementations use forms hosted by ESPs. After forms post to vendors, however, scripts can be implemented to redirect users to branded landing pages that have relevance to mailings.

- **Check the unsubscribe.** When evaluating a vendor's forwarding capabilities, consider what the forwarded message looks like. Make sure the forwarded message does not include the Unsubscribe link from the initial recipient. If it does, the initial recipient could be mistakenly unsubscribed by the friend who received the message. As the recipient forwarding the message, is your unsubscribe information still contained in the recipient's email message? Also, ensure that the recipient of the forwarded message knows they have not yet been opted in to your email campaigns. Promote opt-in: If you were to take a sample of these Forward to a Friend messages as we did, you would be amazed just how many do not promote opt-in to the forwardee recipient. This seems like a no-brainer, but ensure that in the forwarded message you are including a big opt-in link for the new subscriber.

With these rules in mind, you should be able to harness the viral power of your audience and increase your opt-in rates while better understanding just who makes up your list of customer advocates.

Week 4: Promoting Your Email Results Within Your Organization

At this point, you should be approaching rock star status in your organization—if you are promoting your results effectively within your organization. In the following sections, we will provide some suggestions for further leveraging and promoting your email marketing results within your organization. These will help you bridge organizational gaps and processes in order for your company to make the most out of its email marketing dollar.

Monday: Effecting email used in other parts of your organization
Tuesday: Sharing results with your online peers
Wednesday: Sharing results with your offline peers
Thursday: Using your email results for PR purposes
Friday: Looking ahead to dynamic content

Note: The topic of building an effective organization is outside the scope of this book, but if you are not familiar with how to build a spirit of togetherness to ensure that everyone in your organization is on the same page, we suggest you review the proven rules of Total Quality Management and the McKinsey 7S model that people such as Tom Peters established long ago.

Monday: Effecting Email Used in Other Parts of Your Organization

As marketers begin the slow adoption of tactics such as targeting to improve the relevancy of their mailings, the use of email throughout the enterprise is also increasing. However, many companies are not yet centralizing their email initiatives, and even fewer maintain rules to control message frequency, analyze subscriber behavior, or coordinate their messaging initiatives across channels and business units. Although the market will continue to expand, this lack of sophistication and centralization will amplify the volume of messages that subscribers receive. Without centralization, marketing strategies will be undermined to the detriment of their brands. Today's hour provides insight into the current state of messaging deployments and guidance for how enterprises can best organize their email initiatives.

It is always better to ask for permission than forgiveness, particularly when it comes to email marketing. One mistake that marketers make is using a subscriber list for inappropriate cross-marketing. The customer who opted into mortgage offers, for example, may or may not want that used by a different division, such as making them a credit card offer. In companies such as the Time Warner or Sony empires, permission is not transferable across various divisions. Still, it may be appropriate for you to promote new products or product divisions to subscribers in the hope they will opt in or participate in marketing messages advocating those other areas. However, this must be done in a coordinated manner. The following are some general rules for expanding your email marketing efforts across the broader organization.

Purpose

Do the basic constructs of relevancy indicate that an offer from one product team might be relevant to subscribers who exist on a list from another product team? If the answer is yes, then potentially there is an opportunity to cross-pollinate these lists in hopes of creating a company-wide cross-selling effort. However, the rules of relevancy are built on customer preference—what the subscriber has indicated either through their choice to opt in or through their behavior to demonstrate affinity for other products.

Frequency

As we discussed earlier, the primary reason for subscribers opting out is content they don't find relevant, while the second is frequency. If you have agreed with your counterparts that there is a just reason for you to begin to cross-market to your joint subscribers, you must have a master frequency rule in place that ensures that customers are not marketed to too often. Typically most marketers will market to their subscribers no more than four times per month. In some instances, it may be more frequent, such as mortgage interest updates, but even then the best practice is to realize that the customer's interest in getting messages from you on a more frequent basis is tied to the life cycle of a product. For example, Wells Fargo will automatically opt out customers who do not sign up for the mortgage interest rate alerts after 45 days. In this instance, Wells Fargo has determined that clients are usually in the market for a mortgage or refinance for a finite period of time. Wells Fargo will send the customer a series of final messages stating they will be removed from the mailing unless the subscriber says they want to continue to get the information.

Platform

One of the largest challenges that marketers cite is the lack of enterprise coordination as it relates to email marketing. In fact, a JupiterResearch executive survey found that as few as a third of marketers agreed it was easy for them to understand how often their companies sends email to their customers as a whole. This underscores the need to not only be synchronized with your co-workers but, if possible, to be using the same email marketing technology platform to manage frequency caps, suppression rules, and common reporting and metric methodologies. Companies must centralize email technology and management to assert better control and refinement of multidepartment mailing coordination, frequency controls, deliverability and message bounce handling, list management, use of messaging to meet multiple company goals and purposes, and oversight of the production process.

Accordingly, if you are considering a centralized email messaging platform, seek to implement the following tactics to ensure the investment is being properly leveraged and optimized:

- **Synchronize user and publishing controls.** Seek out a platform that allows different users to have different rights and privileges across a wide set of message types (transactional, promotional, service, and so on). It is imperative that companies control email and manage the ability of users to send email, all while adhering to the federally prescribed CAN-SPAM rules. Such an approach not only mitigates these legal risks but also allows the organization to leverage the investment by taking advantage of scale and widespread usage.

- **Implement frequency controls to optimize relevancy.** Frequency must become the arbiter of relevancy; companies must commit to limiting their customer email communications to a certain number each month. Companies must think of email frequency and the associated mailing as inventory. Take into account all transactional, service, and relationship email, and determine the number of promotional messaging opportunities that exist each month for every subscriber segment. Leverage email goals, such as viral campaigns, account reactivation, and conversion, into all messages, particularly transactional messages, which JupiterResearch finds often go underutilized.

- **Focus on behavior to drive engagement.** Marketers must begin to use subscriber behavior to tailor the tone, content, and frequency of their messages. Previous research by JupiterResearch has found that more than two-thirds of marketers do not use click-through data as an attribute to target subscribers. Additionally, marketers who do target subscribers by behavior generate mailings that on average are nine to ten times more effective than mailings that are simply broadcast. Past behavior is the best predictor of future behavior, and executives must begin to leverage this in their messaging strategies.

- **Implement infrastructure improvements to aid in delivery.** The delivery of email is becoming more complex every day. ISPs and corporate mail gateways alike are constantly tweaking their rules to limit the amount of email they receive, and they are always adjusting their spam algorithms. To maximize message delivery, it is important to implement improvements that can be more easily managed from a central platform, such as these:
  - Sending different classes of mail (transactional versus promotional) from different IP addresses
  - Throttling the sending volume of messages
  - Limiting connections to specific ISPs so as not to overload them
  - Measuring and handling bounced messages consistently
  - Implementing authentication schemes in the headers of messages
  - Optimizing mailing patterns by learning from previous mailings

- **Build testing and optimization into all processes.** Marketers must begin to test on a more regular basis. The importance of being able to leverage previous tests (subject line, and so on) from marketing and apply those tests or their outcomes to other forms of messaging such as transactional or service-related messages should not be underestimated. Testing must be built into each mailing so executives are able to optimize their practices in real time. Determining optimal frequency patterns as well as the tone and content of messages can be determined only through testing.

Lastly, it is important to know and understand the goals of the other divisions seeking to implement email marketing. It is necessary to understand those organizational and perhaps political differences with your co-workers before a true consensus can be built.

Tuesday: Sharing Results with Your Online Peers

Your co-workers will respond best to what they are most interested in, for example, the metrics and goals by which they are judged and rewarded.

Earlier in this chapter we gave you some insight on how to build a customized dashboard for your own purposes. However, here is an opportunity to build a separate dashboard that focuses on the metrics that most interest your co-workers. The following are common measures of success that are applicable company-wide.

New Subscribers from Paid Search Listings

For your co-workers who are focused on search engine marketing, you want to be sure that you first have insight into how they are measuring both paid and organic search traffic. This is typically done with page tags from the various search engines. Be sure your peers have given you the insight to tag your subscription page(s) with that data so you can, in turn, provide them with a customized report of how their efforts and marketing spending is impacting the opt-in rate of your email marketing program.

Call Center Data

As with new subscribers from search engines, if you are working with the call center to gather or confirm email addresses, be sure to indicate how those efforts are paying off. Before we got involved in the Internet and email marketing, we both had a long tenure working in call centers and running that facet of direct marketing operations. One thing we found to be very beneficial when being the "internal customer" to other groups, namely the broader marketing organization, was to ensure that the call center was meeting the goals of the marketing team.

One tactic that worked particularly well for us was to do random quality assurance taping of call center phone calls and grade the call center representatives on a 10-point scale on how well they did meeting the company objectives. We would randomly select three calls over the course of the month and have an objective quality assurance representative (not their manager) fill out this evaluation. Although the first tendency with this approach is to grade representatives on areas such as tone and their overall "helpfulness" to clients, those measures often ended up not being objective.

Instead, we created quality assurance programs that would grade the call center representatives only on objective measures—did they confirm the customer's credit card? Did they ask for the source code on the back of the catalog? Did they ask for and/or confirm the customer's email address? This last one is the gem that you need to focus on with your call center peers because it will serve to benefit the company as a whole. In our call center days when we did this quality assurance, we would actually place more value or emphasis on those items that supported marketing and that grade for the call center representative. We suggest doing what we were able to accomplish, in that those call center representatives that scored above an aggregate score of 90 or better on their monthly evaluations were given small bonuses.

Although this might seem like rewarding people just for doing the job they were hired to do, it enabled us to focus people on the tasks that mattered most. Using such an approach will allow you to broker a better relationship with your call center peers and ensure they are working to support your goals. Although you need to report how well the call center is doing in providing new addresses, your co-worker can provide a measure of how well or how consistently they are asking for the client's email address. We would imagine at this point that your email marketing is becoming so profitable that you could use the profits of your program to fund the incentive plan, staff, and extra talk time that is required to ensure the success of the integration of the call center and your email marketing program. This program can be particularly effective in industries that are prone to higher call center contact ratios, such as insurance and banking.

Wednesday: Sharing Results with Your Offline Peers

Coordinating and sharing your successes with your offline counterparts throughout the organization is an important part of building a cross-channel integrated marketing strategy. The following are some tips to build corporate relationships by sharing the results of your programs with your offline peers:

Store or Other Channel Information

The same rules of collaboration as described for your search engine and call center peers apply here; be sure clear incentives are in place for those business units to participate and advocate the use of email throughout your organization.

Support, Fulfillment, and Service

Are email subscribers more or less satisfied with your customer support and service than those who aren't email subscribers? Do they return products or complain at the same frequency as non-email customers? Only you can provide that answer, but it will most likely require a little help from your friends. Although every company selling hard goods has customer-specific return or customer service reporting in place, can yours be enhanced with the availability of email subscriber data? If you can demonstrate that email subscribers are more satisfied and return fewer products than non-email customers, then we are sure you'll convince your co-worker in the warehouse to put a piece of paper in every outbound shipment that promotes subscribing to your email marketing newsletter. After all, since that package is already going in the mail and the client has paid or at least deferred the postage cost on that shipment, it would be worthwhile to put such a promotion in the box—even in an untargeted manner—simply for the clients who were unaware they could subscribe to your awesome email promotional newsletter.

Banners That Do Not Appear in the Browser

Does your company do offline "in-person" events? Like most organizations, does your company still do a lot in the non-connected world that is not ruled by browsers and media companies? If so, then it probably is in your interest to do the following:

- Pay for new banners or posters that promote your newsletter.
- Report on the effectiveness of customers acquired through and subsequently marketed to via email.

Your event organizers will quickly become your best friends, because you offer them the only measurable link to retention. After all, when someone walks away from a booth at a trade show or a picnic table at summer outing, how can one expect to measure their interest, presence, or intent to interact with your brand? Email. Make email a part of their event; and be sure that when you do that, you can measure the acquisition source of them differently than you would through your other acquisition tools; and, of course, report to this person each month on the performance of those subscribers who they helped bring into the email fold.

Adjust not only reporting but your welcome campaigns as needed to recognize the source of acquisition. It might be very useful to remind a subscriber that they are getting an email because they stopped by your tent at the Texas Old Town Cookout where your company just happened to have a booth. Context is everything and will help endear you to the subscribers you are courting.

Thursday: Using Your Email Results for PR Purposes

What follows are our rules for leveraging your email experience thus far for your promotional efforts. Not all of them are press-release-worthy, but in time your actions and involvement in the greater industry can help your email program get there.

- **Get involved.** Although we are both involved in a board and/or advisory capacity to many of the marketing- and email-specific associations across the industry, we want you to know we are not stating this to serve the purpose of any of those efforts that we undertake in the spirit of benevolence on our own time. We suggest you get involved for the same reason we got involved with associations and continue to stay involved—which is sharing, learning, and collaborating with professionals in our field who are passionate about what they do. Now, there are a couple of upsides to getting involved with industry associations:

- You will learn a thing or two.

- You will share a thing or two.

- You might find the next member of your email marketing team in such a forum.

- Finally, your successful program may just get noticed. Often, as a member of an association, you will be offered the opportunity to speak at events, write a case study on your successes, or be an interview resource with the press, any of which might be material for a press release from your organization. At this point in your email marketing career, you might be thinking that your expertise with email is not quite pressworthy. But it wasn't so long ago that we were just learning how to hit the Send button ourselves. So, clearly anything is possible, but getting involved helps.

- **Become friends with your vendor.** Although this might seem like a foreign concept to some, think back to those simpler days when your neighborhood grocer or butcher was your friend. They were a vendor, too, right? Although your expectations must be the arbiter of vendor trust and reward, your email technology vendor is always looking for a success story. Sure, they too have something, potentially more, to gain from your success on their platform, but if they helped you get here and if they helped you achieve success, why not share it for all to see? We know, competitive pressure and corporate pressure might prevent you from going on record, but still there is a balance in sharing your secret sauce and the notion that you can say just enough about your successes. Explore this option to boost your results.

- **Talk to a third-party analyst at a research or advisory service.** Although coming from us this appears to be self-serving, we know that companies will want to come in and brief analysts on the successes they have achieved. Although there might be some tough questions—how many people do this? Are you satisfied with your vendor? How did you execute your X, Y and Z?—know that companies that open up in this format are often the ones that are written about by the analyst firms and subsequently the press. As with associations, this can lead to speaking opportunities at events and on webinars.

- **Start a blog.** Certainly, check with your company on its rules of engagement that involve such sharing publicly. Still, companies can endear themselves to their constituents by sharing the inner workings. The marketing team at online shoe retailer Zappo's has begun to twitter about their internal workings. Although this might not seem conventional, it could be very much in keeping with your key demographic, that is, if it is younger consumers who are highly engaged with the Internet.

Friday: Looking Ahead to Dynamic Content

Dynamic content has been around in some fashion since the mid-1990s. Dynamic content is typically constructed using JavaScript coding, but don't worry, you don't need to be a computer programmer to make this feature work within your marketing campaigns. Most ESPs have this functionality available in a simple template or provide intuitive wizards to walk you through the process. Essentially, dynamic content is the use of rules to marry specific pieces of content (images or text) with subscriber attributes.

Dynamic content is useful when you want to change one content block or section in an email so that it best matches the interests of the subscriber. In the most basic example, you could have an email message where one content section is variable. Let's say it has three options. Option 1 is an offer that is geared toward everyone on your list with a ZIP code that is west of the Mississippi River, and option 2 is an offer that is for everyone on your list with a ZIP code east of the Mississippi River. Option 3 is a generic offer that will render for everyone who does not meet the rule. For example, in this scenario, the subscriber might live outside the United States or the ZIP code field on their subscriber record is blank. (This third rule is often referred to as the *null rule*.)

Dynamic content can become quite complex, with multiple content blocks and multiple options for each content block. In these instances, where so many rules are driving your dynamic content, it is often easier to upload those rules outside the ESP's dynamic content editor and instead create an integration table that matches the rules to the content assets. In fact, the entire body of an email could be swapped out dynamically, as illustrated in Figure 7.8.

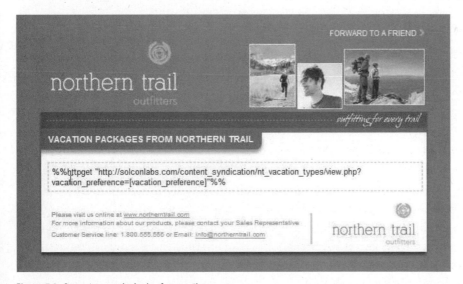

Figure 7.8 Swapping out the body of an email message

The rules you deploy for your dynamic content can be as easy or as sophisticated as you need them to be. Figure 7.9 shows a rather complex query that is doing an inclusion of subscribers based on state.

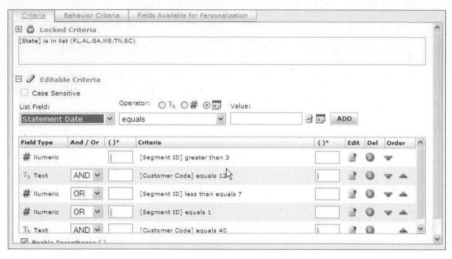

Figure 7.9 Query to develop rules for dynamic content

Dynamic content presents some interesting measurement challenges, because you may have to run multiple versions of the same report to identify which dynamic content version performed best. Don't look just at click-through; also look at the total number of clicks of that dynamic content version in relation to the entire list size. That is, one version of the mailing or that content block may have a very high click-through rate, but that content block may have reached only ten subscribers. Be sure to look at the click rate as a percentage of the entire list.

With this introduction to dynamic content, you are now ready to learn how to put other objects into your email, such as polls and surveys, which we cover in the next chapter.

Test Your Knowledge

Can you get a score of 3 out of 3 and correctly answer these questions?

- What is a seed list, and what are four types of email addresses that should be included in it?
- What are feedback loops, and why are they important?
- What is a control group?

Month 3: Adding Bells and Whistles

8

For the past two months, you have focused on setting up budget requests, technology, creative, and messaging strategies. You have pored over reports and test campaigns. Now it's time to have some fun! This final month enables you to reap the benefits of all your hard work and effort and add some bells and whistles to your program. This is the month where you get to explore ways in which you can make your campaign sizzle by employing some of the latest trends and tactics.

Chapter Contents

Week 1: Using Email as a Feedback Tool

So far, you have been focusing on creating the most strategic and effective email campaigns. The design of your message template, deliverability testing, and reporting and analytics have been your main concerns. But now that your first few email messages are behind you, it is time to have some fun.

In addition to eliciting responses and purchases, email also works very well in a myriad of other areas. For example, you can use it to garner feedback about your company's services or products. In this coming week, you'll learn about five great ways you can use your email campaigns to help solicit active feedback and content:

Monday: Leveraging email surveys

Tuesday: Designing an email survey

Wednesday: Polls in emails

Thursday: Email focus groups

Friday: Email-driven testimonials

Monday: Leveraging Email Surveys

How would you rate this book so far? This is a question you can assume you will be asked at some point in time. In fact, our professional lives are full of surveys of different types. You are asked to rate your performance and the performance of those who work for you annually; you are asked your thoughts on products and services you buy and use; you are asked about your opinions on the economy; and you are even asked how well you think your insurance company has handled your recent claim. Yes, surveys are one of those critical elements businesses use to determine how well a product is being perceived.

 Write This Down: A Google search indicates that more than 167 million surveys were conducted in 2007.

Surveys can be expensive, though. Acquiring enough data to make your survey efforts statistically significant is key. Not only does your survey data have to reflect your target or user audience appropriately, but it also needs to reflect data from an adequate number of members from each of your various target segments. Because of the high number of survey programs in effect, adequate response rates for these programs can be challenging to garner. In fact, a good rule of thumb is that for every four hours after a transaction has happened, the chance of getting someone to complete a survey is reduced by 40 percent.

The two main barriers to generating large volumes of survey feedback—time and money—can be drastically reduced or even eliminated by leveraging email as a means to solicit feedback. A survey can be sent through email in real time, possibly in response to some triggering event or action.

The process of creating a survey to be offered through an email is fairly similar to that of creating any survey, whether it is presented on a website or through any other venue. Some companies choose to embed their entire surveys within the email. This works well with email clients that allow forms to be completed within the client (see Chapter 6 for a list of these clients). Other companies simply refer readers to a link to complete the survey. The choice you make should be based on the responsiveness of your current email database. In either situation, you should keep in mind a number of best practices when designing an email survey, covered in the next section.

Tuesday: Designing an Email Survey

For today's hour, we'll describe the strategy for designing an email survey as a series of steps:

1. Determine the end objective of the survey, and don't go data crazy. Many people think about all the questions they would love to have answers to. They forget that the person filling out the survey is going to expect to hear how your company will change or respond to concerns in reference to any question that is asked. If you do not have the time or resources to change the way in which you do business, do not ask your customer or prospect for feedback. It's as simple as that.

2. Target your survey audience. You can select a demographic segment of your database (for example, men 25 to 40) or select actions or lack of (for example, purchased a product or canceled a reservation). Choosing whom you are targeting will be important. Answers to survey questions may change dramatically based on the audience you target. You can't afford to have results that lead to larger company misperceptions.

3. Create your questions. VerticalResponse, an email marketing and survey company, created a series of survey best practices for creating surveys. Its best practices for the type of questions you should create are summarized in the "Survey Best Practices" sidebar.

4. Determine whether you need an offer to drive higher response to your survey. In some cases, offers like those illustrated in Figures 8.1 and 8.2 can increase response rates.

Figure 8.1 FlowerStore.com used this offer to boost the response to its survey.

Figure 8.2 BusinessWeek used this offer to boost the response to its survey.

Survey Best Practices (Source: VerticalResponse)

The clarity and conciseness of your questions, the questionnaire length, the number of items per page, and the way you group your questions can all contribute to a better experience for the respondent. This will lead to a higher completion rate and increase the likelihood that people will choose to take your future surveys.

- **Make sure each question is clear and concise.** Keep your questions as short as possible without making them so short that they're hard to understand. If each question on a page begins with the same phrase, consider using that phrase as the beginning text on the page so that it doesn't have to be repeated as part of each question. Introductory text that asks, "How likely is it that…" can be followed by questions like, "Would you use our service again?" or "Would you recommend us to a friend?"

  There should be no ambiguity about what a question means. If a question is complex in some way, you should provide a brief explanation or provide some clarifying examples within the question itself (in parentheses). Be sure to use terms that will be familiar to your respondent, and avoid technical jargon.

- **Be careful with acronyms.** Don't use acronyms without an explanation of what the acronym means. If you use an acronym several times, spell it out the first time and place the acronym in parentheses. If we were creating a survey that asked respondents several questions about their ISPs, we'd want to write the first question as "Which Internet service provider (ISP) do you currently use?" We could then follow up with questions like, "Are you happy with your ISP?"

- **Avoid stating questions in the negative.** It can be confusing if a phrase is negative and the respondent has to say "yes" in order to confirm that negative statement.

- **Make sure your questions and answers are mutually exclusive.** If you have different categories of content, make sure they are distinct from one another. This can also refer to answers that use numerical ranges. For example, a question that asks the age of your respondent should not have overlapping answers like 18–24, 24–30, 30–38, and 38–45. The 24-, 40-, and 38-year-olds wouldn't know which group to choose. The answers should instead be written as 18–24, 25–30, 31–38, 39–45, and so on.

- **Be sure not to ask leading questions that suggest a certain answer to your respondents.** An example of this would be to state a conclusion in the question and then ask for feedback ("We just redesigned our website to become a leading destination…"). If you present a list of options that allows the respondent to select one or more, be sure the most common or important items do not appear at the top of that list. A possible way to group such options without bias would be to list them alphabetically.

It's important you feel confident the respondents will understand your questions and be able to give you their honest answers. If you are not sure that all respondents will be able to answer each question, be sure to include "N/A" or "Don't Know" as options. If you ask sensitive questions like age or income range, offer "Prefer Not to State" as an option.

5. Guide your respondents through the survey. Some of the best surveys convey a sense of brevity. By showing people that they are on page "3 of 5" or have "3 more questions left," your respondents will feel like they are making progress and will be more apt to complete your entire survey. Some of the best emailers even choose to start the survey inside the email and then give readers a button to click to continue to the remainder of the survey on a landing page or website.

6. Always send an email immediately after someone completes a survey, thanking them for their involvement and letting them know what the next steps, if any, will be. Even if your survey is captured on the website or is completed on a website, don't rely on the "thank you" page to make your participant feel satisfied with their experience. They just took time out of their day to share their thoughts with you. The least you can do is send them an email to thank them for their support.

Wednesday: Polls in Emails

In some cases, you want to solicit feedback from your client or prospect base, but you don't have enough time, don't have enough resources, or don't have a large enough database to justify an email survey. In this situation, you may want to simply take a poll in an email. Polls are also a really good way to increase click-throughs, readership, and general interaction.

Email polls do not need to be longer than one question. For example, "Did you find this article helpful?" Companies have seen up to a 36 percent increase in long-term readership when poll questions were introduced one week, with the answer to that poll included in the next week's email. The ongoing sharing of information provides a compelling reason for people to keep reading your emails.

You can use a few different tactics to create your email polls.

Using a mailto Link for Active Polling

Although many ESPs include polling tools, some do not, so we're covering mailto for anyone who needs to use it. Using mailto links is the most basic tactic to create a poll. It is very manual and should not be used when a large number of responses is expected.

You can implement the mailto link in two ways. You can use a pre-filled subject line for each choice of the answer, or you can use a different mailto email address for each different response. In both situations, you ask the reader to click the link that best corresponds with their answer. For example: "Have you ever tried this type of poll before?"

In the pre-filled subject line example, the link response would look like this:

```
Yes, I have tried this type of poll before: mailto: email@marketing.
com?subject=Yes%20Poll

No, I have not tried this type of poll before: mailto: email@marketing.
com?subject=No%20Poll
```

For the responses to different emails, the links would look like this:

```
Yes, I have tried this type of poll before: mailto: yesemail@marketing.com
No, I have not tried this type of poll before: mailto: noemail@marketing.com
```

Using an HTML Link in the Email

Many companies will find some use for the first tactic but quickly run out of the resources to manage this type of effort. If you are using HTML in your email campaigns and want to move to the next level of sophistication without employing a special survey tool or service, you can simply create links and track the clicks for each of the link answers.

The only downside of this effort is that there is one additional requirement. With the mailto option, the participant clicks a link that launches their email browser. There is nothing you need to do regarding the poll. With a link, however, people will need a place to land after they click. If you are going to employ this method to implement your polls, you will need to create a simple landing page that says "thank you" or refers people to your email.

Voting Using a Form

This is the type of poll that most large email marketers employ. Many ESPs include basic polling tools inside their email software. In Chapter 6, you'll find a table showing which email clients will render forms and which will make them operable.

This is an example of a form question: "How often do you poll your readers?" The options for answering might look like the following:

Whichever tactic you choose to employ, including polls can help improve the lifetime value of a customer as well as short-term results.

Thursday: Email Focus Groups

Once you master basic polls and surveys for email, you are ready to maximize responsiveness and impact by reaching out to a broader segment of your audience by creating an email focus group.

Email-based focus groups typically run outside your current email program and reach out to a representative sample of your customer set. In most cases, email focus groups are used to keep a pulse on your customer base's feelings about a variety of elements including the economy, your company's products or services, and even future product performance potential.

There are many different designs of an effective email focus group. This book does not explore which type of focus group is the most effective for your company to use. That is up to you. Instead, we will outline two of the most popular options you can take advantage of.

Net Promoter Score

There is a good bit of buzz around a metric called the *net promoter score*. This score relies on answering one simple question: "Would you recommend us to a friend or colleague?" This question allows companies to track promoters and detractors and produces a clear measure of an organization's performance through its customers' eyes.

With a net promoter score approach, this first question is asked via email and then a series of questions are asked, enabling the respondent to provide additional insights as to why they answered the way they did.

Email Discussion Group

Another type of email focus group that is very popular enables participants to discuss general topics of interest in an email-driven discussion forum. In this scenario, a question is posed to a group of participants, and an open dialogue ensues. In Chapter 4, we included an example of how some members of these types of groups have become very clever in the way they use subject lines to ensure that emails are read with various levels of urgency.

Friday: Email-Driven Testimonials

In addition to surveys, another way to garner ongoing feedback and communication is to include a request for email-driven testimonials. In this scenario, a product or service is displayed in the email, and instructions on how to leave a comment or testimonial about the product are included.

Amazon does this very well (and frequently) in the email presented in Figure 8.3.

In this example, you can see that once a purchase is made, feedback is requested. One of the biggest benefits of placing this type of request in an email is that the recipient can file away the email in a folder until they are ready to actually place the review of the product. In certain circumstances, some companies will even send testimonial reminders to ensure that maximum feedback is received.

Figure 8.3 Amazon uses this email to drive testimonials.

The key to making these types of emails successful is to include the request in the subject line. A subject line like "Thank you for your purchase; please provide us a review" ensures that the recipient knows this is not just a "thank you" email and that an action is required.

One reason this type of email is so frequently used by marketers is that it establishes a database of user-generated feedback. This feedback is also very highly regarded in the eyes of your consumer. Two recent Jupiter Research statistics demonstrate this impact:

• Twenty percent of online buyers post on average nine product reviews a year.

• Seventy-seven percent of the online population finds reviews more useful than email.

Yes, feedback is very good to solicit. And, if done right, it can even be turned into a large database of customer-generated content that can grow from feedback and ratings into its own email program.

Customer-Driven Content

Now it's time to really turn up the fun. You've done a poll, you've included a survey, and you have even pulled together an email focus group along with reviews and testimonials. Now what? Now, it's time to take all the highly trusted research and feedback you have and make it do the hard work for you.

It is fairly simple to leverage customer content in a way that enables the automated creation of a stand-alone email program or campaign. The very best example we have of this comes from a recent search we did for information on a travel destination in Spain. We were asked to visit Spain on business and were told we would have a day or so free. The local employees of the company we were visiting suggested going to the Canary Islands. Not knowing anything about these islands, we decided to do a Google search on the area.

The Google search took us to the TripAdvisor website (`www.tripadvisor.com`). We landed on a page about the Canary Islands (not the home page). This page was a perfect picture of best practices. As you can see in Figure 8.4, the page asked us to opt into email information about these locations. We did. In addition to the email opt-in pop-up page, we also noticed the ability to add photos, videos, and even testimonials or content about the locations that were listed within the Canary Islands. We knew that this was going to be a very informational visit from an email marketing standpoint.

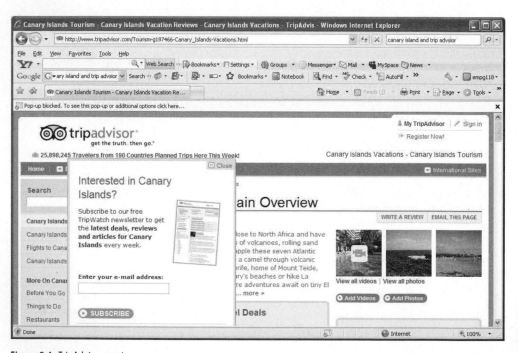

Figure 8.4 TripAdvisor opt-in

We received the standard "thank you" email, which we liked quite a bit. But better than that, two days later we received an email about the Canary Islands that was completely consumer-generated. You can see that email in Figure 8.5.

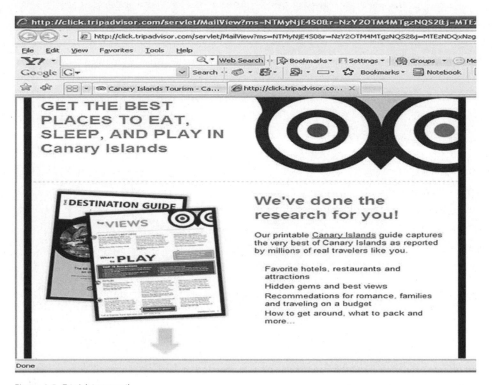

Figure 8.5 TripAdvisor email

This email was simple and included one link to download the content. The impressive part comes with the eight-page consumer-generated content document (done on demand) that had feedback about every aspect of this trip in which we could be interested.

We were so impressed that we are posting the full eight pages at www.sybex.com for you to review; Figure 8.6 shows the first page. If your email marketing program can act this seamlessly, you will know you have made it to the level of email marketing expert. Take a look at this document, and your mind will end the week thinking all about ways you can creatively include customer-generated feedback to your program.

Figure 8.6 First page of the Canary Islands Guide generated in response to our interests

Week 2: Creating Video- and Audio-Enabled Emails

Surveys and polls help engage your email recipients in a type of dialogue that will help boost lifetime value and provide insights. That said, continuously returning to the same person time and time again to solicit feedback can begin to feel very one-sided. Be sure to consider the frequency with which you are sending surveys and polls. This is not to suggest that the frequency in which you ask for feedback needs to be reduced. Instead, you may want to consider timing your requests for feedback and information with emails that carry what is often called *unanticipated rewards*.

Unanticipated rewards outside the world of email marketing can be defined as any special offer or gift that a person who does business with your company receives. Sometimes these rewards are coupons, sometimes they're small gifts or free trials, and sometimes they can be even better. In the world of email, though, it is quite challenging to deliver unanticipated rewards that are seen as having tangible results. These rewards must live inside the emails themselves.

Creative email marketers, however, have found ways to increase the level of surprise and delight they include in their emails by enabling the use of audio and video inside their messages. Creating and sending this type of content via email can surprise, delight, and entertain your customer or prospect in many ways.

Travel companies tend to use video or audio well inside large campaigns. In their case, they use the videos to educate people about what to expect on their trip. Retailers use video to demonstrate a product line or offering. Even pharmaceutical companies have started using video and audio emails as part of a larger campaign to drive home a consistent brand message and impact throughout every touch point.

If your company is large enough to build multifaceted campaigns, then video or audio email could be the one element you need to bond all the other elements together.

This week we will explore when and how to successfully use video and audio inside your emails. We must start this week with a word of caution. Audio and video emails are either highly successful or highly annoying. If you are not 100 percent sure that using one of these tactics is appropriate for your audience, you could be tempting the email gods. So, as you read this section, consider each element you read carefully, and apply it with caution. Follow the rules and do it the right way, and you can increase results by more than 700 percent. Ready to explore the pros and cons of video and audio usage inside your emails? Here we go.

Monday: Deciding whether using audio or video is right for your emails
Tuesday: Building the five layered emails
Wednesday: Making your video email viral
Thursday: Making your video email an integrated part of a larger campaign
Friday: Allowing your reader to create their own video email

Monday: Deciding Whether Using Audio or Video Is Right for Your Emails

The first step in successfully implementing audio and video in your emails is deciding whether it is right for your audience. Knowing when to use video and audio is almost as important as knowing how to build the message.

To help you make your decision with ease, we have included this questionnaire to use as a reference.

Should I use audio or video in my emails?

Question	Yes or No
1) Can you communicate your key message points in 20 seconds or less?	
2) Will audio or video help explain your offering better than photos with text?	
3) Does your product/service thrive from referrals (from colleagues/businesses)?	
4) Will the recipients of your emails be connected with broadband?	
5) Will the recipients of your emails have sound cards on their computers?	
6) Will the recipients of your emails have access to the Internet?	
7) Do you have access to preshot content?	

If you answer "yes" to at least five of these questions, then you have a pretty good reason to explore using audio or video in your emails. Whatever you do, don't use these emails as a gimmick to make an impulse sale or to attempt to drive a significant volume of referrals. Instead, use them to inform, educate, introduce, or even train readers on new talking points and content.

Whether you are using email for B2C or B2B messages, the justification for active content is the same. If it will significantly increase the levels of response to your messages, it should be done.

Tuesday: Building the Five Layered Emails

Once you have decided to move forward with audio or video in your emails, you can get ready to create those elements. To ensure that your message will be received and viewed in the best manner possible, you (and your HTML developer) will need to create five layers of interactive content within your email message:

- A flat HTML version

- A version with animated GIFs but no sound

- A version with animated GIFs and sound

- A Flash or video version without sound

- A Flash or video version with sound

Today, the entire focus is on how to create those five layers.

Layer 1: The Flat HTML Version

The assumption with this layer is that no matter how good you are at designing a rich-media email, someone somewhere on some email client will not be able to see it. For those viewers, it is important to have a basic email design that will still get across all the essential points of your message.

Layer 2: The Animated GIF Version (with No Sound)

The simplest form of visual animation is a timed series of GIF images, often "thumbnail" size, that create the appearance of, say, a person dancing or a globe revolving. (We're sure you can think of other examples you've seen, because the effect can be really eye-catching.)

Many businesses provide employees with PCs or laptops without sound cards. If you work in a cubicle environment, you might already know that it is difficult to concentrate when your cubicle neighbor is blasting music next door. Imagine how annoying it would be if this happened when someone simply opened an email. For this reason, you should anticipate that some viewers will see your animated email move but never hear the sound; for these viewers, you need to make sure that no essential information is found only in the audio. To determine whether a computer has a sound card at all, you can include some basic code in the HTML for the email. This version will play if there is no alternative.

Layer 3: The Animated GIF Version with Sound

For PCs with sound, you can create a version of your animated email that adds a voice to your message. A little-known fact about Hotmail users is that they can accept sound while most other animation and noise is filtered out. If you have a high number of Hotmail users on your email list, sound emails may be something you want to test.

Layer 4: The Flash or Video Email (with No Sound)

Designing an email that truly enables an animated feel often requires the use of Flash and/or video. In these cases, some email clients allow the animation through but block the audio code. As with the emails designed with no sound, it is always best to design a Flash version that supports frames, with text taking the place of audio so that the reader can get the full experience.

Layer 5: The Flash or Video Email with Sound

If you are lucky, your recipient's email client will support both Flash or video animation and audio. This means you are ready to roll! As you design your email for the most optimal experience, here are a few tips to keep in mind:

- Always allow your reader to start the animation. If not, your reader may miss the first ten seconds of your email message and not understand the point.

- Never send an email video or flash that is longer than 30 seconds. People don't have that much time to watch videos. Keep it short and simple.

- Make sure you have an ending frame. All too many times we have seen the best videos end on a black screen. No URL, no call to action—just black. Don't let your emails fall into the black hole; make sure you end with a clear action message.

Following all these design guidelines will help you make sure you have a technically effective email. Testing these five layers across the email deliverability and rendering platforms is key. Once you have a solid design and message, you are ready to move on to the next effort, making your emails viral.

Wednesday: Making Your Video Email Viral

If you like YouTube, you will love video emails. Unlike YouTube content, video emails are typically advertisements that are built in a way that will drive business for a company. Many times these videos are educational. Sometimes they are funny. Rarely do they encourage someone to forward the email along to a co-worker or friend. Internet content that is compelling enough to get forwarded along is described as spreading "virally."

Those of us who have been in email marketing for a long time can tell you that video email made a hugely successful debut in early 2000. Broadband penetration was not high enough to enable massive consumer adoption, but the novelty and interest levels were there. These first video-enabled emails often got high pass-along rates. They were new and exciting to us all. But as time went on, the interest in video email started to wane because of the delivery challenges we've outlined. In fact, in a recent conversation with Keith McCracken, chairman of video email company Vismail America, he reflected on the way video email first died and is now coming back to life with a vengeance:

> *"Some advertisers have all but written off email as a video delivery mechanism because mass streaming in the past has caused more problems than opportunities. And yet, because email is so ubiquitous and so popular in our society, it really should be the greatest of advertising tools on the Web.*

> *"Combine this thought with the 'elephant in the room,' with the elephant being the precipitous decline of TV audiences.... Advertisers must simply go elsewhere to deliver their [video] ads to consumers, and right now, all they can buy are pre-rolls, mid-rolls, and post-rolls on video sites presupposing that consumers will be any more disposed towards such interruptions on the Web than they are now on their TV sets.*

> *"The answer is a version of ads on demand via email. Consumers do enjoy some ads, but they need to be relevant, amusing, and useful. Email opt-in lists of consumers who've already said to advertisers, "Send me information about your brand," will not only watch the video ads but welcome video ads sent by email."*

But how do you take this newfound interest and make it viral? Here are some suggestions for making sure you can help your email live longer:

- **Test funny.** We know this sounds crazy, but it just could work. In fact, Centrum did this a while back when it created a video commercial and posted it on YouTube. You can watch it at `www.youtube.com/watch?v=wjPfJ8LHOB4`; Figure 8.7 shows one of the milder frames.

Figure 8.7 Centrum Silver video

This video is pretty "off brand" for standard Centrum ads, but it was well received by the video email crowd. People who received this email were so surprised with the content that it was forwarded like crazy.

- **Ask your viewers to forward the video.** Earlier we spoke about including instructions on the final frame for the video. This space can also be used to include a request to send it to a friend. In some cases, these requests can even include a special offer or incentive.

- **Try a serial set of videos.** There is nothing better for forwarding email than seeing a set of video emails that tells a story over time. In Figure 8.8, Unilever's I Can't Believe It's Not Butter brand created a series of videos outlining a murder mystery in the refrigerator (see the whole series at `www.free-spraychel.com/freespraychel/default.asp`). The company later made it into a sweepstakes. Emails were sent with a video box showing one of the frames in it and driving you to the landing site. Videos like this typically become very viral.

Figure 8.8 A webisode viral video

Creating a video that will become viral is a challenge. Many factors will play into its success (or lack of success), some of which you simply don't have control over. Viral videos require a good bit of testing and learning to see what resonates with your brand best.

Thursday: Making Your Video Email an Integrated Part of a Larger Campaign

Whether or not you are able to design a video email that goes viral, sticking to the best practices covered earlier will be key. Your email message, including its enclosed video, Flash, and/or audio, must be flawless, especially if it is going to be included as part of a larger initiative.

IBM conducted a fantastic campaign that leveraged video email, online search tools, its own website, and the websites of many other properties when it launched a program called Scavenger Hunt.

In the Scavenger Hunt campaign, targeted viewers were shown a video email clip, supposedly recorded by IBM's two spokespeople at the time, Ned and Gil. Ned and Gil were making the video email from their cell phone as they were stuck in a server room and wanted you, the viewer, to go to the website, get the clues, and help them escape.

This integrated campaign included all the best practices for video and audio email you could think of. It offered the five layers of messaging, there were three video emails sent to keep interest, and the landing destinations encouraged people to share the videos with others.

This campaign was a best practices success. IBM even saw an unexpected number of people blogging about how to solve the mystery and generating additional social buzz.

Friday: Allowing Your Reader to Create Their Own Video Email

If you are thinking about using video or audio email, just as with general email content, testimonials work very well. They increase the quality of the message and boost the "forwardability" of the message as well. Building a platform and process to capture user-generated video email can be one way to achieve lifelike testimonials.

You can access user-generated video content in a few ways. You can ask someone to post it on YouTube, or you can store or send it via other social networks. Some companies even build unique applications to drive and store user-generated content.

The volume of user-generated video content is growing like crazy. AccuStream iMedia Research released a report in January 2008 about online video usage for 2007 and its predictions for 2008. The market grew by an estimated 70 percent in 2007, up from a total 13.2 billion views generated in 2006. **It predicts an increase of about 50 percent in 2008 to a total number of video views of 34 billion.**

This prediction is startlingly large. And although it does not identify how much of the video content is being recommended using email, or being shared using email as the main channel for communication, one thing is certain: User-generated video content can drive revenue and results.

According to a recent McKinsey & Company study, more than 90 percent of consumers regard word of mouth as the best source of information about products and services. Everyday brand evangelism works. Happy customers constitute a powerful army of word-of-mouth advocates. And the opt-in friends of those satisfied customers are, in the David Mamet vernacular, "the Glengarry leads."

So, how do you get there? How do you make online word-of-mouth programs happen and figure out whether they're a viable part of your marketing mix? If you are looking to capture, leverage, or help design user-generated content, there are a few key techniques that our friends at Mass Transit use to assist their clients when developing successful viral campaigns that leverage user-generated content:

- **Get behind a good product or offer.** Give potential brand advocates something to talk about. A great product gets attention; so does a super-cool prize. This doesn't mean you will always have a choice what you market, but it doesn't mean you should strongly recommend against a viral email if the product or offer is not strong.

- **Make it easy.** The most powerful part of a successful email campaign is the four-word link at the top and/or bottom of the page: Forward to a Friend. Every email should have one. The form should be simple, intuitive, and honest, and the time required to fill it out should be miniscule compared to the reward to you and your friend.

- **Be transparent.** Marketers need to be clear about benefits, prizes, and privacy. Brand advocates need to be transparent about their relationship to the marketer—who they are, and why they think people they send this message to should sign up, enter the contest, or buy the gizmo. As a marketer, you should consider helping define these benefits on landing pages and in emails.

- **Plan your next move.** Have a strategy for sending a welcome email to new opt-ins, running contiguous promotions, eliciting feedback from new demographics, and executing future word-of-mouth initiatives.

- **Measure.** Although you cannot send emails to a recipient who receives a tell-a-friend message from your site, you can count how many of such messages were sent. You can also ask those recipients to opt into future emails so you can determine the growth of your opt-in database. You can then benchmark and compare this number to, say, your SEM universe or direct marketing campaign. One ROI equation might look like this:

  Cost of email design and transmission + cost of incentive/number of new opt-ins = cost per buzz-generated subscriber (CPB, if our acronym sticks)

Week 3: Creating Mobile Email

Bells and whistles in email can generate a tremendous amount of fun. They allow you to be creative and think outside the box. This week, we challenge you to think way outside the box. In fact, think outside the inbox of emails. Recent research and trending reports indicate that an increasingly high number of emails are being read in a mobile environment. Whether someone is reading the emails on a BlackBerry, iPhone, Treo, or other type of device, the message is not being seen with the same level of integrity or design that was originally intended. This week's focus is on leveraging your email campaign for those readers who are seeing your message on a mobile device. Whether it is because of travel or simply life, this week should enable you to refocus.

Monday: Why your email needs to be mobile

Tuesday: The mobile email creative

Wednesday: How many readers in your database are reading "on the run"?

Thursday: Defining your mobile email preference center

Friday: Making Your Current Email Strategy Work in a Mobile World

Monday: Why Your Email Needs to be Mobile

In 2007, ExactTarget released a white paper that spoke to many of the latest demographic trends and statistics in mobile email marketing.

Young adults, they found, are the primary users of mobile devices. Of the 4,202 mobile phone users ExactTarget surveyed, 7 percent identified themselves as mobile email users, and another 6 percent said they planned to purchase a new mobile device with email capabilities within the next six months.

The survey also found that "mobile users tend to be 18–44, employed full-time or self-employed, affluent, and highly educated." They also tend to read mobile email with divided attention. Remember, these people are on the go. Of mobile email users identified in the survey, the following is true:

- Seventy-five percent were ages 18–44.
- Sixty-two percent were working professionals (either employed or self-employed).
- Eighty percent access their mobile email at home.
- Forty-six percent check mobile email at dinner.
- Thirty-nine percent admit to checking email while driving their cars.

Users are also a wealthier demographic—19 percent of mobile phone users with an annual household income of more than $100,000 regularly use their mobile devices to access email. For households earning $200,000-plus, that number doubles to 38 percent.

We know these numbers are changing fast. ExactTarget's research was conducted prior to the release of the first-generation iPhone, which accelerated the adoption of mobile email. According to Gartner, worldwide smartphone sales increased 29 percent in the first quarter of 2008 over the first quarter of 2007. In North America, the increase was 106 percent. As mobile devices grow simultaneously more sophisticated and less expensive, adoption will continue to grow.

Another key point is that people use mobile email differently. Primarily, it's to stay on top of matters that users deem urgent. According to Morgan Stewart, director of research and strategy for ExactTarget, the key advantage of mobile email is simple—it's mobile. It frees people up from their desks, and it allows them to feel productive during downtime. Poor rendering, small screen resolution, hard-to-use keyboards, and limitations when working with attachments all make mobile less desirable than desktops or laptops for accessing email. The majority of people access the same email accounts from both their mobile devices and through a computer at home or work, but some do maintain a "mobile-only" email address provided through their mobile carrier for personal communication.

To date, fierce competition between mobile phone manufacturers in North America has stymied the development of mobile email standards. Apple, BlackBerry,

Microsoft Windows Mobile, and Palm offer different mobile email experiences and show few signs of standardizing. Outside North America, Symbian is the dominant operating system followed by Linux. "This market is a moving target because everyone is trying to beat everyone else in terms of putting out the next cool device," Stewart says. "Email is a key selling point for many of these phones, especially in North America. We are seeing the mobile email experience look more and more like the PC experience, so, in time, many of the rendering issues will resolve themselves. Until then, I recommend marketers incorporate text alternatives as the lowest common denominator."

Tuesday: The Mobile Email Creative

Creating email for a mobile device is a challenge. Without standard viewing-window sizes or a consistent way to determine which device your message is being rendered on at the time it is read, you need to be very careful about each creative decision you make, from the subject line down to the HTML code.

To ensure that your messages are as readable as possible, we recommend considering these four points:

- **Always design two versions of your email, and send messages as multipart/ MIME.** This lets the email client determine which version to show. Ideally, the PC client will display the HTML version in its intended beautiful layout, and mobile clients with limited functionality will display the text version. But remember, this is not always the case. Design your HTML version with links at the top that provide both HTML and text alternatives. (See the Sam's Club example in Figure 8.9, in the next section.) This way, if the email does not render appropriately, the user has options to improve their experience. For more specific creative hints, refer to Chapter 5.

- **Use SMS length (160 characters or less) for urgent messages.** When sending time-sensitive messages or alerts, consider using short message formats to allow recipients to react to the message quickly. In today's world, where Twitter is becoming more popular, messages that the user can read in the window of a BlackBerry without needing to scroll down are key. Preliminary studies conducted by the authors indicate that 72 percent of those who read emails do not scroll down if they think the message is completed when the content is above the fold. This means you need to keep your message to 100 total characters, or 20–25 words.

- **Type URLs; do not try to code them as hyperlinks.** Symbian or BlackBerry devices do not support coding that makes your links appear "friendly." Instead of a simple "click here," you need to type the entire link, as in "http://www.abc.com."

- **Use action copy.** If your reader opens their email on a mobile device, it will show as opened or read on their desktop email system. Using action-oriented copy in your text can help ensure they do not skip over the message when back at the desktop.

Five Common Mobile Email Scenarios

The various mobile platforms all display email differently. Here's how ExactTarget and Pivotal Veracity summarized the differences.

Apple iPhone

The iPhone has the richest email experience and displays the HTML part of MIME messages. Images are on by default, and links are enabled.

BlackBerry

Some versions show text only, while others show text contained in the HTML part of MIME messages. No images are displayed. The BlackBerry displays links and image URLs.

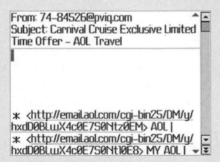

Continues

Five Common Mobile Email Scenarios *(Continued)*

Palm/VersaMail

These devices display the HTML part of MIME messages but do not support images.

Symbian

These devices display text contained in the HTML part of MIME messages. Only full links are clickable (for example, "`http://www.abc.com`").

Windows Mobile 6/Outlook

HTML, links, and images are supported. The default is for images to be turned off.

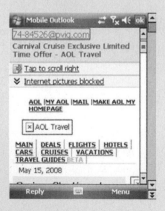

Source: ExactTarget and Pivotal Veracity, 2008

Wednesday: How Many Readers in Your Database Are Reading "on the Run"?

Whenever we speak about mobile marketing to email marketers, we always get weird looks at first. Many marketers think about their database and company product/service offering and assume their readers are not reading anywhere other than on their home or work computer. The use of mobile devices to read email has increased 400 percent within the last year, and there is no end in sight. This means that even if you are selling a product or service that is typically going to be seen by someone who is homebound, you can't be sure.

For this reason, when considering mobile marketing techniques, we recommend you conduct this simple test:

1. Add a line on the top of your email instructing readers to "click" to see a mobile version or a web version of the email, as shown in Figure 8.9.

Figure 8.9 Sam's Club and mobile email

Before moving on to step 2, make sure you actually have an email creative designed for readability on a handheld device. The two common screen sizes for BlackBerry models are 320×240 pixels for the newer versions (8700/8800 series and 8300/the Curve) and 240×260 pixels for 8100 (also called the Pearl) and 7100 series. Mobile phone screens tend to be even smaller. You can use a BlackBerry simulator to check your design. Two of the more popular simulators are available here: `http://na.blackberry.com/eng/developers/downloads/simultors.jsp`

2. Check your reports. You will want to look for two different types of clicks in your email reports.

The first thing to look for is the number of people who clicked the top link. This will enable you to identify the percentage of your recipients who are viewing your email on a handheld device. This will provide you with the benchmark you need to know how seriously you should consider designing a separate strategy for this group.

The second thing to look for is the number of clicks on links that reside on the mobile version of your message. This number will be fairly small but will enable you to get an idea whether your emails are simply being read in a mobile environment or whether they are also being acted on there.

Once you have these two data elements, you are ready to take your email strategy and results to the next level through the design of a mobile preference center.

Thursday: Defining Your Mobile Email Preference Center

You can consider adjusting your current customer preference center in a number of ways to allow for high-frequency mobile email reading.

The first way is to ask subscribers whether they want to begin reading your emails on a mobile device, with an input field for their mobile phone number or an indicator of their mobile reading device. Although this technique is probably the simplest to employ on the front end, it requires a tremendous amount of work and commitment on the back end. We do not recommend you start with this strategy unless your company is already fairly seasoned in mobile messaging strategies in general and has a few programs already set up. Reading an email on a mobile device and opting in to receive mobile marketing messages are two different decisions. Each has a different strategy, different goals, and different mannerisms used to drive response.

The second way is also fairly sophisticated but can really drive results to boost your bottom line. In this method, you set up a triggered email message to be sent once someone clicks the "view this email on a mobile device" link three times in a row. The three times is a good indicator that your reader is constantly on the go or at least reading your messages consistently in this manner. The automated email that is sent asks the reader whether they want to change their preferences to receive only the mobile versions of the message in the future (this would change your database from an HTML option to a text option). If the person says yes, they receive the mobile-enabled content from the start.

Many people who test this strategy take the time to include a link at the bottom of the text email that says, "Want the HTML version of this email back again? No problem; just click the link http://XXX.com, and your next email will be sent in HTML." In some cases, these companies also set up a second automated query that sends a stand-alone email asking the same thing if no links in the mobile version are clicked after three emails are sent.

Mobile-driven preference questions outside the standard "HTML or text?" are still very new to the world of email marketing, so there are no good examples to show you. However, this is a growing trend that will continue to make a huge dent in your ability to drive results. You will need to think about the creative- and preference-based aspects of this issue, and you may need to change your email marketing strategies to account for viewers reading emails while on the go.

If you are still not convinced, consider this. A recent study conducted by the Pew Internet & American Life Project indicated that more than 62 percent of people read their email on a mobile device. These people do not fall into one specific category of users. They are a racially and economically diverse segment of people whose main commonalities lie more within their love of the Internet than anything else. This means that regardless of the business you are in, or your target segment, you may need to revisit all aspects of your email program to ensure it is primed for mobile reading.

Friday: Making Your Current Email Strategy Work in a Mobile World

On Monday of this week we said, "If your reader opens their email on a mobile device, it may show as opened or read on their desktop email system." You may have skimmed right past this statement, but whether you decide to design your emails for mobile reading or not, it impacts the effectiveness of your basic email strategies. So, let's explore its implications further.

Think about your own email inbox and how simple it is to gloss over an email that appears to have already been read in lieu of those bolded and high importance flags. Your email could be at risk if it was read on a handheld device and your reader assumed they would get to it later. Unfortunately, if they were mobile, they were probably doing something else at the same time; therefore, the chances of them remembering to act on your email at a later time is less than 10 percent.

This phenomenon is not the end of the world for your campaign. It is a gift of insight that you should be excited to have. Now, you can take advantage of the new realities used in communication to test the following elements of your campaign strategy:

- **A/B test of subject lines.** Putting an action-oriented word first to allow handheld readers to understand the urgency (for example, "Click now for 20% off.")
- **A/B test of short copy versus long copy.** If you have ever wondered whether teasers linking to long content are more appealing than long copy that paints a full picture, now is the time to test it. Mobile reader research is weak in this area. We are unsure whether people appreciate short tidbits or have the time to scroll for the whole story so they can act now and don't need to save for later. You can determine this for your own readers fairly easily.
- **Mobile-supported landing pages.** Once you get out of the world of email and into the world of the mobile browser, detection capabilities are vastly improved,

and the user's experience can be significantly more positive. A number of detection systems exist that will be able to present your reader with an optimized landing experience. The challenge here is to make sure you have created the key elements to support the dynamic presentation of each of those landing pages.

- **Increased reminder emails.** Once, while one of us was at a meeting, a client was gushing over how proud they were to have increased their open rate to 40 percent. But that meant 60 percent of this audience was not engaged. Although engagement strategies are covered in other chapters of this book, the impact that mobile reading can have on engagement is big. Reading emails on the run generates email ADD. People read them and think they will remember to respond later, but they then get preoccupied with other facets of the day. Now is a good time to test sending stand-alone reminder emails that will enable you to engage your readers at various times or stages of purchase.

Now that you understand why awareness of the level of readers using mobile or handheld devices to read emails is important and you have access to a few key tips and strategies to make sure your design is on target, you are ready to roll. To wrap up the week, we wanted to prepare a consolidated checklist that you can employ with your future email efforts.

Your Mobile Email Success Checklist

Making sure your email campaigns will be successful regardless of where they are read or how they are read is contingent on the following elements. Please make sure you've done all of the following to organize your efforts:

- Determine how your emails currently look on BlackBerry devices and other handheld devices by using one of the rendering tools.
- Get a benchmark of how many people (or what percentage of your database) are actually reading your emails using a handheld device in one of two ways:
  - By adding a link asking people to click it to see a mobile-readable version
  - By tracking the links in the text version to see who is clicking where
- Assess your current subject line strategy, and make sure it is optimized for mobile reading (short and to the point).
- Review your messaging strategy and test reminder emails for nonresponsive readers (to battle the "opened" status emails appearing in the inbox).

Now that you are ready to tackle the world of email being read on the run, it is time for the weekend, as well as a quick break. Next week's focus opens the doors to an even more exciting and trendy topic: social email.

Resources for Mobile Email Viewing

We asked frequent email blogger and expert Mark Brownlow for some tips on mobile email design. He referred us to a post he wrote in 2007 (`www.email-marketing-reports.com/iland/2007/07/mobile-email-whos-right.html`) listing a number of YouTube links that can help you with a realistic picture of how your email looks. You may find these both interesting and helpful:

Nokia 770

`www.youtube.com/watch?v=tb8LaRgLzNE`

Another Nokia 770

`www.youtube.com/watch?v=4P9tvl_DLmo`

Mobile Gmail on a cell phone

`www.youtube.com/watch?v=qTZE3yPA2AE`

iPhone (at Apple)

`www.apple.com/iphone/features/`

Samsung D600E

`www.youtube.com/watch?v=Do6SCnONjJE`

Motorola Q

`www.youtube.com/watch?v=BoE0YVcvJ8Q`

LG enV

`www.youtube.com/watch?v=fxRoD5T2PW8`

Misc cell phone

`www.youtube.com/watch?v=eKSLaScpvfA`

BlackBerry Pearl

`www.youtube.com/watch?v=WM2YFwoJrog`

BlackBerry 8700g

`www.youtube.com/watch?v=x1n7clhSzGM`

Week 4: Creating Social Email

The world of social networking is very supportive of email marketing. This last week, we will explore the way in which the worlds of new media collide, yet how email remains the backbone of all digital communications. Social email offers us the ability to drive a better and expansive response to our email programs by being able to enact some of the elements of viral email just discussed, without even trying.

Monday: When email is used on social networks

Tuesday: Response guidelines for social email

Wednesday: Reviewing results for social email

Thursday: Social messaging: thinking inside the box

Friday: Keeping the use of social email in "check"

Monday: When Email Is Used on Social Networks

When social networks first came into play, they took the buzz away from blogs and RSS feeds and quickly became the next "great" new invention intended to doom email to its death. People could send messages and posts to their friends and families without even opening the email inbox.

If you are not familiar with social networks, you should take a few minutes and check out at least some of the more popular networks: Facebook (`www.facebook.com`; you can even add us as your friends to get started); Gather (`www.gather.com`); and LinkedIn (`www.linkedin.com`).

For a while, the email industry was scared when social networks grew in popularity. This new convenient method of messaging, such as using SMS, was faster, easier, and reached more than one person. You didn't need to worry about delivery, open rates, click-throughs, or eyeballs. Social networks like LinkedIn, Facebook, MySpace, and even Friendster offered a new, fun, and trendy way to communicate, and it was adopted very quickly by the younger generation.

JupiterResearch provided this research on the usage trends for social networks in late 2007:

- Eighteen percent of the online population has used social sites (MySpace, Facebook, and so on) for personal communications instead of email.

- There's a massive skew in usage by age. Half of 18–24-year-olds use social networks instead of email. Thirty-two percent of 25–34-year-olds use social networks instead of email.

Yet, even with the growing adoption of social networks, email didn't die. Instead, it became more widely used. The reason social networks have been able to increase the success of email is fairly simple. Emails received from your social networking site are trusted emails. You as a subscriber have signed up for notifications when someone in your social network sends you an email. You receive emails on your social network only from your friends, so they are messages you want. When you receive these emails, often they get priority to be opened and read. And, in many cases, the email notification triggers you to go into your social network and respond, which generates more emails.

This means that if you can expand your concept of email marketing to include not just those messages you have sent to your opt-in house list but to your social network fans as well, you could drive even higher results for your email campaign.

If you still need a concrete example of how social networks can impact response and increase the use of email, you will enjoy the next case study.

Case Study: The Email Marketing Industry Uses Social Networks

There is a pretty large list of 100 email marketers who frequently talk on social networks. One of the big benefits of social networks is that they notify you when someone on your list is having a birthday coming up. For example, recently, it was one of our "friend's" birthdays one day, and a simple email was generated from the social networking group to the list saying, "Happy Birthday, XXX." This email generated over 62 emails in direct response to the original message, and over 20 more of new conversation. A few of these strings actually turned into business discussions, which generated new business for the group members.

Simply put, one note on someone's social networking profile generated a highly read and responded-to-conversation. This is an example of email at its best—trusted, responded to, and shared with others. And thanks to social networking, it was able to happen.

So now that you know the impact and potential benefits of social networks, you can learn how to take advantage of them for email campaigns. Tomorrow, you'll see how to design creative that will work for social networks yet do a good job in promoting your brand.

Tuesday: Response Guidelines for Social Email

Once your company has a social networking site, like the one in Figure 8.10, you can begin inviting members (this is done through an email) and then sending updates to them (again, through email) to keep them coming back to your site and getting engaged.

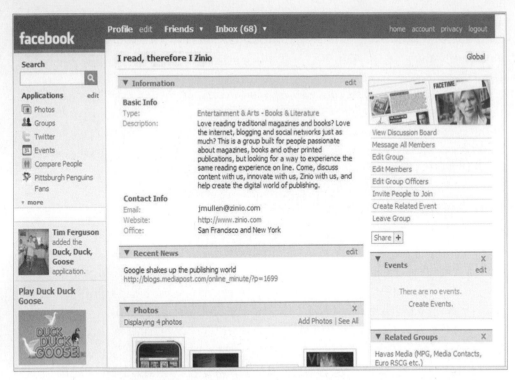

Figure 8.10 Sample Facebook group

There are a tremendous number of best practices and tips for building an effective social network. That subject deserves its own book and will not be covered here. What we will focus on are the top five ways you can make sure your social marketing email elicits the biggest response:

- **Do not design a message in HTML.** Most social network messages are sent from one person to another, so your email needs to look and feel just like a personal email. Designing a message in text is your most successful route.

- **Write your message in the first person.** Again, social networks originated so that people could connect with other *people* who have similar interests. People who are members of social networks wants to be informed and not marketed to. Your emails should contain a very personal feel and tone. Figure 8.11 shows an example.

This email is a marketing email. It is driving registrations for an event. Yet, it is written in a very personable manner. The tone is light. The message is informational, not pushy, but it does get a message across. And, since these people opted to join a group that holds events, this email gets a high read rate. Aaron Kahlow, founder of the Online Marketing Summit, often speaks about the positive impacts his social networking emails derive.

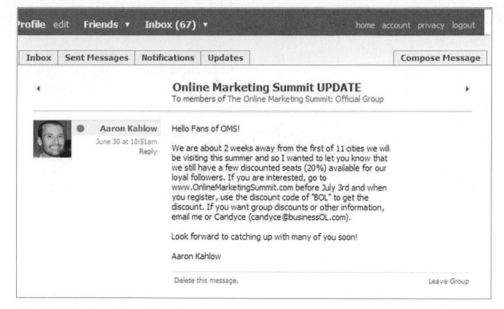

Figure 8.11 Sample social network email

- **Send people to the social networking site to get more information, not to your website.** One of the things you will find about your social network emails is that people will either want to reply to you directly or want to go to the network for more information. In most cases, they do not want to receive an email that sends them to a marketing landing page.

- **Be ready and available to respond to replies your social emails receive.** Once you send an email to your social networking list, you will receive personal replies. You or someone on your team will need to respond to these replies within 24 hours or lose credibility of your messaging.

- **Make sure you send an email to your social networking group every six weeks or so to maintain an ongoing dialogue.** Sending messages to your social networking group only when you have a promotion to talk about will turn your readers off. Sending emails that include informative tips and news on occasion (but not too frequently) will be seen as very helpful and will often initiate that viral effect that we spoke about earlier in this chapter.

Now that you have the basics of creating emails from social networks that can drive response, it is time to look at ways to evaluate whether your social messaging efforts are effective.

Wednesday: Reviewing Results for Social Email

When your social email goes out, there is no tracking. No delivery notices, no opens, no clicks. It's kind of like putting an ad on TV: either it works or it doesn't. For email marketers, this is a huge change in behavior. Email marketers can measure elements of success down to the impact of the number of characters in a subject line.

So, with social email, you need to rely on alternative forms of measurement. The great news is that with social email, there are so many different but interesting ways to measure responsiveness to your social email campaigns. Table 8.1 will help get you thinking in the right direction.

▶ **Table 8.1** Social Email Response Measurements

Email Measurements	Social Email Equivalent
Delivery rate	Group size
Click rate	Number of people who reply or post
Viral rate	Number of new people who join group within three days of your message being sent

Although the elements of this chart are not comprehensive ways to evaluate and measure the success of your social email, they should help get your mind thinking in new directions. After all, social email has a strong viral and branding impact that has a focus on results. For example, when someone gets an email from a person in their social network, one of the first things they do is check out that person's profile. Once they look at the profile, other networks they belong to suddenly become trusted recommendations of actions to take. This by itself can sometimes generate ancillary results.

"The good news is that deliverability for social networking messages is 100 percent," explains Gather CEO Tom Gerace. "On a closed messaging network, we can eliminate spam, which improves the user experience. They know that almost every message in their inbox was meant for them." Open rates for social network messaging can be as high as twice industry averages for the same reason.

The challenge for marketers is that members do not expect purely promotional messages in their inboxes on social networking sites. Therefore, highly designed, image-laden messages are out. Simple notes related to brand experiences on Gather with a handful of text links to shopping opportunities at the bottom are in. Consider Figure 8.12, an example from the Paralyzed Veterans of America.

Measurement systems are still evolving. "Candidly, we have yet to develop measurement tools for testing variations and quantifying success rates that are on par with email systems," Gerace explains. "Marketers will know how many messages were delivered (100%) and will be able to measure their click rates, but we do not yet allow easy rotation of messages, open rates, or link-by-link reporting. That will come in the future, but we just aren't there yet."

Figure 8.12 A paralyzed Veterans of America social email

As social network messaging grows, companies like Gather are working with email marketers to create more robust solutions for messaging. A/B testing and detailed analytics will be forthcoming. The good news is that because social sites know a lot about their members, this reporting will automatically be broken down by demographic and psychographic classifications. That will make social networks a great place to test and learn.

Thursday: Social Messaging: Thinking Inside the Box

Messaging systems on social networks are increasingly being used as a substitute for email. On social networking sites, users do not need to know friends' email addresses to contact them. Friends find friends through friends. Mailboxes are more easily kept free of spam and other unwanted mail. And messages are connected to profiles and photos that friends have shared, creating a more robust connection between people.

As people divide their attention between email and social messaging, marketers must reach customers in both locations. There are two challenges:

• Most social networks prohibit bulk mail from being sent on messaging systems.

• List building requires engagement.

"To reach gain access to these mailboxes, marketers must create experiences on social networks," explains Gerace. "Social networks like Gather allow the creation of groups or company pages by marketers (with the approval of the social network). The challenge for marketers is to create an experience that engages and involves members. Then their experience grows virally."

On Gather, for example, Amtrak has created a group (`http://allaboard.gather.com`) where train travelers can share experiences from the small towns and sights they encounter when riding the rails. Amtrak used a train photo and essay contest to engage the community and encourage the first few hundred members to join. About 4,600 people have now shared train experiences in the Amtrak group. Each time they do, their friends are notified, bringing them into the Amtrak experience. Some marketer-created Gather groups exceed 50,000 members and continue to grow, creating hundreds of thousands of notifications of group activity each week. Figure 8.13 shows an example.

Figure 8.13 Amtrak social network

To build an initial list, marketers must do the following:

- Create an experience that people want to join and explore together (product reviews, contests, recipe sharing, parenting tips, and health maintenance, for example).

- Make it cascade by integrating it into the social platform where you are building.

- Invite your email lists to it. Your customers are your best advocates, and when they join, they will invite their friends.

- Use onsite messaging systems to announce new group experiences to people who have joined, bringing them back to the experience and encouraging them to do things that cascade.

Once your group has been created, you have the ability to send messages to that group using the social network's messaging platform. You can use messaging to announce new experiences, alert members to special shopping opportunities, or call out some of the great things that members are doing in the group. These messages, while basic in format, can have embedded links to your site encouraging shopping or exploration.

Friday: Keeping the Use of Social Email in "Check"

As you can see, social networking is changing the way we communicate about things and with each other. And it has a growing impact on the way email is being used as a communication device. Recently, JupiterResearch did a number of studies that show the growing usage of social networking that could be useful to keep in mind when you are creating your marketing strategies.

One of the most interesting statistics showed that when asked which media they had used for personal communications instead of email within the past year, more than half of 18–24-year-olds chose social networks. You can see the details in Figure 8.14.

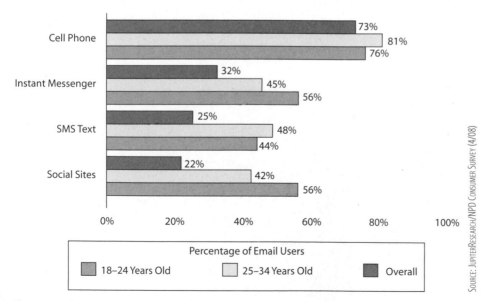

Figure 8.14 Changes in communication patterns compared to email

Does this mean that as these 18–24-year-olds grow up their use of email will die? Not really. Remember that these 18–24-year-olds have not entered the workforce yet, where email remains the predominant communication channel. However, these statistics do offer us a clear indicator that communication preferences vary, by age, by interest, and by access. And it is up to us as intelligent email marketers to determine whether our audience is more inclined to respond to service emails, newsletters, direct marketing, video-enabled emails, surveys, or even social emails.

Understanding the motivators for your audience will enable you to make an intelligent choice for moving forward, especially as you move into year 1 of your email efforts and begin to reforecast the impact and needs for year 2, which will be discussed in more detail in the next chapter.

Test Your Knowledge

This chapter contained a ton of information that is important for you to know. A score of 5 out of 5 will ensure you are on your way to email marketing success.

- Name two bells and whistles you can try with your email.
- Does an email client need to accept forms in order to send a survey to them?
- What percentage of people are reading their email on a mobile device?
- How many layers of a video email do you need to produce?
- Should email and social networking be thought of separately?

Getting Ready for Year 2 and Beyond

You've learned all the critical aspects of email marketing, from building a staff and selecting the technology that is right for you, to segmenting your audience and analyzing your results. We trust you are off on your successful journey. However, email marketing is a continual process of optimization through trial and error. In this last chapter of the book, we cover how to plan for the long-term with future testing, so get ready.

9

Chapter Contents

Iterative Financial Analysis: Analytics
   Over Time
ESP Refresh: Evaluating Your ESP and
   Technology Partners
Assessing Future Trends
Journey On

Iterative Financial Analysis: Analytics Over Time

Trending your email marketing campaign data over time will be one of the most useful tasks you do as an email marketer. As we've mentioned in previous chapters, there are no industry-standard metrics or methodologies for measuring this data; everyone uses their own. This underscores the need for you to build a benchmarking framework that can serve as a point of comparison for your campaign's success. You should avoid benchmarking to "industry-wide" metrics from other marketers because they will not be as informative as your own historical performance. In the following sections, we'll show a report that will allow you to analyze all your key measures over time.

A Top-Down View of Annual Performance

By building average aggregate annual measures for key metrics such as delivery, opens, clicks, and conversions, you'll be able to see the key differences in these measures over time. In years past, many marketers have seen their open rates decline, in part because image blocking in email clients has increased. In the example report shown in Figure 9.1, you can see the delivery rate increasing, the unique open rate modestly declining, the unique click-through rate increasing, and the conversion rate increasing slightly. The bars represent each year of your email marketing performance. Keep in mind this is a sample report and the actual numbers should not be used as a comparison tool.

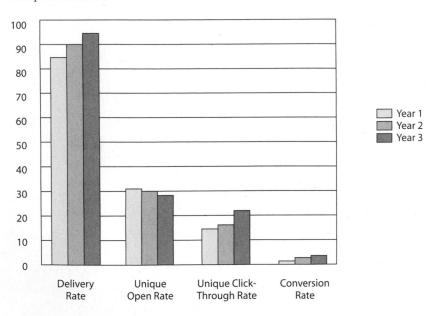

Figure 9.1 Annual email performance comparison

Analyzing Individual Subscriber Segment Performance

Using recency, frequency, and monetary measures, you should be monitoring your subscriber performance on a year-over-year basis. Understanding differences at this level will detail how well your subscribers are performing over time. This report allows you to measure the following in a comparative year-over-year view:

- Dollars per email subscriber
- Number of orders per email subscriber
- Average order size
- Average dollars per mailing

List Health

You should measure the number of new subscribers (or opt-in rate) each year, the average opt-out rate per year, the number of spam complaints, and the average number of active subscribers. *Active subscribers* are most commonly defined as subscribers who, on average, have clicked links in at least six mailings over the course of the year. You may want to have three measures of active subscribers: those who clicked once during the year, those who clicked two to six times, and the very active who have clicked six times or more in a year. These measures will help give you a macro view of your list health. You can also apply this approach for recency, identifying, for example, those subscribers whose most recent click was in the past month or six months. Using the techniques covered in previous chapters, you should already be well versed in measuring and understanding the performance of your most active and inactive subscribers.

Financial Performance / Budget to Plan Performance

Are you meeting your goals? Are you exceeding them? What are your cooperative email marketing-partner departments (stores, call centers, emerging channels) doing to meet your goals? Which of those partners are underperforming, and which are exceeding their goals? Are you accounting for all the necessary costs, including integration and personnel?

All the variable components such as CPM should be performing better by year 3, because your volume should be up sharply and your costs should have decreased by as much as 10 percent. We have found that over ten years, mailing costs per thousand on the whole have decreased. As your list grows, you will have more sending volume, and you'll be able to negotiate a better price with your ESP partner. We have encountered many marketers who have had this experience, and wise marketers reinvest those new-found dollars from an improved cost basis back into the medium, for example, in new features (such as dynamic content) or channels (such as print integration). And part of that reinvestment will consist of additional personnel needed to implement these new features and channels.

So, whether those additional dollars are being gained by bottom-line savings or generated as revenue at the top, ask yourself what you are doing with them. How much are you using automation, such as a triggered continuity campaign? That automation component of email marketing should be considered a big financial lever, because it has been proven to reduce costs over time. However, there is typically a higher cost for setting up those campaigns the first time, and they will require a quarter to a third of an FTE (Full-Time Equivalent) to monitor and manage the creative refreshes and analytics required to optimize those campaigns (see Chapters 5 and 7). As campaigns become more advanced, email marketers will find themselves managing more complex budgets, additional staff members, and new features. Don't be overwhelmed by the additional management this requires. The new complexity will pay off with lower costs and more effective campaigns over the course of the year.

The Necessity of Rebudgeting

Although we have never heard anyone speak favorably of the budgeting process, it is something you will need to plan more time for each year; and that added time will also have an impact on your ability to do the things you have done in years past. Rebudgeting and its requirements may take up to three months to complete. So, consider that this can impact your personnel needs by a quarter of an FTE. What follows is a list of what you should be doing over those three months to become a master of email marketing. Re-evaluate the following:

Planning for Personnel We have probably convinced you by now that you will probably need at least half an FTE to get your email checklist accomplished. So, why not ask for a full body, a full FTE? This person will likely be a novice, and as such, their learning curve will be slower (much like yours was when you started with this book) because they take the time to learn and do all the things you can do now. So, budget for at least one person because although you will teach them to do what you or another staff member does (and please introduce them to this book if it has helped you), they will do these things at a slower pace at least to start.

Planning for New Media, Technology, and Integration Costs Have you planned or are you planning to use such media as mobile and social, to integrating email and print, to creating a call center? Again, ask yourself which tactics are working. The good news is that emerging technologies or communication media typically cost less to adopt. This is either because of a charter "be the first to use this" reduction in cost or, if it is budgeted on a CPM basis, because of the volume of messages to that medium will likely be low. But you still need to understand those volume and integration requirements and costs, and budget for them accordingly.

Planning a Creative Refresh A creative refresh may include the use of a focus group or eye-tracking study. This will certainly take some time and some additional expense. How much will depend upon the scope of the creative refresh. It most likely will involve re-evaluating the wire-frame layout of your email template and may extend to logos or simple usability improvements.

Planning for an ESP Refresh This is one activity that is so important to do in year 2 that we are devoting the next section of the chapter to it.

ESP Refresh: Evaluating Your ESP and Technology Partners

What is an *ESP refresh*? If you have been with your ESP partner for a couple of years, it is probably time to re-evaluate its capabilities against its small core competitor set. As we see it, if you have been with your ESP or technology partner for two years, that means you either signed a two-year contract or did not do an exhaustive vendor reassessment in year 1. (Probably that's because your program was exploding, and you were just trying to keep up with your burgeoning and successful campaigns.) So, now is the time to do that ESP refresh. We recommend comparing at least two other vendors to your incumbent vendor at least once every two years. Chapter 3 described the process of vendor selection, but here are additional items to dig into, again adding to the time it will take to review even three vendors. (Believe us, vendor evaluations of this sort are a very time-consuming process.) But at this stage of the game, you must make time, because you might not have the opportunity to do this for another two years.

> **Write This Down:** Thirty-six percent of email marketers stated they are considering switching ESPs in the next 12 months. (Source: JupiterResearch)

So, here is that list of additional items to evaluate in a refresh:

Advancement in Their Features Has your ESP shared its product map with you, either at your request (as we recommended earlier) or by previewing product development plans at a user conference? Did it deliver what it promised on its product road map? Did those features meet your expectations of what was promised? You might not have any new requirements, but at this point in your email marketing career, your more sophisticated campaigns might be consuming more features, more integration points, and more challenges (such as staffing). In other words, your skills have matured, so it is likely you will want to use more advanced features. Pay particular attention to features such as dynamic content and content management integration.

Innovation Is your ESP thought of as cutting-edge? Is that important to you? *Cutting-edge* may mean the need to integrate mobile, social, and/or networked affiliate marketing into your campaigns. Or it may mean understanding what effect these "cutting-edge" integration points and channels are having on your email program. RSS may become passé, but we are sure that even as you are reading this book there are new email marketing start-ups emerging to complement and create new innovations in the email channel. Is your vendor capable of delivering the innovation required to achieve the integration you need? Is it exceeding the market threshold in the features race? Is your ESP challenging you to do more with email and to become more innovative? It should be.

Service Do you feel loved? What does your client love meter say? That sounds pretty subjective, but service can be measured by hard data, such as response time, availability, and creativity. What is your ESP's track record in its commitment to the truth? And how knowledgeable is its services staff? What is its skill set? Does it understand email at least as well as you do? Does your ESP have a solid understanding of your industry? Again, this is an area that requires you to draw on your experience—the "gut check"—but you need to moderate this by factoring in those noticeable consequences, such as slow service time or difficulty getting the proper number of resources allocated to your account from the ESP.

Price Although price is always a factor, it should not be the only or even the most important one. Evaluate the price in combination with this entire list of attributes. By year 2 and beyond, your CPM should generally be lower. It might be slightly higher if you've adopted further features from your ESP. Your overall spending could also be the same or slightly higher if you've kept the same ESP features but reallocated your spending on personnel. If you're looking for specific integrations, you may end up paying more to another vendor because of those integrations. Evaluate all those costs to offset any real perceived savings in your CPM as a whole.

Deliverability If your campaign is facing deliverability issues, you and your vendor should be responding to them quickly—long before year 2. But let's assume they have occurred. Perhaps there was one bad delivery experience that you had because an ISP suddenly changed the rules and stopped accepting large quantities of inbound mail (this actually happened while we were writing this book). How quickly did your vendor respond? Was it proactive? Is it being informative about delivery changes and challenges, or should the company be better informed in this area than it is? Although that is probably unlikely, these are all things to evaluate. Additionally, is it keeping up with the latest deliverability and reputation requirements? Does the company have good integration with DSPs (Delivery Service Provider)? Is it fulfilling its earlier promise that likely led you to this vendor?

Deliverability should not be a serious issue for you at this stage of the game. If it is, you have to consider whether the problem is with your own mailing practices or failure to apply list hygiene tactics (see Chapters 5 and 6), or with ESP infrastructure issues that prevent an optimal and consistent pattern of email delivery? In the area of deliverability, there have likely already been several changes or improvements industry-wide since the writing and publishing of this book. Seek out sources such as Deliverability.com, the Email Experience Council, or your favorite industry expert source to stay abreast of the latest news in this field.

Uptime, Reliability, Security Deliverability is just one of the areas where your vendor should be demonstrating competency. Although we are both familiar with vendor faults across the whole Internet and technology economy, we have found that it is those vendors who acknowledge these momentary lapses in ability that can be most trusted. Obviously, if there have been consistent issues in any one of these areas, you should have abandoned the provider or technology before year 2. Uptime is the issue that has most likely come across your desk by this point at one time or another.

So, again, come to the vendors with a set of questions. What is your service level? Your uptime track record? What is your response to unplanned outages? How many planned outages do you have on your calendar for this year? You need the quarterly and monthly breakout. Preferably you should be told the actual dates. If there are planned outages such as upgrades, the vendor should have these dates pinpointed. What is its upgrade plan? How many version releases does it have planned this year? Upgrading also feeds into those innovation and feature questions mentioned earlier in this section. Unplanned downtime affects your bottom line and can ruin a complete mailing campaign.

Redundancy What are your ESP's backup plans? How many data centers does it utilize? Does the company utilize its own staff to monitor its data centers around the clock, 24/7?

Ease of Use Choose two of the vendors that are being called the most usable by independent analysts, take the creative best practices discussed in earlier chapters, and apply those rules to the applications those vendors provide. But also consider the overall usability of an application or feature (such as dynamic content). How easy is it to use? Is the application's navigation easy to use? Is it intuitive? Has it been easy for you and your staff members to learn? These are the attributes that embody usability.

Create a test mailing you can run on the top ESPs you are evaluating. Can you complete the same mailing on all three applications in a demo WebEx environment over a given time period, such as 90 minutes? Which vendors had time to spare, and which just barely finished or didn't finish at all? To do this, send them a list of seed accounts just before the WebEx demo, as well as the HTML and creative needed to execute the mailing. Have them do that mailing start to finish with you watching and instructing. A good test mailing will require basic personalization, two dynamic content elements, and a subject line test on a sample of all dynamic content elements. Deliberately provide some mismatched data in the sample, or include some data that is incomplete such as missing values in one column. How does the vendor handle that?

Integration Evaluating integration requires that you look at the vendor's entire ecosystem and the greater list of technology integration points. Is it integrating to the vendors that you utilize in other areas, such as web analytics, search, and content management? What are the additional costs for this integration? Does the company use a standard connector to this vendor's platform, such as Omniture's Genesis offering or Coremetric's LiveMail 2.0 integration? Vendors that use a standard connection reduce your switching costs, as disconnecting and reconnecting a standard integration is easier than starting from scratch again with a custom integration. Repeatability of the integration is a big thing to evaluate. Is this a core competency for the ESP? How many of these integrations does it currently do, and what percentage of its overall client base does that represent? There is always some pain when switching a vendor that is integrated into one of your systems; it is not dissimilar from redoing a bathroom and being without a working shower or toilet for a day or weekend. So, ask lots of questions about the downtime and the time it takes to complete this integration to ensure that your data will be flowing when those pipes come back online.

Assessing Future Trends

To avoid future shock, you need to know how to assess future trends and determine which trends create maximum leverage for you. What is the biggest and latest trend in online marketing, in traditional direct marketing, and in emerging media marketing? Since we hope this book will stand the test of time, it is up to you right now to explore and confirm the latest trends. Here are few places that we have mentioned throughout the book that are great resources to stay abreast of the latest trends. You'll find a complete list of resources in Appendix A of this book, but here are some of those sources that track the latest trends:

- **Clickz.** This is an email marketing newsletter, published by Incisive Media (www. clickz.com).

- **MediaPost.** This is an email insider newsletter, published by MediaPost (www. mediapost.com).

- **Associations.** Try the Email Experience Council (EEC) and its Digital Lifestyle Roundtable (www.emailexperience.org).

- **Research firms.** These include JupiterResearch (www.jupiterresearch.com), MarketingSherpa (www.marketingsherpa.com), and Forrester Research (www.forrester.com).

- **Events and webinars.** Although we are partial to the EEC Evolution Conference, the Email Insider Summit, and vertical industry events such as the Shop.org Innovation Summit, there are dozens of events and webinars—some of which are free! That should make keeping up to date about the latest happenings and trends in the industry easy.

- **Blogs.** Look to the experts in the field and vendors that often maintain blogs that publish frequently, including the website for this book. Check there for a list of blogs that we recommend.

So, with all this expected continued evolution and sophistication in email marketing, how can you be sure these trends are right for you? Well, evaluate them against this four-part scale:

Target Customer Overlap What is the breadth of your target customers' overlap with this new trend? Look at a segment level, usually with new technology or channel adoption that typically exhibits clear age- and gender-based demographic segments. What is the breadth of the demographic overlap of the new trend to your historically best customers? To what extent is growing this segment is part of your new budget initiatives, your goals, and your targets? If spending on this new trend is in your budget plan, then you most certainly must do this.

Cost of Entry Is this a budget breaker or something that can easily be entered at a low cost? What is the total cost, including the technology, the necessary integration, and the custom development to the marketing dashboard and analysis? Lastly, what is the cost impact in terms of personnel? Will this require a person of special skills and cost? Expertise is a step of this process all unto itself. Remember to budget appropriately each year to have a new-media slush fund so that you have some funny money to dabble in new areas.

Expertise Do you know anything about this new trend? What do you know? What are the resources you can use to learn more about it? Although it will likely be new for everyone, is this an area you feel confident that you or your staff can become familiar with? If not, what are the training and personnel costs in this domain, including training and travel to events and seminars? This is typically a hidden chunk of the cost to entry.

Appropriateness Is this an appropriate channel for your brand? Does it support all your marketing efforts? Is it integrated to them? What percentage of the population is playing with this new-fangled thing, and how does that overlap with your target customer audience? You can see we have gone full circle, going back to step 1 to continually analyze whether this is moving the needle of your target-customer overlap.

Any one of these four points could be weighted differently, more significant or less, to fit your specific situation. You could even score each point on a scale where +1 is a positive, 0 is neutral, and −1 is a negative to counteract the extra effort or cost it may take. If you score a 4, then you know it might be for you. If, on the other hand, you have a −4, then you might want to put the project on the back burner.

Journey On

At this point, we'd like to offer some closing thoughts to inspire your journey of continual improvement. We are so glad you undertook this project and decided to select our book to aid you on your journey to become a professional email marketer. As with all skills, it is a journey that is steeped in continuous improvement, and it's an approach that will allow your skills to grow. With that in mind, in closing, we remind you of some of our favorite passages from each chapter in the book to inspire you to work yourself out of a jam or continue to speed down the road to optimization:

- Drive all the potential subscribers you want; if they aren't qualified, consider it a waste of marketing dollars (Chapter 1).

- Every email impacts your company's brand equity (Chapter 2).

- Understand the value that email subscribers represent to your organization (Chapter 3).

- A good email strategy, strong analytics, and a solid budget will often reap rewards far beyond the implementation of a few emails (Chapter 4).

- Create key performance indicators that detail performance across three distinct categories: barometer, engagement, and infrastructure/list measures. (Chapter 5).

- Determine how the access to email assets you have can best support your company goal. Pick the most impactful effort, and begin your strategy there (Chapter 6).

- To be comfortable with the concept of testing, you must be comfortable with the notion of failure (Chapter 7).

- Leverage customer-created content in a way where you enable an automated creation of a stand-alone email program (Chapter 8).

- We both thank you for your Hour a Day.

Vendor Resource List

This appendix lists the resources and companies that were mentioned throughout this book.

Associations, Events, and Publications

The following are resources for newsletters on market developments, best practices, and events:

ClickZ (Incisive Media): www.clickz.com

Direct Marketing Association: www.the-dma.org

EmailStatCenter: www.emailstatcenter.com

Email Experience Council: www.emailexperience.org

Email Insider (MediaPost): www.mediapost.com, www.mediapost.com/blogs/email_insider

Internet Advertising Bureau: www.iab.net

International Association of Privacy Professionals: https://www.privacyassociation.org

Internet Retailer: www.internetretailer.com

MarketingCharts: www.marketingcharts.com

MarketingProfs: www.marketingprofs.com

Network Advertising Initiative: www.networkadvertising.org

Email Service Providers

The following are Email Service Providers (ESPs) and email technology vendors. Some of these vendors offer their applications on a hosted-on-demand basis, while others are deployed in an on-premise-software manner. Many vendors listed here also offer strategic and production-oriented tactical services.

Acxiom Digital: www.acxiomdigital.com

Adestra: www.adestra.co.uk/email_marketing

Alchemy Worx: www.alchemyworx.com

BlueHornet (Digital River): www.bluehornet.com

ClickSquared: www.clicksquared.com

Constant Contact: www.constantcontact.com

Datran Media: www.datranmedia.com

e-Dialog: www.e-dialog.com

EmailLabs (Lyris): www.emaillabs.com

eRoi: www.eroi.com

ExactTarget: http://email.exacttarget.com

Experian CheetahMail: www.cheetahmail.com

MailChimp: www.mailchimp.com

Merkle: www.merkleinc.com

Puresend: www.puresend.com

Responsys: www.responsys.com

Silverpop: www.silverpop.com

StrongMail: www.strongmail.com

SubscriberMail: www.subscribermail.com

VerticalResponse: www.verticalresponse.com

WhatCounts: www.whatcounts.com

Yesmail: www.yesmail.com

Delivery Service Providers and Reputation and Accreditation Management Services

These vendors offer tools and services to measure and manage email deliverability. Often these vendors' services are sold in combination with the vendors listed in the preceding section.

Habeas: www.habeas.com (Habeas is now a part of Return Path)

Goodmail: www.goodmailsystems.com

Iconix: www.iconix.com

Lyris: www.lyris.com

Pivotal Veracity: www.pivotalveracity.com

Return Path: www.returnpath.net

UnsubCentral: www.unsubcentral.com

Market Research, Agencies, and Consultants

Consultants, agencies, and market research providers can offer additional knowledge about the email industry, and many listed here offer strategic advisory services or specialized consulting services, such as creative optimization and privacy expertise.

Chapell & Associates: www.chapellassociates.com

Center for Marketing Research: www.umassd.edu/cmr/

comScore: www.comscore.com

Eyetools: www.eyetools.com

Forrester Research: www.forrester.com

FreshAddress: http://biz.freshaddress.com

JupiterResearch: www.jupiterresearch.com

MarketingSherpa: www.marketingsherpa.com

McKinsey & Company: www.mckinsey.com

Ogilvy: www.ogilvy.com

Prospectiv: www.prospectiv.com

Radicati Group: www.radicati.com

Smith-Harmon: www.smith-harmon.com

Think Eyetracking: www.thinkeyetracking.com

Technology Vendors

Although the vendors listed in this appendix deal with technology in one way or another, here a few vendors that we mention in the book text:

Microsoft: www.microsoft.com

Technorati: www.technorati.com

Zinio: www.zinio.com

Web Analytics Vendors

Web analytics vendors help to measure site traffic—specifically, visitor behavior—that can be used to further optimize email mailings.

Coremetrics: www.coremetrics.com

Google: www.google.com

Lyris: www.lyris.com

Omniture: www.omniture.com

Unica: www.unica.com

WebTrends: www.webtrends.com

Yahoo: www.yahoo.com

Email Checklists

In an effort to broaden the education and awareness of email marketing best practices, members of the Email Experience Council have committed to creating a series of checklists. The following checklists were created by the Direct Marketing Association's Email Experience Council (DMA/eec's EEC's) Email Design Roundtable. To learn about additional email checklists being produced, or to download new checklists, visit www.emailexperience.org/resouces/email-checklists/. *These checklists are guides to ensure that you are addressing the basics and adhering to the latest best practices as it relates to email design.*

B

Email Design

You need to know what to check to maximize your email creative's performance. Compare each of your designs against the following checklists before approval and coding.

Content

Don't assume your message is compelling! Ask yourself the following questions:
- What is this message about?
- Why should my subscribers care?
- Is it clear what action I want my subscribers to take?

Subject Line

The subject line is the mechanism to get your readers to open your message. It should be compelling, drive interest, and tease the subscriber.
- The key message should be clear in the first 50 to 60 characters so that if the rest is truncated, the message still makes sense.
- Avoid using words, symbols, and punctuation that might trigger spam filters.
- Make sure the subject line describes what the email contains and how it will benefit the reader to open it.

Preheader/Header

This is the information at the very top of the message body. Reserve this space to reinforce important tactics, such as the following that will assist with image rendering:
- Include a text content teaser to inform your reader of the message content.
- If you include "add to address book" language, make sure the address is correct.
- Add links to mobile and hosted versions, if applicable.

Preview Pane

In many email client software applications, such as Microsoft's Outlook, there is a preview pane which shows a portion of the message's body.
- Make sure the primary message is visible "above the fold."
- Make sure the call to action is visible "above the fold."
- If this is a longer-form newsletter, did you include a table of contents with anchor tags linking to each body content section?

Message Construct

Review your message prior to sending to ensure that it is constructed properly.

- Spel-check the copy.

- Confirm all punctuation is in place.

- Verify that as much text as possible is system/HTML text instead of graphical.

- Make sure the primary call to action "pops."

Recovery Module

Just above the footer of the message, you have one last chance to inspire the subscriber and drive the call to action.

- Include a recovery module as a last chance to inspire engagement.

- Consider using alternative links to categories.

- Consider including incentives.

Footer

Just because it is last, footer's are certainly not least. An important space to include legal information, navigational elements, and the aspects of the CAN-SPAM requirements, including an unsubscribe link and your company's physical address.

- Update any disclaimers referencing promotions or special offers mentioned in the main message of the email.

- Check for the correct copyright date.

- Include an Unsubscribe link.

- Include your company's physical address

- Consider including a Forward to a Friend link.

- Consider including a social sharing mechanism so that the message can easily be pushed out to social networking sites such as Facebook and Gather.com

Code QA Testing

You need to know what to check to make sure your email looks and acts exactly like you intended. Compare your code against the following lists before sending it.

Precheck HTML File

A great marketing message can be easily lost if the message is poorly formed or if the HTML is "Broken."

- Confirm that the coded HTML file matches the approved final creative proof:

    - Check the text for inconsistencies.

- • Check the graphics for inconsistencies.
- • Make sure that all sub-messages are included in the coded file.
- Spell-check all of the content.
- Check every link:
  - • Confirm the links match the products/landing pages on the site.
  - • Confirm the prices in the coded file match the prices on the site (if applicable).
- Validate the HTML using an HTML validation tool.
- View the local HTML file on Windows using Internet Explorer and on a Mac using Safari and Firefox.
- Using Internet Explorer, check the rollover alt text:
  - • Make sure important images have alt text associated with them.
  - • Make sure the copy in the alt text matches the imagery.
  - • Make sure the price in the alt text matches the pricing in the product imagery.
  - • Confirm the capitalization and punctuation in the alt text works well within the context.
- Make sure there are no empty link tags; search for `href=""` and `href="#"`.
- Confirm the image path has been properly updated; search for *images/*.
- Check the header and footer legal verbiage for any inconsistencies or mistakes.
- Check that the `<title>` tag is correct. Make sure it works within the context of the current message.

Precheck Text File

Once your HTML message has been laid out, you can scrape the text out of it to create a text version. Some applications can do this automatically, but even then, be sure to scrutinize your text version even if you are manually constructing it.

- Compare the text file against the HTML file to ensure all primary and sub-messages have been included in the text file.
- Spell-check all of the content.
- Review all the links:
  - • Confirm the links match the placement.
  - • Make sure that all the links are included in the text file.
- Make sure all the lines break before 65 characters (except for links that may be longer depending on tracking information).
- Make sure all blank lines have two spaces.

- Check for special characters that may not render correctly in plain-text format—em dashes and en dashes, smart quotes from Microsoft Word, and so on.
- Check the header and footer legal verbiage for any inconsistencies or mistakes.

Conduct Rendering Testing

Ensuring that your message renders correctly on a variety of email software clients and mobile devices is a vital part of the pre-sending process. Vendors such as Return Path, Pivotal Veracity, and Lyris have tools that can automate this process. However, this task requires human capital to eyeball the message on a variety of clients.

- Send the message to your QA test list.
- Use an email content–rendering tool or send the message to major email readers to ensure consistent rendering.
- Check for rendering errors:
  - Check all web-based email clients on Windows using Internet Explorer 6 and 7 and Firefox.
  - Check all web-based email clients on a Mac using Firefox and Safari.
  - Check the message in Outlook 2007.
  - Check the message on multiple mobile devices that have email-reading capabilities.
  - Correct any rendering issues, and resend tests as needed.

Glossary

Although we have tried to avoid jargon as much as possible in this book, some of the terminology used will be unfamiliar to some readers. This glossary defines the terms all readers should be familiar with to get the most out of this book—and to look smart and sound knowledgeable when talking to colleagues and prospective business contacts.

A/B split A test to compare two different versions of an email. Specifically, an email list is split into two groups; half is sent one version of the email, while the other half receives a second version. See also *Nth name*.

above the fold The part of an email message or web page that is visible without scrolling; this comes from a printing term for the top half of a newspaper above the horizontal fold in the paper. Material in this area is considered more valuable because the reader sees it first. Unlike a newspaper, email and web page fold locations aren't predictable. Your fold may be affected by the user's preview pane, monitor size, and monitor resolution, as well as any headers placed by email programs such as Hotmail and other factors.

acquisition cost In email marketing, the cost to generate one lead, newsletter subscriber, or customer in an individual email campaign; typically, this is the total campaign expense divided by the number of leads, subscribers, or customers it produced.

affirmative consent An active request by a reader or subscriber to receive advertising or promotional information, newsletters, and so on. Generally, affirmative consent does not include the following: failing to uncheck a preselected box on a web form, entering a business relationship with an organization without being asked for separate permission to be sent specific types of email, or opting out.

authentication An automated process that verifies an email sender's identity.

autoresponder Automated email message–sending capability, such as a welcome message sent to all new subscribers when they join a list. It may be triggered by joins, unsubscribes, or all email sent to a particular mailbox. The autoresponse may consist of more than a single message, and it can be a series of date- or event-triggered emails.

blacklist A list developed by anyone receiving email or processing email on its way to the recipient, or by interested third parties, that includes domains or IP addresses of any emailers suspected of sending spam. Many companies use blacklists to reject inbound email, either at the server level or before it reaches the recipient's inbox.

bounce A message that doesn't get delivered promptly is said to have bounced. Emails can bounce for more than 30 reasons; for example, the email address is incorrect or has been closed, the recipient's mailbox is full, the mail server is down, or the system detects spam or offensive content. See also *hard bounce* and *soft bounce*.

bounce handling The process of managing email that has bounced. Bounce handling is important for list maintenance, list integrity, and delivery. Bounce handling is managed by adjusting the cadence of the retried email message attempts.

bounce message A message returned to an email sender, reporting that the message could not be delivered and why. Not all bounced emails result in messages being sent back to the sender, and not all bounce messages are clear or accurate about the reason the email was bounced.

brand equity Refers to the marketing effects or outcomes that accrue to a product with its brand name compared to those that would accrue if the same product did not have the brand name. This consumer perception of the brand's value over another one is referred to as brand equity.

broadcast The process of sending the same email message to multiple recipients.

bulk folder Where many email clients send messages that appear to be from spammers or contain spam, or are from any sender not in the recipient's address book or contact list. Some clients allow the recipient to override the system's settings and direct that mail from a suspect sender to be routed directly to the inbox. Also called *junk folder*.

CAN-SPAM Popular name for the U.S. law regulating commercial email, updated in July 2008. (The full name is the Controlling the Assault of Non-Solicited Pornography and Marketing Act of 2003.)

cell A segment of your list that receives different treatment specifically to see how it responds compared to the control, which receives the standard treatment. Also called *test cell* or *test version*.

churn A measure of how many subscribers leave a mailing list (or how many email addresses go bad) over a certain time, usually expressed as a percentage of the whole list.

clickstream The collection or *stream* of clicks that a user makes when visiting a website.

click-through When a recipient clicks a hotlink included in an email. See also *uniform resource locator (URL)*.

click-through rate (CTR) The total number of clicks on an email link divided by the number of emails sent. Some email broadcast vendors or tracking programs define CTR differently. The term is slightly inexact because some clicks "get lost" between the click and your server. Also be sure to determine whether your CTR is unique, meaning that each individual user is counted only once no matter how many times they click a link.

click-through tracking The data collected about each click-through link, such as how many people clicked it and how many clicks resulted in desired actions such as sales, forwards, or subscriptions.

confirmed opt-in Inexact term that may refer to double opt-in subscription processes or to email addresses that do not hard bounce back a welcome message. Ask anyone using this term to define it more clearly.

content All the material in an email message except for the codes showing the delivery route and return-path information. This includes all words, images, and links.

conversion When an email recipient performs a desired action based on a mailing you have sent. A conversion could be a monetary transaction, such as a purchase made after clicking a link. It could also include a voluntary act such as registering at a website, downloading a white paper, signing up for a web seminar, or opting into an email newsletter.

co-registration An arrangement in which companies collecting registration information from users (email sign-up forms, shopping checkout process, and so on) include a separate box for users to check if they would also like to be added to a specific third-party list.

CPA Cost per action (or acquisition). A method of paying for advertising, or of calculating equivalent results from other payment models, where the publisher is paid each time someone completes an action (such as making a purchase).

CPC Cost per click. A method of paying for advertising. This is different from CPA because all you pay for is the click, regardless of what that click does when it gets to your site or landing page.

CPM Cost per thousand.

cross-campaign profiling A method used to understand how email respondents behave over multiple campaigns.

CTR See *click-through rate (CTR)*.

data center A physical location that consists of servers used to store data and execute your email campaigns. Email Service Providers often run multiple data centers to create redundancy and scale.

delivered email The number of emails sent minus the number of bounces and filtered messages. This is a highly inexact number because not all receiving ISPs report accurately on which emails didn't go through and why not.

display name See *email-friendly name*.

DomainKeys An antispam software application being developed by Yahoo and using a combination of public and private "keys" to authenticate the sender's domain and reduce the chance that a spammer or hacker will fake the domain sending address. The latest version is referred to as DKIM.

double opt-in A process that requires new list joiners to take an action (such as clicking a link to a personal confirmation page) to confirm they want to be on the list. Interpreted incorrectly by some email broadcast vendors to mean a new subscriber who does not opt out of or bounce a welcome message.

dynamic content Email newsletter content that changes from one recipient to the next according to a set of predetermined rules or variables. Dynamic content often reflects past purchases, current interests, or where the recipient lives.

ECOA Email change of address. A service that tracks email address changes and updates.

email address The combination of a unique username and a sender domain (`JohnDoe@anywhere.com`). The email address requires both the username and the domain name.

email appending A service that matches email addresses to a database of personal names and postal addresses. Appending may require an "OK to add my name" reply from the subscriber before you can add the name to the list.

email client The software recipients use to read email, such as Outlook Express or Lotus Notes.

email domain Also called simply the *domain*, the portion of an email address to the right of the @ sign. Comparing your list to common domains can be a useful hygiene tool; for example, you can identify all records where the consumer entered `name@aol` as their email address and correct it to `name@aol.com`.

email filter A software tool that categorizes, sorts, or blocks incoming email, based either on the sender, the email header, or the message content. Filters may be applied at the email client, the ISP, or a combination.

email-friendly name The portion of the email address that is displayed in most, though not all, email readers in place of, or in addition to, the email address. Also called the *display name*; see also *From name*.

email harvesting An automated process in which a robot program searches web pages or other Internet destinations for email addresses. The program collects the addresses into a database, which frequently gets resold to spammers or unethical bulk mailers. Many U.S. state laws forbid harvesting. CAN-SPAM does not outlaw it by name but allows triple damages against violators who compiled their mailing lists with harvested names.

email newsletter Content distributed to subscribers by email on a regular schedule. The content is seen as valued editorial in itself rather than primarily a commercial message with a sales offer.

email prefix The portion of the email address to the left of the @ sign.

enhanced whitelist A super whitelist maintained by AOL for bulk emailers who meet strict delivery standards, such as receiving fewer than one spam complaint for every 1,000 email messages. Emailers on the enhanced whitelist can bypass AOL 9.0's automatic suppression of images and links.

event-triggered email Pre-programmed messages sent automatically based on an event such as a date or anniversary.

eye tracking The process of measuring either the point of gaze ("where we are looking") or the motion of an eye relative to the head. A device is used for measuring eye positions and eye movements. This research process is applied to marketing creative and general usability projects.

false positive A legitimate message mistakenly rejected or filtered as spam, either by an ISP or by a recipient's antispam program. The more stringent an antispam program, the higher its false-positive rate.

feedback loop (FBL) Information provided by a variety of ISPs (AOL, Microsoft, Yahoo, and so on) about which subscribers are marking your email as spam, as well as overall insight into your reputation with that ISP.

footer An area at the end of an email message or newsletter where you can place information that doesn't change from one edition to the next, such as contact information, the company's postal address, or the email address the recipient used to subscribe to mailings. Some software programs can be set to place this information automatically.

forward Also called *Forward to a Friend*, the process in which email recipients send your message to people they know, either because they think their friends will be interested in your message or because you have offered incentives to forward messages. Forwarding can be done through the recipient's own email client or by giving the recipient a link to click, which opens a registration page at your site in which you ask the forwarded visitor to give their name and email address, the name/email address of the person they want to send to, and (optionally) a brief email message explaining the reason for the forward. You can supply the wording or allow the forwarder to write their own message. The act of forwarding to a friend is commonly called *viral marketing.*

frequency value See *recency, frequency, monetary (RFM) score.*

From name Whatever appears in the From line in your email recipient's inbox. Chosen by the sender, it may be a personal name, a brand name, an email address, a blank space, or alphanumeric gobbledygook. This is not the actual "from" contained in the header, and it may also be different from the email reply address. It is easy to fake; it's also called *email-friendly name.*

full-service provider An email vendor that also provides strategic consulting and creative support in addition to sending messages.

hard bounce Message sent to an invalid, closed, or nonexistent email account.

header Routing and program data at the start of an email message, including the sender's name and email address, originating email server IP address, recipient IP address, and any transfers in the process.

heatmap A visual depiction of data. Marketers use heatmaps to learn more about what visitors to their site are viewing. A heatmap can show things such as the frequency of clicks, the length of time spent on a particular page, and which tags and news subjects are most popular. A color scale is usually used to illustrate the variation in the data.

hotlink See *uniform resource locator (URL).*

house list The list of email addresses an organization develops on its own.

HTML message An email message that contains any type of formatting other than text. This may be as simple as programming that sets the text in a specific font (bold, italics, Courier 10 point, and so on). It also includes any graphic images, logos, and colors.

hygiene The process of cleaning a database to correct incorrect or outdated values. See also *list hygiene.*

IMAP Internet Message Access Protocol, a standard protocol for accessing email from a server.

impression A single view of one page by a single user, used in calculating advertising rates.

IP address A unique number assigned to each device connected to the Internet. An IP address can be dynamic (changing each time an email message or campaign goes out), or it can be static (unchanging). Static IP addresses are best for email marketing, because dynamic IP addresses often trigger spam filters.

landing page A web page displayed after the user clicks a link within an email. Also may be called a *microsite*, *splash page*, *bounce page*, or *click page*.

linkrot What happens when links go bad over time, either because a website has shut down or because a site has stopped supporting a unique landing page provided in an email promotion.

list The email addresses to which you send your message. This can be either your house list or a third-party list that sends your message on your behalf.

list fatigue The effect of diminishing returns from a mailing list whose members are sent too many offers, or too many of the same offers, in too short a period of time.

list hygiene The act of maintaining a list so hard bounces and unsubscribed names are removed from mailings. Some list owners also use an email change-of-address service to update old or abandoned email addresses (ideally with a permission step included) as part of this process.

list management How a mailing list is set up, administered, and maintained. The list manager has daily responsibility over the operation of the list, including processing subscribes and unsubscribes, bounce management, list hygiene, and so on. The list

manager can be the same as the database manager but is not always the same person as the list owner.

list owner The organization or individual who has gathered a list of email addresses. Ownership does not necessarily imply that the addresses were collected "with permission."

list rental The process in which a publisher or advertiser pays a list owner to send its messages to that list. This usually involves the list owner sending the messages on the advertiser's behalf. (Tip: If someone hands over their list to you, take such a list with caution because it is likely a privacy policy violation and could lead to unsubscribe CAN-SPAM issues.)

list sale The actual purchase of a mailing list along with the rights to mail it directly. Permission can be "sold" only if the subsequent mailings continue to match the frequency, brand name, content, and "from" of the past owner's mailings—and even then this is a somewhat shaky procedure on the spam front. You are in effect buying a publication, not just a list.

mailto A code to make an email address (in either a text or an HTML email) immediately clickable (for example, mailto:JohnDoe@anywhere.com). When the link is clicked, it usually opens the user's email client and inserts the email address in the To field of a blank message.

monetary value See *recency, frequency, monetary (RFM) score*.

MTA Mail transfer agent. A computer that forwards email from senders to recipients (or to relay sites) and stores incoming email.

multipart/MIME Also known (confusingly) as an *email sniffer*. This is a message format that includes both an HTML and a text-only version in the same message. Most (but not all) email clients receiving messages in this format will automatically display the version the user's system is set to show. Systems that can't show HTML should show the text version instead. This doesn't always work for many Lotus Notes users. Also note that tracking information about which version a recipient ended up viewing is limited; only HTML open rates and (possibly) link click tracking are transmitted to the sender.

Nth name The act of segmenting a list for a test in which names are pulled from the main list for the test cell by number, such as every fifth name on the list. See also *A/B split*.

open rate The number of HTML message recipients who opened your email, usually expressed as a percentage of the total number of emails sent. The open rate is considered a key metric for judging an email campaign's success, but it has several problems. The rate indicates only the number of emails opened from the total amount sent, not just those that were actually delivered. Opens also can't be calculated on text emails. Also, some email clients allow users to scan message content without actually opening the message, which is falsely calculated as an open. See *preview pane*.

open relay An SMTP email server that allows outsiders to relay email messages that are neither from nor addressed to local users. Often exploited by spammers and hackers.

opt-in A specific proactive request by an individual email recipient to have their own email address placed on a specific mailing list. Many list renters and buyers now require

list owners to provide proof of opt-in, including the actual email or IP address opt-in date and time the request was received.

opt-out A request to remove an email address from a specific list or from all lists operated by a single owner. Also, the practice of adding an email address to a list without the addressee's prior approval, forcing those who don't want to be on your list to actively unsubscribe.

pass-along An email recipient who received your message via forwarding from a subscriber. (Some emails offer Forward to a Friend links, but the vast majority of pass-alongs happen using email clients, and not that technique.) Pass-alongs can affect the formatting of the email, often stripping off HTML. See also *viral marketing*.

permission The implicit approval given when a person actively requests to have their own email address added to a list.

personalization A targeting method in which an email message appears to have been created only for a single recipient. Personalization techniques include adding the recipient's name in the subject line or message body or having the message offer reflect a purchasing, link clicking, or transaction history.

personally identifiable information (PII) Any piece of information that can potentially be used to uniquely identify, contact, or locate a single person.

phishing A form of identity theft in which a scammer uses an authentic-looking email to trick recipients into giving out sensitive personal information, such as credit card or bank account numbers, Social Security numbers, and other data.

plain text Text in an email message that includes no formatting code. See *HTML message*.

POP Post Office Protocol, which an email client uses to exchange messages with an email server.

postmaster Whom to contact at a website, ISP, or other site to request information, get help with delivery, or register complaints.

preferences Options a user can set to determine how they want to receive your messages, how they want to be addressed, to which email address messages should go, and which messages they want to receive from you. The more preferences a user can specify, the more likely you'll send relevant email.

Pretty Good Privacy (PGP) Software used to encrypt and protect email as it moves from one computer to another; it can also be used to verify a sender's identity.

preview pane The window in an email client that allows the user to scan message content without actually clicking the message. See *open rate*.

privacy policy A clear description of how your company uses the email addresses and other information it gathers via opt-in requests for newsletters, company information, third-party offers, or other functions. If you rent, sell, or exchange your list to anyone outside your company or if you add email addresses to opt-out messages, you should state so in the privacy policy. State laws may also compel you to explain your privacy policy and may define where to put the policy statement so people will see it and even in what form the policy should be displayed.

proof list List of email addresses, usually production and marketing department employees who receive a copy of the email when it is deployed. This proof list may also include email addresses at a variety of domains or webmail accounts. See also *seed list*.

queue Where an email message goes after you send it but before the list owner approves it or before the list server gets around to sending it. Some list software allows you to queue a message and then set a time to send it automatically, either during a quiet period on the server or at a time when human approval isn't available.

read email A type of data that is not measurable. Only opens and clicks can be measured in any way. You can never know whether a recipient simply read your message.

recency, frequency, monetary (RFM) score Commonly referred to as *RFM analysis*, this approach is used to segment customers into different groupings based on how much they've spent (the monetary value), how frequently they've purchased, and how recently. Marketers will often use this to create groups of six-month buyers, meaning those buyers who have purchased in the past six months. The approach can also be applied to email click and or site visit behavior, as in those subscribers who may have clicked within the past six months.

registration The process where someone not only opts into your email program but also provides some additional information, such as name, address, demographic data, or other relevant information, usually by using a web form.

relationship email An email message that refers to a commercial action—a purchase, complaint, or customer support request—based on a business relationship between the sender and recipient. Generally, this is not covered by CAN-SPAM requirements.

reply-to The email address that receives messages sent from users who click Reply in their email clients. Can differ from the From address, which can be an automated or unmonitored email address used only to send messages to a distribution list. Reply-to should always be a monitored address.

reverse DNS The process in which an IP address is matched correctly to a domain name, instead of a domain name being matched to an IP address. Reverse DNS is a popular method for catching spammers who use invalid IP addresses. If a spam filter or program can't match the IP address to the domain name, it can reject the email.

rich media Creative content that includes video, animation, and/or sound. Rich-media emails often collect high open and click rates but require more bandwidth and are less compatible with different email clients than text or regular HTML messages. Some mailers also consider transactional email "rich."

seed email Email addresses placed on a list (sometimes secretly) to determine what messages are sent to the list and/or to track delivery rate and/or visible appearance of delivered messages. Seeds may also be placed on websites and elsewhere on the Internet to track spammers' harvesting activities.

seed list A collection of email addresses that act only as seed emails.

segment The ability to slice a list into specific pieces determined by various attributes, such as open history or name source.

select A segment of a list determined by any number of attributes, such as source of name, job title, purchasing history, and so on. CPM list renters pay an additional fee per thousand names for each select on top of the base list price.

selective unsubscribe An unsubscribe mechanism that allows a consumer to selectively determine which email newsletters they want to continue receiving while stopping the sending of others.

Sender ID The informal name for a new antispam program combining two existing protocols, Sender Policy Framework and Caller ID. Sender ID authenticates email senders and blocks email forgeries and faked addresses.

Sender Policy Framework (SPF) A protocol used to eliminate email forgeries. A line of code called an SPF record is placed in a sender's Domain Name Service information. The incoming mail server can verify a sender by reading the SPF record before allowing a message through.

sent emails The number of email names transmitted in a single broadcast. This does not reflect how many were delivered or viewed by recipients.

signature A line or two of information found in the closing of an email, usually following the sender's name. Signatures can include advertising information, such as a company name, product, brand message, or marketing call to action.

SMTP Simple Mail Transfer Protocol, the most common protocol for sending email messages between email servers.

snail mail A slang term for postal mail.

soft bounce Email that is sent to an active (live) email address but is turned away before being delivered. Often, the problem is temporary—the server is down, or the recipient's mailbox is over the quota. The email might be held at the recipient's server and delivered later, or the sender's email program may attempt to deliver it again. Soft-bounce reports are not always accurate because they don't report all soft bounces or the actual reason for the bounce.

spam The popular name for unsolicited commercial email. However, some email recipients define spam as any email they no longer want to receive, even if it comes from a mailing list they joined voluntarily.

SpamCop A blacklist and IP address database, formerly independently owned but now part of the email vendor Ironport. Many ISPs check the IP addresses of incoming email against SpamCop's records to determine whether the address has been blacklisted because of spam complaints.

spoofing The practice of changing the sender's name in an email message so that it looks as if it came from another address.

subject line Copy that identifies what an email message is about, often designed to entice the recipient into opening the message. The subject line appears first in the recipient's inbox, often next to the sender's name or email address. It is repeated in the email message's header information inside the message.

subscribe To join a mailing list, either through an email command, by filling out a web form, or offline by filling out a form or requesting to be added verbally. (If you accept verbal subscriptions, you should safeguard yourself by recording each one and storing it, along with a time and date, in a retrievable format.)

subscriber The person who has specifically requested to join a mailing list. A list has both subscribers, who receive the message from the sender, and pass-alongs.

subscriber data table A database table that holds all your email subscriber information, including their demographic attributes and profile information.

suppression file A list of email addresses you have removed from your regular mailinglists, either because they have opted out of your lists or because they have notified other mailers that they do not want to receive mailings from your company. More broadly, marketers may choose to suppress subscribers from a mailing for many reasons. Required by CAN-SPAM. Also called *do-not-email list*.

test A necessary step before sending an email campaign or newsletter. Many email clients permit you to send a test email before sending a regular email newsletter or solo mailing, in which you would send one copy of the message to an in-house email address and then review it for formatting or copy errors or improperly formatted links. Email marketers should also send a test campaign to a list of email addresses not in the deployment database to determine likely response rates and how well different elements in the message perform.

throttling The practice of regulating how many email messages a broadcaster sends to one ISP or mail server at a time. Some ISPs bounce email if they receive too many messages from one sending address at a time.

transactional email Also known as transactive email. A creative format where the recipient can enter a transaction in the body of the email without clicking to a web page first. Transactions may be answering a survey or purchasing something.

UCE Unsolicited commercial email, also called *spam* or *junk mail*.

uniform resource locator (URL) The web address for a page, always beginning with http:// (or https:// for a secure page), followed by www (or variations, although some URLs are set up not to include this information), the domain name, and the domain suffix. This is commonly referred to as a *link* or *hotlink*.

unique reference number A unique number assigned to a list member, usually by the email-broadcast software, used to track member behavior (clicks, subscribes, unsubscribe) or to identify the member to track email delivery. Also referred to as the *primary record key*.

unsubscribe To remove oneself from an email list, either via an emailed command to the list server or by filling in a web form.

verification A program that determines an email came from the sender listed in the return path or Internet headers; this is designed to stop email from forged senders.

video email An email message that includes a video file, either inserted into the message body, accessible through a hotlink to a website, or accompanying it in an attachment. (The latter is the least desirable because

many ISPs block executable attachments to avoid viruses.)

viral marketing The process of marketing a product or brand through an existing social network. This is a tactic that is not exclusive to email marketing.

virus A program or computer code that affects or interferes with a computer's operating system and gets spread to other computers accidentally or on purpose through email messages, downloads, infected CDs, or network messages. See *worm*.

web bug A 1-pixel-by-1-pixel image tag added to an HTML message and used to track open rates by email address, as well as other behaviors. Opening the message, either in the preview pane or by clicking it, activates the tag and sends a signal to the website, where special software tracks and records the signal as an open. Also called *web beacon*.

webmail or web mail Any of several web-based email clients where clients have to go to a website to access or download email instead of using a desktop application. Some examples are Yahoo Mail and Hotmail.

welcome message A message sent automatically to new list members as soon as their email addresses are added successfully.

whitelist A list of email addresses authorized in advance, held by an ISP, subscriber, or other email service provider, which allows email messages to be delivered regardless of spam filters. See also *enhanced whitelist*.

worm A piece of malicious code delivered via an executable attachment in email or over a computer network and which spreads to other computers by automatically sending itself to every email address on a recipient's contact list or address book. See *virus*.

Index

Note to reader: **Bolded** page numbers indicate definitions and main discussions of a topic. *Italicized* page numbers indicate illustrations and tables.

More Advance Praise for
Email Marketing: An Hour a Day

"More and more of our members tell us how they are using multiple channels to reach consumers. And why? As all marketing goes direct and multichannel, consumers have learned to adapt differently to media. A marketer who does not embrace the power of email is missing an important touch point with consumers."
>   —JOHN A. GRECO, Jr., president and chief executive officer,
>   Direct Marketing Association

"In Email Marketing: An Hour a Day, *David and Jeanniey offer a must-have guide for every marketer that is filled to the brim with insider tips and practical tactics on improving the effectiveness of email marketing. As tenured champions of the email channel, they deftly explore email's intersection with social and mobile marketing, making this a critical resource for every marketing professional."*
>   —DEIDRE BAIRD, president and CEO, Pivotal Veracity

"If there was one book this year that I would give to all of my employees and clients, it would be this book that Jeanniey and David have created. It puts all the years of experience, research, and knowledge that they have gathered into one place to make it easy for my team to do their jobs better. It will become the book that all new hires at eROI will be given along with their offer letters and that all new clients will receive when they decide to work with us. Having this resource in print will allow most email marketers to do their jobs better, resulting in sending out emails that are relevant, compliant, and in the end more successful to their bottom lines."
>   —DYLAN T. BOYD, VP of sales and strategy, eROI

"There's no one I'd rather talk email with than David and Jeanniey—their knowledge of the channel is an invaluable resource. This book will help improve the overall quality and performance of the email marketing we all send and receive."
>   —JEANNE S. JENNINGS, email marketing strategy consultant;
>   author of *The Email Marketing Kit*; ClickZ columnist on email marketing

"Jeanniey Mullen and David Daniels have done the impossible: they present sophisticated strategies in an accessible and easy guide for all types of email marketers. Ignore this book at your peril."
>   —DAVE HENDRICKS, EVP of Operations, Datran Media

"Jeanniey Mullen and Dav *il marketing, and now finally they wrote the book."*
>   —NICK FRIESE, president, Digital Media and Marketing Events